# The Manager as Change Agent

# The Manager as Change Agent

A Practical Guide for
Developing High-Performance
People and Organizations

New Perspectives in Organizational Learning,
Performance, and Change

Jerry W. Gilley
Scott A. Quatro
Erik Hoekstra
Doug D. Whittle
and
Ann Maycunich

PERSEUS PUBLISHING
Cambridge, Massachusetts

Many of the designations used by manufacturers and sellers to distinguish their products are claimed as trademarks. Where those designations appear in this book and Perseus Publishing was aware of a trademark claim, the designations have been printed in initial capital letters.

CIP record for this book is available from the Library of Congress.
Copyright © 2001 by Jerry W. Gilley

Perseus Publishing is a member of the Perseus Books Group.
Find us on the World Wide Web at http://www.perseuspublishing.com

Perseus Publishing books are available at special discounts for bulk purchases in the U.S. by corpora-tions, institutions, and other organizations. For more information, please contact the Special Markets Department at the Perseus Books Group, 11 Cambridge Center, Cambridge, MA, 02142.

Text design by Tonya Hahn
Set in 9 point by Times

First printing, June 2001
1 2 3 4 5 6 7 8 9 10—03 02 01

# Publisher's Note

Organizations are living systems, in a constant state of dynamic evolution. New Perspectives in Organizational Learning, Performance, and Change is designed to showcase the most current theory and practice in human resource and organizational development, exploring all aspects of the field— from performance management to adult learning to corporate culture. Integrating cutting-edge research and innovative management practice, this library of titles will serve as an essential resource for human resource professionals, educators, students, and managers in all types of organizations.

The series editorial board includes leading academics and practitioners whose insights are shaping the theory and application of human resource development and organizational design.

v

# Contents

# List of Figures

# Becoming a Change Agent

Organizations are in crisis, in a constant state of change, but largely lack the internal wisdom and fortitude to embrace and drive change with energy and vision. Moreover, it has become perfectly clear that organizations will never again be stable and predictable (Preskill and Torres, 1999, 3). In fact, some organizations have described the current situation of constant change as *permanent white water,* characterized by continuous surprises, increasing complexity, poorly organized and ambiguous work units, and ever costly interventions (Vaile, 1996).

Several factors incite organization change, including higher costs, market competition, regulatory environment, financial disasters, declining revenue or profits, and changing technology. For example, changes in technology require learning new ways of thinking and working. The total quality movement requires employees to monitor their own work, reduce errors, and contribute suggestions for making the organization more competitive. The quality customer service movement requires new learning to understand and satisfy customer needs and expectations. Additionally, competitive pressures require organizations to reduce unnecessary work processes and steps in production, and globalization prompts organizations to adopt new human resource philosophies to enhance their competitive readiness and renewal capacity.

Technology is a major force affecting organizational change (Preskill and Torres, 1999). Increasing reliance on technology has revolutionized the world's production and consumption capacities and needs, as well as the way work is accomplished. This requires people to change how they make things, provide services, and communicate with one another.

The result is that many organizations look to external change agents (i.e., management consultants) to fix the problem of the day, with disappointing

1

long-term results. Let me illustrate. A large, nationally known insurance company, which I'll call Forlorn, Inc., was experiencing mediocre results (flat sales, minimal growth) in the mid-1980s. Forlorn's president and executive cabinet decided to enlist the aid of an outside change agent, Will, to isolate areas of opportunity and to provide the company with direction. The change agent, a consummate salesman with impressive credentials, seduced upper management with promises of dramatically improved performance and growth as a result of his services. Upper management was so enamored with this change agent that he was hired as an executive vice-president at a six-figure salary. Will was given broad power, nearly carte blanche, to analyze the firm, make recommendations, and implement activities necessary to put his advice into action, including the ability to hire additional "experts," who coincidentally were his friends and colleagues.

The change agent's analysis of the company and industry predicted that major growth loomed, provided that the firm was able to seize the opportunity. Will recommended hiring financial and market analysts to stay abreast of industry potential, along with about a 20 percent increase in production, processing, and customer service staff. After two years, Will's predictions had failed to materialize and Forlorn's business remained flat. The company was burdened by top-heavy management and too many employees, which forced layoffs of nearly 20 percent of its workforce in an effort to avoid financial disaster. The company's reputation as a dependable, solid employer in the community suffered greatly, and its management and employment practices were criticized as being insensitive. "Hurricane Will" is credited with bringing the company to the verge of bankruptcy; change agents are no longer welcome at Forlorn, Inc.

The above example (a true story) reveals many of the problems associated with outside change agents. Like Will, many change agents make grandiose promises of dramatically improved business results that are directly attributable to their services. External change agents, however, are foreign to the organization and initially are unfamiliar with its problems, opportunities, and capabilities. Their short-term orientation and lack of accountability act as insulation, shielding change agents from the consequences of ineffective, misguided, or inappropriate advice. The businesses they serve are often left with hefty bills and disappointing results, similar to what Dorothy and her friends experienced in *The Wizard of Oz* upon their initial discovery that the Wizard was an illusion, a fake.

Organizations should look within to develop the talent they already have; to identify, develop, and nurture internal change agents rather than hope that the Wizard of Oz will magically appear to solve all their problems. Change agents may take the form of human resource personnel, managers at any level

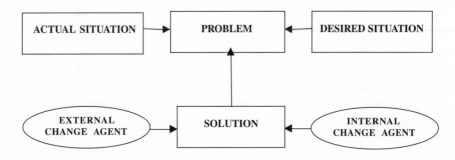

FIGURE 1.1   The Problem and the Solution

in the organization, or anyone who has a stake in the organization's future, the means to influence others, and the motivation to take on an active and creative role. This means "you."

In Figure 1.1, we summarize why becoming a change agent is appropriate. First, organizations have a problem that they need to resolve, which is the difference between the actual and desired situation. Organizations use one of two approaches to resolve this problem: external and internal change agents. Although using external change agents is an appropriate solution, it has its drawbacks, as we just illustrated. Using internal change agents is a possibility because these individuals have an understanding of the organization, existing relationships, and knowledge of policies and procedures that help them improve their organization.

It takes courage to become a change agent and requires a new mindset toward individual and organizational performance and a willingness to take risks, wrestle with ambiguity, deal with conflict head-on, and so forth. Becoming a change agent is not for the weak. The role requires one to possess certain expertise such as sales aptitude, problem-solving skills, and the ability to tolerate rejection, even failure. When you accept the responsibilities of a change agent, you may be considered "an outsider" who must overcome organizational apathy, politics, and inertia. Further, change agents are often thrust into the latest organizational "political hot topic," for which they may be conveniently blamed, at some future date, for its failure or less-than-satisfactory impact on the firm.

Courage also involves the ability to say no, to decline a specific assignment, or to provide employees with answers they don't particularly want to hear. Change agents who are unable to say no often find themselves engaged in activities for which they are not well suited, and then find themselves resorting to smoke and mirrors to get by. Change agents may be unable to devote sufficient time to these mismatched activities; they may be outside their scope of expertise, or the subject matter may simply lack appeal. Participating in such engagements often leads to frustration, and occasionally failure.

Whether you are already an experienced change agent (and just didn't know it!), a human resource professional, or a manager looking to take on new challenges and contribute in new ways to your organization, *Manager as Change Agent* will be your guide

## How Can I Make a Difference?

As a manager, you may sometimes feel helpless as your organization does stupid things, operates in a dysfunctional manner, or treats employees unfairly or unprofessionally. In fact, you may be polishing your résumé right now in order to escape the insanity. Unfortunately, there is no place to escape to—all organizations are dysfunctional. How many of the organizations that you've worked for operate in a purely rational, professional, humanistic, nurturing, commonsensical, supportive, and developmental manner? None? Based on this awareness, the only remaining question is the degree of your organization's dysfunction. Naturally, some organizations are more dysfunctional than others, but there is no Valhalla.

You may believe that you are in an out-of-control organization. You may feel frustrated because of an inability to influence your boss or impact the organization as a whole. In fact, many of you do not believe that you have the opportunity to change your organization, which ignores a wonderful opportunity. Consider your organization for a moment. How many people are employed: 100, 1,000, 10,000, 50,000? Regardless of the number, how are they organized? Most likely, organization is by departments, divisions, or work teams consisting of ten to fifty individuals. In fact, you may be the person responsible for their performance or output. These employees represent your span of control, and are the people with whom you interact every day and have the opportunity to influence. Some of you may have an opportunity to regularly interact with another twenty-five to fifty people, but this is generally your limit. In short, you have the opportunity to influence a small but important group of people, who in turn are part of additional networks across the entire organization. Your responsibility is to help them cope with the daily insanity created by the organization. Additionally, you are responsible for their growth, development, efficiency, performance, and quality. In essence, these people are your organization and you are their leader.

Although you may recognize the need for drastic change within your organization, your circle of influence impacts only individuals, processes, and procedures within your control. Thus, the focus of this book is to this end. We will share with you a variety of techniques proven successful for making a difference in your employees' lives, along with strategies for improving your small but important piece of your organization.

We are advocating that you make the transition from manager to change agent—a transformation that we believe is the most effective way of addressing the dysfunctional nature of today's organizations. This transformation, however, requires you to accept different responsibilities and acquire new knowledge, including understanding and managing change (Chapter 2), facilitating and directing change (Chapter 3), overcoming and managing barriers to change (Chapter 4), adopting a new philosophy that embraces employee development and enhances employee motivation (Chapter 5), creating a climate for change (Chapter 6), developing change agent's expertise (Chapter 7), executing change agent responsibilities (Chapter 8), and developing the competencies required of a change agent (Chapters 9–12).

## Six Critical Questions About Becoming a Change Agent

To help clarify your responsibilities during change, we would like to address six critical questions that will help you define the role of a change agent (Figure 1.2). Afterward we introduce the change agent blueprint, which encompasses the remainder of this book.

### What Is a Change Agent?

The *American Heritage Dictionary* defines *change agent* as "a person who gives expert or professional advice." Some believe that consultation is "fundamentally the act of helping" (Block, 1999), that the essence of the change process involves a relationship designed to help an employee facilitate, implement, and manage change to improve performance. Note our emphasis on *change*. Organizations engage change agents to effect some form of change—to enable the organization or employee to achieve a previously unattainable outcome. The key is that employees must live the change—the change agent cannot do it for them. Recall that Glinda, the good witch in *The Wizard of Oz*, guided and offered advice to Dorothy and her friends, but didn't deprive them of the vast learning opportunities the journey offered—even though she could have done so quite easily. Whether hired for your content knowledge, vast experience, process expertise, access to resources, or objectivity, the result is the same—change, and hopefully for the better. As a result, we will use the terms *consultant* and *change agent* interchangeably.

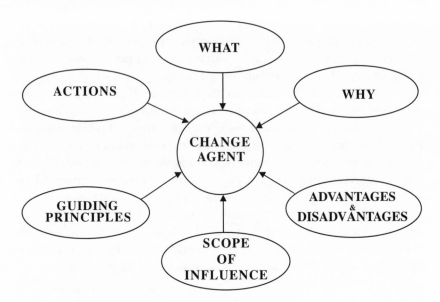

FIGURE 1.2   Change Agent Questions

A change agent's effectiveness depends on his or her ability to *influence* others, *discover* and mobilize *human energy* (both within oneself and within the employee organization), maintain a *sense of humor* and *perspective,* have *self-confidence,* and be *interpersonally competent* (Burke, 1992). Although most of these abilities can be learned, individuals have difficulty making the transition from manager to change agent because they are not prepared for the complexity, ambiguity, and uncertainty common in the world of the change process. To make the transition a consultant must have the following abilities:

- Understand and apply the objectives of the change process,
- Adopt change agent roles and responsibilities
- Design and develop change activities
- Demonstrate change agent competencies and skills
- Implement and evaluate change initiatives

The three dominate models describe how change agents function within an organization: *purchase, doctor-patient, and self-directive* (Schein, 1992). The purchase model represents the most common form, in which your expertise is used (purchase) by the organization to gather information or identify a need. An example would be asking you to conduct organizational analysis for the organization (see Chapter 9). By contrast, the doctor-patient approach is used when the organization shares the symptoms of a problem with the change agent ("turnover is too high," "lack of resources to do an adequate job,") and then asks him to prescribe a remedy.

Others contend that the change agent should be used to help employees as well as an organization diagnose their own strengths and weaknesses more effectively, view organizational problems more clearly, and propose a remedy (Schein, 1992). This approach is sometimes referred to as *self-directive analysis*. When this approach is used, your primary responsibility is to encourage self-diagnoses on the part of employees for the purpose of identifying what may be wrong, and encouraging them to actively generate a remedy. This approach is based on the belief that only the employee ultimately knows what is possible and what will work in his culture and situation (Senge, 1990). Thus, the primary outcome is that employees learn how to help themselves more effectively.

As a change agent, you will engage in a variety of activities. They are as follows:

- Motivational systems (Chapter 5)
- Compensations and reward programs (Chapter 5)
- Work environment culture transformation (Chapter 6)
- Organizational communications (Chapters 6 & 7)
- Employee development (Chapter 7)
- Job design (Chapter 7)
- Performance management systems (Chapter 7)
- Performance and causal analysis (Chapter 8)
- Problem solving (Chapter 8)
- Strategic and change partnerships (Chapter 9)
- Organizational analysis (Chapter 9)
- Change alignment (Chapter 10)
- Performance coaching (Chapter 11)
- Conflict resolution (Chapter 11)
- Vision setting (Chapter 12)

Each will enhance your credibility within the organization as well as help improve organizational effectiveness. Moreover, these activities are used to facilitate employees, change.

## Why Do Organizations Need Change Agents?

Organizations reap many benefits when change agents are used to improve individual and organizational performance and effectiveness. As a change agent, you become a true partner within the organization, functioning as sources of information and expertise on subjects, processes, or both. Organizations enlist the services of consultants for a variety of reasons:

*Lack of expertise or experience in a particular area.* Although external change agents are commonly used to fill this void, internal change agents can also be used if they demonstrate that they have the necessary competencies and interest. In fact, many small organizations may lack the financial resources to hire external consultants and must rely on internal talent.

*Objective perspectives.* Organizational leaders often desire fresh, objective perspectives regarding their opportunities, problems, processes, and challenges. Unfortunately, some employees are too close or "married" to the problem to be objective. However, individuals who are able to assess problems and opportunities without bias can provide a fresh perspective regardless of the department in which they work. They help their organization approach problems openly and without scripted solutions. These change agents function as objective observers, which is one of their fundamental roles.

*Improved communications and interpersonal relations.* Change agents are often charged with "getting to the heart of the problem," "learning what the troops are really feeling," or "helping us maximize our potential." Accomplishing any of these tasks requires change agents to function as unbiased listeners who promote open lines of communication throughout all levels of the organization—and maintain confidentiality in the process. Conflicts, for example, arise for numerous reasons, such as organizational restructuring, mergers, acquisitions, and so forth. As a change agent, you act as an independent, unbiased mediator to help resolve differences.

*Facilitating change.* In essence, change agents deliver change. Improving performance requires individuals and organizations to step outside their comfort zones—*to change*—which may require the assistance of an unbiased change agent. As a change agent, you are engaged to effect significant change in the form of positive, substantial improvements previously elusive to the organization.

## What Are the Advantages and Disadvantages of Internal and External Change Agents?

Traditionally, internal change agents are centrally housed in the Human Resource division or elsewhere, offering their services to all units, departments, and divisions of the firm. Occasionally, they may be housed within divisions such as marketing, manufacturing, or customer service, with whom they share product-, function-, or process-specific knowledge and skill. An emerging contemporary phenomenon is the use of managers as change agents, who share their experience and expertise to improve organizational results.

Many organizations focus on maximizing opportunities by enlisting the aid of change agents who offer expertise in critical areas. The contemporary view of change agents stresses seizing opportunities and enhancing efficiency and effectiveness, not "fixing" broken organizations or people.

At this point, several questions remain unanswered. First, when should organizations use internal or external change agents to improve competitiveness and business success? Second, should organizations use both internal and external change agents? Third, can a person serve as both an internal and external change agent?

Typically, organizations use external change agents because its managers lack experience or skill in a critical area. For example, managing organizational change, making use of new technology, restructuring the organization, improving the organizational culture, implementing performance improvement initiatives, and participating in a merger or acquisition are topics commonly reserved for external change agent expertise. Internal change agents are typically used when problems require understanding of an organization's policies, procedures, structure, culture, and practices.

We believe that both internal and external change agents are successful in resolving organizational problems. Internal and external change agents are similar in their focus on helping employees improve performance and facilitating organizational change. Both offer expertise that is external to the project or engagement, and rely on internal members for information and actual implementation. Both must live with their decisions, and are held accountable for results. Their focus, therefore, must be long-term and tailored to the specific needs and capabilities of the organization. However, they each have distinct advantages and disadvantages (Figure 1.3).

Finally, we believe that the same person can serve as both an internal and external change agent. For example, you serve as an internal change agent when you work within your own department. You have several advantages when serving in this capacity, such as established relationships, organizational

| | Advantages | Disadvantages |
|---|---|---|
| **Internal Change Agent** | political savvy | too influenced by politics |
| | existing relationships | lack of respect/credibility |
| | organizational understanding | lack of objectivity |
| | accountability | blamed for failures, problems |
| | trust | perceived lack of confidentiality |
| | job stability | mistrust |
| | ability to hit the ground running | may make assumptions |
| | varied assignments | may not be free to reject assignments |
| | reduced security risk | may be part of the problem |
| | able to spend more time with internal members | pressure to conform |
| | | has a boss and departmental goals to satisfy |
| **External Change Agent** | objectivity | inability to see the "full picture" |
| | "expert" image | greater/false expectations |
| | power due to independence | arrogance |
| | freedom to leave the assignment | lack of accountability |
| | freedom to be candid | potential to create fear or resentment |
| | greater autonomy than internal counterparts | "short-termer" image resentment by employees |
| | varied experiences/ broader perspectives | attempts to apply old solutions to existing problems |
| | high payoff | instability or lack of work continuity |
| | job freedom and variety | high risk |

FIGURE 1.3   Comparison of Internal and External Change Agents

understanding, and political savvy. You may be more cost and time efficient because you are already familiar with the internal workings of the organizational system. You have knowledge of organizational politics, resources, capabilities, and culture, and are committed to the long-term success of the endeavor. At the same time, you have several disadvantages, which include lack of objectivity, perceived lack of confidentiality, and overinfluence by politics.

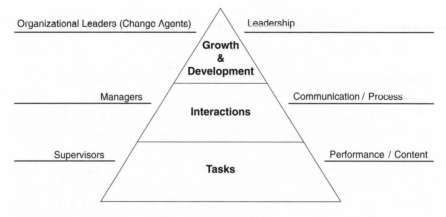

FIGURE 1.4    Change Agent's Scope of Influence

An internal change agent can also serve as an external consultant when working across departmental lines. Even though you may be internal to the organization, you are still external to the specific problem, need, or opportunity of other departments or divisions; thus, you operate just like an external change agent. When this occurs, you benefit by being objective, candid, and independent. You are perceived to be an expert by those who retain your services; thus, you enjoy an instantaneous power base, operate from a fresh perspective, and have greater freedom to reject or leave an assignment. Adversely, you may be disadvantaged by lack of understanding of the "big picture," creating greater or false expectations of success, and generating fear or resentment.

### What Is a Change Agent's Scope of Influence?

As a change agent, you have the potential to affect (influence or impact) any and all areas of your organization. Figure 1.4 illustrates the scope of a change agent's influence. The left side of the diagram indicates which members of management are involved at various levels; the center portion shows the focus of each member of management; and the right side reveals the type of advice (consulting) generally offered.

For example, supervisors, whose primary focus is task completion and efficiency, generally benefit from advice regarding processes, efficiencies, and basic skills such as computer literacy. Other managers often find themselves consumed by interpersonal issues among staff, thereby requiring help with communications, team building, basic managerial skills, and the like. Finally, executives, as leaders, are challenged to promote both individual and organizational growth leading to continuous improvement and competitive readiness; therefore, leadership development opportunities are numerous. As a result, opportunities abound for change agents to help stakeholders improve their business.

The pyramid at the center of the diagram reveals the relationship among tasks, interactions, and growth and development. Independent and interrelated tasks comprise the majority of the activity within most firms, and thus occupy the foundation of the pyramid, indicating the enormity and importance of this segment of business life.

Interactions among associates at the next level contribute to successful task completion. Similarly, leadership talent, effectiveness, and emphasis on growth and development influence interpersonal interactions as well as task performance. Keep in mind that the levels, competencies, and change approaches not only overlap, but also influence each other.

### What Are the Guiding Principles of Change Agents?

Several guiding principles are useful in providing direction for making the transition to change agent.

*Principle 1: Positive Perspective of Employees.*   Change agents have great respect for the ability of employees to improve. As a result, they assume that every employee can be trusted to perform to the best of his or her skills and abilities. They believe employees have the right to be informed about the organization's decisions, mission, and strategy. Further, they contend that employees prefer to be involved contributors rather than passive observers. They assume that employees are willing to take risks if the organization establishes a safety net. Change agents believe that employees enjoy teamwork and group harmony, want to grow and develop, and prefer to feel important, needed, useful, successful, proud, and respected. They assume that employees want to develop a positive relationship with leaders, managers, and coworkers. Further, they contend that employees prefer meaningful work, desire appreciation and recognition for their accomplishments, and prefer responsibility to dependency and passivity. Change agents believe that employees thrive under a self-directed leadership approach versus an authoritarian approach. Finally, they want the organization to meet its strategic business goals and objectives and thus be successful (Maslow, 1998).

*Principle 2: Self-Awareness.*   Change agents continually examine their behavior, decisions, and beliefs, making appropriate adjustments as needed. As a result, they are able to reinvent themselves over and over again, looking inward to discover new awareness and insights, which is essential for change agents to understand who they are, what they believe, their strengths, weaknesses, and growth areas.

Self-awareness is the ability to understand one's values and beliefs and to know why one behaves in a particular manner. Self-awareness implies that change agents understand "why" they do what they do and are able to identify "when" a change initiative violates their guiding principles. Thus, you know when changes are consistent with guiding principles and when they are not. Without this self-awareness skill, you have difficulty maintaining personal integrity. Over time, employees lose confidence in your intentions, which severely damages professional relationships and in turn diminishes employees' productivity, quality, and efficiency.

One way to improve self-awareness is to engage in a value alignment activity, which helps identify what the company considers important—an essential element in making decisions that impact the well-being of the organization. This activity enables change agents to identify their values and beliefs and determine whether they complement those of the organization. First, identify your personal values and beliefs, comparing them to those of your organization. Second, determine the amount of agreement between personal and organizational values and beliefs. Third, identify how personal values and beliefs impact employees on a daily basis. Fourth, make adjustments that align personal guiding principles with those of the organization. If the organization's values and your values are incongruent and you feel that altering your values would be inappropriate, you may need to leave your organization and join one that more closely aligns with your values.

*Principle 3: Personal Accountability.* Far too many managers simply "wash their hands" of their responsibility to their employees. Change agents, on the other hand, understand that they are personally accountable for their own behavior, actions, and business results, including the policies, procedures, incentives, interventions, and plans they advocate and implement. Moreover, change agents live by the Truman philosophy, "The Buck Stops Here," and behave accordingly.

Personal accountability is more than a mere slogan used by managers who want to manipulate a situation or event. It is a way of thinking, guided by internal forces deep within the soul of every change agent. It is part of your personal fabric and remains constant during good times and bad. Personal accountability enables employees to believe in you, which makes them vulnerable by trusting in your words and deeds. In short, personal accountability establishes a connection with employees, which is a necessary ingredient to build trust and honesty.

*Principle 4: Effective Communications.* Effective change agents skillfully communicate with others throughout the organization. Communications is not just the expression of ideas or rhetorical choices made during an interaction, but the ability to use all communication mechanisms available to stimulate and challenge employees to grow and develop, as well as to perform to the best of their abilities. Change agents have a powerful command of the communication process and understand that information is often misunderstood because of inference and distortion. Change agents demonstrate an understanding of nonverbal messages when interacting with employees and use such techniques to emphasize their meaning. By possessing effective communication skills, you are able to deliver performance feedback, conduct performance appraisals, confront poor performance, and provide career counseling and mentoring.

*Principle 5: Employee Advocacy.* All too often, managers are selfish, only concerned about their own careers and how they will advance in the firm. Little regard is given to the respective careers of their employees, so it should come as no surprise that such managers avoid their developmental responsibilities. Consequently, their employees are "on their own" when acquiring or developing the knowledge, skills, abilities, and aptitudes needed to ensure adequate performance and productivity, or to advance their careers. In fact, many employees simply hope to survive.

However, the true test of a change agent is whether he is able to help others to assume new roles and responsibilities. A change agent is responsible for employee growth and development as well as the impact that employees will make as a result of their efforts. Effective change agents realize that employee growth and development fuels their own long-term career success and advancement.

Change agents also understand that their success is dependent on contributions from each employee. They realize that the sum of the parts is greater than the whole, so they advocate and encourage a synergistic approach to problem solving, strategic planning, organizational development initiatives, change intervention, and so forth.

Change agents practice the principle of employee advocacy every time they delegate work tasks and responsibilities. Delegation is a process of appointing someone to operate on your behalf. This implies that you and your employees are interchangeable parts useful in producing desired results. Thus, you serve as replacements for each other, and assume each other's tasks and responsibilities. In reality, delegation forces you and your employees to rely on each other to achieve desired business results.

*Principle 6: Trustworthiness.* Managers have power and authority over employees, but this does not guarantee that they trust you. Without trust, employees avoid risks and will be less likely to participate in growth and development activities or engage in assignments that will improve their skills and competencies.

Establishing trust is a time-consuming, difficult undertaking that is based on respect, honesty, character, and integrity. Respect involves believing in another person and holding them in high regard. When trust is established, open, honest, and direct communication results. Effective change agents are able to avoid hidden agendas that discourage positive working relationships. However, the true test of one's character is what you do when no one is looking. Obviously, trusting employees believe that you will do the right thing. Integrity is essential because employees follow others who do what they say they are going to do, and in an honest, trustworthy fashion.

There are five steps to establishing trust. First, create a work environment free of fear. Second, develop a solid communication pattern with every employee both in terms of frequency and depth. Third, discover the unique characteristics, personality, life experiences, and professional paths of each of your employees. Fourth, engage your employees by accepting them as positive contributors and worthwhile human beings. Fifth, become personally involved with every employee, spending significant time with each one. Trust is granted when leaders have successfully accomplished each of these steps (these principles are further examined in Chapter 6).

## What Actions Are Required to Become a Change Agent?

Becoming a change agent gives you the opportunity to develop personal relationships with employees and leaders. Alliances allow managers and employees to create trust and develop a shared vision of the future through a free exchange of ideas, information, and perceptions. Becoming a change agent demonstrates your willingness to intimately know those you serve, as well as your ability to learn from employees. This role allows you to direct all efforts at satisfying your employees' needs, including designing and developing services in accordance with their employer's expressed interests, and provide change activities that improve the organization and its competitive readiness. Finally, becoming a change agent produces value, which is measured in terms of increased organizational performance, profitability, revenue, quality, or efficiency.

*Establishing Credibility.* Adjusting to ever-changing conditions and circumstances can improve your credibility and influence within your organization although it requires you to demonstrate new expertise (Chapter 7), accept new responsibilities (Chapter 8), and adopt new roles (Chapters 9–12). Managers are capable of establishing credibility within an organization in a number of ways. They include:

- Demonstrating your ability to solve complex problems
- Demonstrating professional expertise along with understanding organizational operations and culture enabling you to establish respect for your insight and particular area of expertise
- Establishing relationships with key organizational decision makers
- Developing a reputation for delivering results, which implies that credibility can be earned

You also enhance you credibility by being accurate in all activities and practices and by being predictable and consistent in actions and decisions. Meeting commitments also improves credibility. Moreover, you can enhance your credibility by establishing collaborative relationships with employees. Appropriate expression of opinions, ideas, strategies, and activities can enhance credibility, as well as to behave in an ethical manner that demonstrates integrity. Finally, you need to demonstrate creativity and innovation, maintain confidentiality, and listen to and focus on employees' problems in a manner that brings about mutual respect.

*Demonstrating Follow-Through.* We are all familiar with the sports concept of follow-through. Whether in a golf swing, a baseball pitch, or a basketball foul shot, follow-through is the all-important difference between mediocre and excellent results. Becoming a change agent is no different. Change agents need to demonstrate thorough and vigilant follow-through when engaging in the change process (Chapter 2), demonstrating areas of expertise (Chapter 7), executing responsibilities (Chapter 8), or engaging in various roles (Chapters 9–12). Follow-through is critical when conducting project audits, analyzing performance problems, evaluating solutions to problems, and documenting performance results. Follow-through is the most overlooked and underestimated process by many change agents. It is essential to credibility and enhances the change agent's image in the eyes of organizational leaders and employees.

Follow-through must be done at every stage of the change process. For example, once you have agreed to participate in a change initiative, you need to check on it regularly for changes in scope and time line, constantly audit performance by asking questions, determine whether employees' needs are being met, and take time to evaluate solutions after they are implemented. Did the solution narrow the gap between prior performance and expected or desired performance? Even if the answer is no, the information gathered and the experience gained are valuable. Employees need to hear this information and understand its worth.

Change agents also build credibility with employees and upper management by completing the change process. Problems have a way of recycling. Follow-through and documentation can prevent reoccurrence of the same issues.

*Developing a Customer Service Strategy.* An effective customer service strategy satisfies your stakeholders' needs and expectations. Such a strategy ensures that jobs are designed in accordance with the stakeholders' expressed interests, deliverables are generated in accordance with stakeholders' expectations, and performance outputs meet or exceed standards and are delivered on time and within budget. Attention to such criteria assures focus on maximizing organizational performance. As a result, your actions and initiatives will be supported as well as defended by senior managers during difficult economic periods. Further, your contributions will be viewed as essential to the organization's long-term success.

A customer service strategy that satisfies stakeholders' needs and expectations consists of six steps:

1. Establishing a customer service philosophy requires you to be willing to place the business and professional needs of your stakeholders above your own (see Chapter 2).
2. Creating a customer service environment demonstrates willingness to listen to stakeholders, respond to their demands, and work with them in a collaborative manner.
3. Creating customer service opportunities requires face-to-face interaction, the result of unwavering dedication to stakeholder satisfaction.
4. Implementing customer service requires you to become active participants with stakeholders rather than passive observers, which

embodies ample questioning, listening, and facilitating skills that lead to viable recommendations and solutions.

5. Evaluating the utility and shortcomings of customer service involves securing feedback from stakeholders regarding their satisfaction with interventions and initiatives.

6. Implementing areas for improvement in customer service is always based on the feedback received from stakeholders (Gilley and Maycunich, 1998).

Ultimately, an effective customer service strategy becomes a guiding principle for managers, which directs their decisions and actions.

*Demonstrating Accountability for Results.*   A change agent's primary responsibility is to help the employee or organization develop a system that supports meaningful, lasting change. Managing results via individual accountability begins with the mutual establishment of specific, measurable, realistic, and time-based goals and objectives, the accomplishment of which is later evaluated by the employee. By the very nature of their job, change agents are held accountable for results—their employers demand it. When they operate as external change agents, conversely, they are often perceived as immune to accountability. This is owing to lack of a reporting relationship; thus, accountability can be disregarded at the end of an engagement regardless of the outcomes. Successful change agents, both internal and external, however, view themselves as partners with the employees and owners of the change effort. They hold themselves responsible and accountable for results, and let the employee know it from the beginning of the relationship. Additionally, change agents (internal and external) keep employees informed of progress and pitfalls on a regular basis, often via formal (written reports, update meetings) and informal communications (notes, e-mail, or impromptu encounters). These competencies and abilities enhance change agents' effectiveness.

## Change Agent Blueprint

Once you have satisfactorily addressed the six issues listed above, adopting a plan of action will enable you to make the transition from manager to change agent. This process consists of eleven steps, collectively referred to as the Change Agent Blueprint (Figure 1.5)

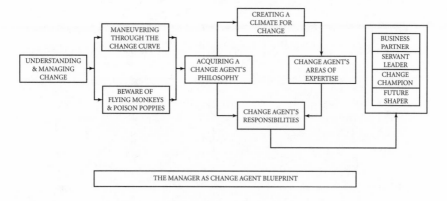

FIGURE 1.5   Change Agent Blueprint

## Conclusion

The ever-increasing complexity of organizations requires you to continuously examine your roles and responsibilities. The outcome of this analysis is the adoption and integration of several new and exciting roles as well as the acceptance of influential responsibilities. With that in mind, you may wonder what you can do to influence or improve your situation. One such role is that of change agent, which can improve your credibility within their organization.

In the remaining chapters we outline how you can personally embrace your effectiveness by adopting the new approach an employee and organizational improvement. The change agent approach is destined to challenge your traditional thinking on management and provoke you to thought. We will provide you with a road map to *becoming a change agent* capable of developing high-performance people and organizations. So let the journey begin.

# Part

# Beyond the Smoke and Mirrors

In this section of the book, we will examine important information that you need to make the transition from manager to change agent. This includes:

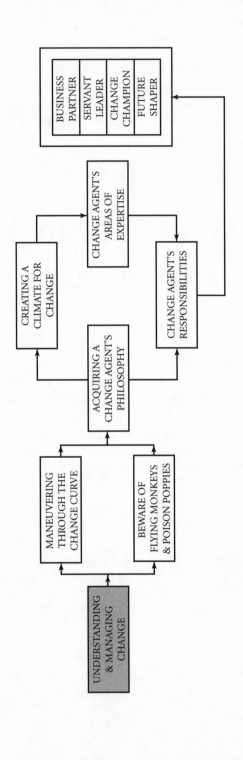

THE MANAGER AS CHANGE AGENT BLUEPRINT

# Understanding and Managing Change

The first step in becoming a change agent is to be able to understand the complexity of change. This requires you to be able to distinguish between differing types of change. You also need to understand the purposes for change, effects change has on organizational culture, barriers to change, and myths that surround change. Next, you need to adopt and implement an approach to managing the change process.

## Types of Change

The majority of changes that occur within an organization deal with routines, activities, problems, issues, and specific circumstances; they are sometimes referred to as *first-order change* (Mink, Esterhuysen, Mink, and Owen, 1993). These are minor improvements and adjustments that occur naturally as an organization and its employees grow and develop. Therefore, the preponderance of first-order changes would not necessarily require organized intervention. However, first-order change does require your attention to ensure that natural employee growth is encouraged.

Another type of change involves a fundamental shift in the organization whereby leaders question their organization's basic assumptions and address new and unknown elements in their work climate and culture. Sometimes referred to as *transformational change* or *second-order change,* this involves a comprehensive examination of an organization's culture, core processes (i.e., structure, management, decisionmaking, and performance management system), vision, mission, values, goals, and strategies (Mink, Esterhuysen, Mink, and Owen, 1993). Further, second-order changes are alterations that are thoroughly integrated into the organization and transform its basic nature.

Organizations require second-order change to embrace long-term change that would alter the way the firm operates. To facilitate this type of change, you will need to make the transition to change agent. Such a transition requires you to examine the type of work environment you provide to make certain that it is conducive to change. This requires you to adopt a developmentally oriented philosophy whereby your efforts are dedicated to employees' continuous improvement based on their strengths (Chapter 5). Additionally, you will need to create work climates free of fear, demonstrate respect for and acceptance of employees, and become actively involved with employees as they integrate change (Chapter 6). Moreover, the transition requires you to develop additional expertise (Chapter 7) and accept new responsibilities (Chapter 8). Finally, you will need to examine your level of competency and determine whether it is sufficient to become an effective change agent (Chapters 9–12). Once this is determined, you will need to create a development plan to build on your strengths and to improve your weaknesses.

## Purpose of Change

Whether the envisioned change is a large, total system, a small division or department within an organization, or an individual employee, the primary purpose of change is to improve the organization and make it more effective. Unfortunately, improving organizational effectiveness is not easy. In fact, evaluating or measuring organizational effectiveness is one of the biggest obstacles that can face an organization. The most common way of measuring organizational effectiveness is to determine whether the company has achieved its strategic and operational goals. Measuring organizational effectiveness in terms of the extent to which the organization accomplishes its goals is but one way to examine this concept. Organizational effectiveness can be measured by your ability to acquire needed resources to accomplish desired results, such as buying computers to improve quality and efficiency or obtaining additional human resources to deliver goods on time. Further, organizational effectiveness can be defined in terms of how smoothly your department and the organization operate (i.e., absence of conflict, turnover, and absenteeism). Organizational effectiveness can be determined by the extent to which you are able to satisfy your stakeholders' needs and expectations (for example, employees, other managers, organizational leaders, and internal and external customers). Using this approach, organizational effectiveness is measured in terms of stakeholder satisfaction with the use of deliverables as well as their perception of the correctness of their decision to have an ongoing relationship with your operational unit.

Although it may be difficult to arrive at an agreed-upon way of measuring organizational effectiveness, it is certainly an important part of organizational life. Consequently, you need to adopt an acceptable or appropriate way of determining organizational effectiveness to serve as a target that all members of the organization strive to achieve.

## Organizational Culture and Change

Most simply, organizational culture can be defined as "the way we do things around here," which refers to the "pattern of basic assumptions invented, discovered, or developed by employees in order to adopt to and share with new members as the correct way to perceive, think, and feel in relation to those problems" (Schein, 1992, 9). Moreover, organizational culture can be defined as the interrelationship of shared beliefs, behaviors, and assumptions that are acquired over time by members of an organization (Conner, 1992, 164). By beliefs we mean a set of integrated values and expectations that provide a framework for shaping what employees believe to be true or false, relevant or irrelevant, good or bad about their work environment. Behaviors are observable actions that constitute the way people actually operate on a daily basis. Although beliefs reflect intentions that are often difficult to identify, behaviors can be verified in a more objective manner. On the other hand, assumptions are the unconscious rationale used in applying certain beliefs or specific behaviors. They are taken for granted perceptions employees have of reality. The prevailing *beliefs, behaviors,* and *assumptions* of an organization guide what are considered appropriate or inappropriate actions in which employees and groups engage. Furthermore, organizational culture is what employees *perceive* to be the pattern of beliefs, values, and expectations that guide behavior and practice within an organization. In short, culture determines the type of institution the organization becomes.

The collective beliefs, behaviors, and assumptions held by employees affect their daily interaction, decisions, and operations on two levels: overt and covert. On the overt level, an organization operates on beliefs and observable behaviors. This level represents observable, intentional, and direct influences on operations (e.g., goals, policies and procedures, and organizational vision and mission statements). The covert level is characterized by unintentional and indirect influences on interactions and operations. At the covert level, the organization is influenced by employees' collective assumptions, which are difficult to change because they stem from personalities, organizational history, biases, and personal views held dear. These assumptions combine to influence oral and written communications, organizational structure, power and status, policies and procedures, compensation and reward systems, and the design and use of physical facilities.

Organizational culture is not only present in every institution; it is used to prevent sudden shifts in operations and practice. For example, organizations are often characterized as organic, living, growing systems in which various units contribute to overall vitality in complex ways, not in simple, linear ways. Thus, organizations constantly struggle to ward off threats to their very existence. Just like other living organisms, organizations are wired to survive by resisting change. More clearly stated, "individuals are what they believe, and groups are their cultures; hence, to require a group to change its shared beliefs is to threaten its very existence" (O'Toole, 1995). Unfortunately, the natural tendency toward resistance typically does not allow organizations to differentiate between necessary and unnecessary change. The natural tendency to preserve the status quo in organizations can pose grave risks for the organization, its employees, and their leaders. It is as though organizations have developed an immune system used to kill off any change inconsistent with their culture, regardless of its positive intent. Consequently, it takes a great deal of time, energy, and resources to implement any change within an organization.

To overcome natural barriers to cultural change, you must first articulate why change is critical to organizational success. Next, define a process to assess the current culture, the desired culture, and the gap between the two. Third, modify the beliefs, behaviors, and assumptions of the current culture to be more supportive of change. Fourth, build an action plan that integrates multiple approaches to culture change.

## Barriers to Change

Many times change initiatives do not bring about change at all. In fact, you undoubtedly have experienced such a phenomenon where your organization engages in a public exercise designed to bring about change, only to discover months later that nothing really changed at all. Quite simply, many change efforts fail because executive and senior managers want "conformation of a problem, not real change." This is because they are either focused on the short term or are unwilling to commit the time, money, and effort needed to bring about real change. Additionally, some leaders are averse to conflict. Thus, they are willing to live with the current situation rather than deal with disruption brought about as a result of change. For example, a human resources department of a major midwestern university was experiencing a serious breakdown in communications between the department and university employees. This created conflicts between employees and caused serious mistakes in the delivery of services. During a meeting to address the problem, the vice president of human resources stated, "Well, I don't know what all the fuss is all about, poor communications is a fact of life . . . anyway, we all know that you can't improve communications." As you can imagine, the problem never was resolved.

Change efforts also fail to occur because managers do not communicate their vision or fail to lead. Some managers are afraid of the unknown, some are unable to mobilize commitment to sustain change, and still others allow political uncertainty to undermine change. Change fails when managers' expectations are unrealistic and when they neglect to generate measurable, tangible results. More important, change does not occur when its initiatives are not tied to organizational strategy or it is seen as a quick fix (see Chapter 4). When these conditions exist, organizational change fails to materialize. Consequently, managers are obligated to overcome these barriers before initiating change.

Another barrier to change is the current structure of most organizations. Most organizations are organized by formal, independent departments, which is like that of silos, tall, thick, windowless structures that prevent interdepartmental communications and interaction (Rummler and Brache, 1995, 6–7). Most employees operate within their respective silos, adopting the culture, language, and customs of their department or division, which prevents cross-departmental cooperation that could improve communications, decisionmaking, performance, and quality. Consequently, employees from different departments fail to communicate or maintain similar language; they tend to be isolated and operate from a narrow, job-centered perspective. All too often, employees are prohibited from working across departmental lines to achieve desired goals. Organizations that promote a silo culture are likely to produce an organizational Tower of Babel, with confusion rampant throughout (Gilley and Maycunich, 1998). Furthermore, the silo culture encourages executive-level decisionmaking that often prevents teamwork, involvement, and cross-departmental cooperation.

Another barrier is the change-for-change's-sake approach, which fosters an environment of learned helplessness (Watkins and Marsick, 1993). This is because people tend to ignore new initiatives that they believe will disappear soon. As a result, employees become passive, which hinders the successful launch and implementation of change initiatives. In other words, employees are rewarded for not embracing organizational change. Organizational stagnation is guaranteed when employees are allowed to passively observe until the change initiative dissipates.

Many employees are familiar only with their own world, not the complexity of the entire organization. When this condition exists, they are experiencing *tunnel vision* (Watkins and Marsick, 1993). Tunnel vision causes employees to react blindly without fully considering the source of change, or become frozen into place because of the overwhelming complexity of change. Furthermore, the inability to see oneself and a situation from a broad perspective and act accordingly prevents long-term systemic change.

## Myths of Organizational Change

Most employees have several unconscious assumptions about organizational change (Conner, 1992, 7). Although these assumptions are firmly held, they are based mostly on fears and prejudice rather than fact. Patterson (1997, 7) believes that seven fatal myths permeate organizational change activities. These include:

1. Employees act first in the best interest of the organization.
2. Employees engage in change because of the merits of change.
3. Employees embrace change when they trust their leaders to do the right thing.
4. Employees opt to be architects of the change affecting them.
5. Organizations are rationally functioning systems.
6. Organizations operate from a value-driven orientation.
7. Organizations can achieve systemic change without creating conflict within the system.

You are better prepared to help your organizations and employees adapt to change when you proactively address these myths and assumptions. Conversely, these can lead to disaster if not appropriately handled.

*Myth 1: Employees Act First in the Best Interest of the Organization.* It comes as no surprise that most employees act in their own best interests, not in that of the organization. They want to know what the change is about and may demand to know how change will affect them personally as well as professionally. Employees want to know how they can possibly fit change into their busy lives with the least disruption. In other words, employees don't care to know the "what" and the "why" of organizational change. They simply want to know what's in it for them. Rather than build a rational case for change based on the benefits to the organization, you need to communicate the personal benefits of change to each employee.

*Myth 2: Employees Engage in Change Because of the Merits of Change.* Most employees engage in organizational change to avoid unnecessary difficulties or personal "pain," rather than implementing change based on its merits (Patterson, 1997). As a change agent, you need to help employees understand the urgency for change by exposing the pain that will result from not changing. In this way, employees will realize that the house is on fire, whether or not the flames are visible. This is an effective metaphor for communicating the importance of taking advantage of the opportunity to solve problems now and manage situations before they spin out of control.

*Myth 3: Employees Embrace Change When They Trust Their Leaders to Do the Right Thing.* Although most employees are outwardly supportive of change, many view change with a great deal of skepticism and cynicism. Many reasons exist for such behavior but the lack of trust in one's manager is a principal cause. Even seemingly *trustworthy* employees question the trustworthiness of those proposing change.

The first step in improving your trustworthiness is to identify actions or events that cause employees to have confidence in you. For example, ask yourself questions such as:

- Did I communicate clearly?
- Did I actually deceive or mislead others?
- Did my conduct in any way prevent employees from accepting my opinions?

These questions will help you determine if you have violated your employee's trust.

Another way of strengthening interpersonal trust is to build an environment that encourages employees to challenge your actions, conduct, or intentions without fear of retribution (Chapter 6). By improving interpersonal communications, you are more likely to be viewed as having good intentions by employees you are asking to initiate change.

*Myth 4: Employees Opt to Be Architects of the Change Affecting Them.* Many employees remain trapped as victims rather than as architects of change because they think and act based on their worst fears. As a result, many employees have a tendency to avoid autonomy and embrace dependency. It is natural, however, for employees to choose the safety of being dependent victims of change rather than to choose the ambiguity and risk inherent in being held accountable for change and its consequences (Conner, 1992). You need to help employees clarify their choices as well as provide support, information, and resources. This will help them make choices that will enhance their growth and development.

*Myth 5: Organizations Are Rationally Functioning Systems.* Most executives and senior managers maintain beliefs that impede change. For example, many executives believe that their organizations operate rationally and are designed to function with a single set of uniform goals that provide organizational stability. Some believe that their organization employs logical decision-making processes, leading to the "best solution" for the firm. Others contend that their organization is independent of their external environment. However, the reality is quite different. Most organizations are guided by multiple, competing sets of goals developed via negotiating, compromise, and synergy. Power and authority are distributed throughout the organization, and decisionmaking is a collaborative process designed to satisfy a number of constituencies. The external environment serves as a filter for the continuing development of the culture. The challenge for you as a change agent is to provide rational leadership in the midst of a seemingly nonrational environment. This can be achieved by identifying and communicating the vision that you have for your organization and employees.

*Myth 6: Organizations Operate from a Value-Driven Orientation.* Far too many organizations enact change as a direct reaction to external pressures, such as an immediate need to achieve greater revenue, market share, or improved profitability. This is because most organizations are event-driven instead of being anchored to a set of underlying values and guiding principles that focus their energy, efforts, and direction. An event-driven approach means that change is characterized by a series of episodes that are unconnected to each other or a core set of principles, and that occur for a short time before being relegated to the proverbial last year's new-thing shelf (Patterson, 1997). You need to make certain that change is consistent with the values and guiding principles of the organization before you embrace and support it. This will help you guard against quick fixes that seldom improve organizational performance (see Chapter 4).

*Myth 7: Organizations Can Achieve Systemic Change Without Creating Conflict Within the System.* Most organizations are unrealistic about the amount of conflict that occurs as a result of change, and naively expect change to be accepted wholeheartedly by employees. Unfortunately, change creates conflict, which creates tension among employees. But conflict is not really the issue; conflict is the condition. The real issue is how you and your employees choose to handle conflict.

However, many managers worry that acknowledging existing conflict may send signals to employees that things aren't under control. Suppressing or denying conflict results in dysfunctional behavior organizationally and interpersonally, which harms everyone (see Chapters 6 and 11).

## Managing the Change Process: An Eleven-Step Model

Managing change is analogous to following the Yellow Brick Road in *The Wizard of Oz*. Like most things, those who follow the road to success adhere to a process. Regardless of whether you are implementing a new compensations program, building a performance management system, transforming the workplace culture, or initiating cross-departmental partnerships, you need to adhere to a proven change process. The following eleven-step model illustrates such a simple, straightforward process (Figure 2.1). Although the phases are distinct, keep in mind that many overlap throughout the process.

### Phase 1: Developing a Readiness for Change

For substantial change to occur, you must first examine your employees' readiness for change. This begins in the same way as addressing organizational culture. First, you must examine your employees' assumptions, which are the set of implicit conditions, principles, ethics, and expectations that define the organization's perception of reality and form the basis for choosing actions and studying the consequences that follow. Another way is to view assumptions as the rules of thumb that guide one's actions. Assumptions are the anchors to which most decisions are linked. Therefore, it is critically important to identify employees' assumptions about circumstances or events prior to engaging in change activities. Unless assumptions are isolated and understood it will be difficult for employees to foster and accept change. This is especially important when adopting a radical change such as organizational transformation.

Another way of understanding the choices your organization makes is to analyze the decisionmaking process: how decisions are made, who partici-

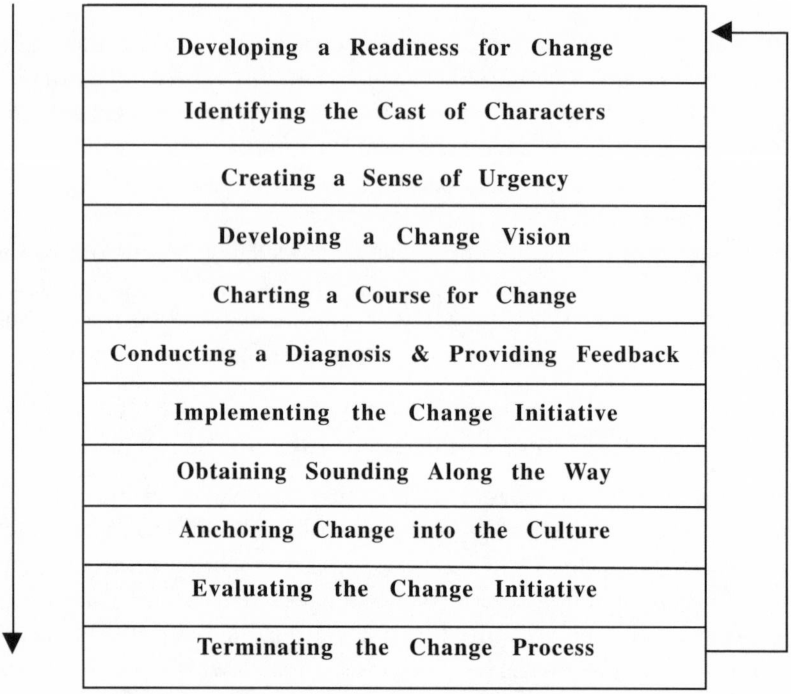

| |
|---|
| **Developing a Readiness for Change** |
| **Identifying the Cast of Characters** |
| **Creating a Sense of Urgency** |
| **Developing a Change Vision** |
| **Charting a Course for Change** |
| **Conducting a Diagnosis & Providing Feedback** |
| **Implementing the Change Initiative** |
| **Obtaining Sounding Along the Way** |
| **Anchoring Change into the Culture** |
| **Evaluating the Change Initiative** |
| **Terminating the Change Process** |

FIGURE 2.1    Managing the Change Process

pates in them, what criteria are used to reach a definitive outcome, and what consequences follow. Once this analysis has been undertaken, you are in a better position to determine how long-term systemic change can take place and whether important organizational members are really interested in *change* or *only interested in confirming that there is a problem*. This is an essential exercise in determining the organization's readiness for change, confirming the organization's capacity for critical reflection.

When employees understand "why" they do what they do, they will be able to differentiate between change-for-change's sake and change initiatives designed to improve organizational performance, competitive readiness, and the capacity for renewal.

## Phase 2: Identifying the Cast of Characters Responsible for Change

In the bar scene in the original *Star Wars* movie, we were introduced to a unique cast of characters. Most of them were unrecognizable, spoke in different languages, and maintained different customs, dress, and worldviews. Although many filmgoers were taken aback by this bazaar cast of characters, they typify today's organization. Let us illustrate. Take a few moments and think about your organization and the unique people that work there. They come in every shape, size, and color, from all over the world. It's overwhelming. Now consider trying to get this eclectic group to pull together in an effort to initiate change. The process of change begins one person at a time and there is a way to group this complex myriad of people during the change process.

Establishing the employee–change agent relationship lays the foundation for the success of any change effort. Positive employee relationships are built on trust and honesty. Once established, the way is paved for exploration and partnership. Needs, opportunities, and problems can then be mutually explored, resources identified, methodology clarified, and the various parties' roles and expectations defined.

*Conduct a Stakeholder Analysis.* People and organizations often fail to face reality. They resist or deny change or fail to accept responsibility for their actions or lack thereof. Failure to face reality or take personal responsibility has grown rampant in our society. "It's not my fault" or "It's not my problem" has become more acceptable to individuals and organizations. This acceptability feeds the failure to see reality.

Change agents must extract themselves from false realities and illusions that others have created to cope with their environment. One avenue for filtering reality from illusion is to gather frequent feedback from *stakeholders.* Honest feedback, even if sometimes painful or disappointing, helps create a more accurate picture of reality. The more sources that are used for feedback, the more accurate it is likely to be.

A stakeholder can be defined as anyone who has something to gain or lose as a result of an interaction with you. In other words, a stakeholder is a person who has a vested interest in your department or organization. That interest can range from those who are simply observing and watching what is happening to those who are impacted most directly by the change. Stakeholders include every one of your employees, the formal leaders and power sources who have approved your budget or provided resources vital to your success, and individuals that provide you with essential information and support along the way. Stakeholders can be your friends or they can be your most dangerous adversaries.

Many managers operate as though they do not have any stakeholders' needs and expectations to satisfy. Since stakeholders are individuals and groups who have something to gain or lose as a result of an interaction, you should focus their efforts accordingly.

However, expectations differ from needs. Expectations are outcomes desired by stakeholders as a result of their efforts, whereas needs are requirements that stakeholders must have met in order to be satisfied. In other words, needs are the minimal or baseline conditions that must be met for the stakeholder, and expectations are the outcomes that stakeholders hope to achieve as a result of their interaction with a change agent. Effective change agents identify the needs and expectations most prevalent among their stakeholder groups and design strategies to fulfill them.

A simple tool called a stakeholder analysis will help you identify the key details you need to know that will align these individuals as supporters of your endeavors, rather than adversaries lurking in the dark. Use the following questions to help you identify your primary stakeholder groups.

- Who needs to know your goals and priorities?
- Why do they need to know? Can they help you achieve success or could they interfere with your progress?
- How would you like them to collaborate with you?
- What information or help do you need from them?
- When will you needs their help?
- What contingencies should you consider and discuss with them?

Typical stakeholders include:

- Other managers—a primary customer because they rely on your employees' outputs to carry out their responsibilities.
- Employees—who perform for you.
- Senior managers—who expect deliverables to return value and help the organization achieve its goals.
- The organization—who need the skills, abilities, and capabilities of employees to produce and deliver high-quality products and services at a profit and rely on employees' capabilities to remain competitive.

Identify the major groups of individuals who have a vested interest in your department, organization, work unit, or change initiative. Ask for one (or a very few) points of contact among your stakeholders' group who can provide you with ongoing direction and simple decisions. Narrow the playing field to as few people as possible—as long as you're sure everyone will live by their decisions and choices. This will ensure that you are not caught in conflicting opinions or that you spend inordinate amounts of time chasing after decision makers who must officially sign off. For each group, complete the following worksheet (Figure 2.2).

Stakeholder analysis for: _____

What is the perceived level of support now? (low, medium, high)

What do you want from this stakeholder?

What is important to this stakeholder?

How could this stakeholder block your success?

What do you want to offer or exchange?

How can you enhance your stakeholder support?

FIGURE 2.2    Stakeholder Analysis Worksheet

*Cast of Characters.*    Once you have conducted a stakeholder analysis, will you be able to identify all those involved in the change process? Typically there are four distinct types of players who participate. Each is critical to the success of the change process. Moreover, identifying them, their respective responsibilities, and expectations allows you to set the stage for an effective change effort. They include change sponsors, implementers, technical analysts, and coaches.

## Change Sponsors

These people have the power or influence to sanction, support, or legitimize change. They determine when change will occur, how it will be achieved, and in what form it will be presented. Change sponsors are responsible for communicating new priorities to the organization, providing the resources needed to foster change, and providing the reinforcement needed to assure success. Typically, change sponsors are the executives and senior managers who are in control of financial resources and who are most accountable for corporate performance. Moreover, you can serve as a change sponsor when change is within your area of responsibility, among your employees, or among people you have direct influence over.

Effective sponsors have established either the formal or informal organizational power to legitimize change within the organization. They are able to communicate the urgency for change and even create a level of discomfort with the status quo that makes change attractive. Effective sponsors have a clear vision of what they want to accomplish (see Chapter 12). They have a thorough understanding of the resources (time, money, people) required to implement change and possess the ability and willingness to commit them. They have the capacity to fully appreciate and empathize with the personal issues major change raises. Effective sponsors have the ability and willingness to meet privately with key individuals or groups to convey strong personal support for the change. They promptly monitor and reward those who facilitate change and express displeasure with those who resist it. Finally, effective sponsors have the capacity to demonstrate consistent support for change, reject any short-term action inconsistent with long-term change goals, and are *willing to make sacrifices* to bring about change.

### Implementers

Individuals who actually implement change are known as implementers. When change resides within your department, your employees are typically implementers. Implementers need to be able to comprehend the changes they are expected to execute. Since an implementer's world is the daily pursuit of performance improvement while using limited resources, their motivation for change is the most pragmatic of any of the cast of characters. Implementers' most frequently asked question is: "How will the change affect our daily lives?" For them, change is personal.

When implementers sincerely think change is unnecessary, they can find a thousand ingenious ways to withhold cooperation. Consequently, you should make every attempt to reassure implementers that the proposed change is practical and beneficial. You need to clearly communicate your commitment to the change in order to reassure implementers. In addition, you should clearly communicate the benefits of the change for implementers and how it will help employees improve their performance and career advancement.

### Technical Analysts

During every change initiative, there are individuals that the change sponsor asks to provide him with technical advice. They are asked to examine the technical specifications of a solution and determine if it is a logical approach. Additionally, they assume the role of gatekeeper by judging the quantifiable aspects of change solutions. They often believe that it is their responsibility to screen out change solutions and eliminate those that will not work. During decision-making activities, they do not have the authority to grant final approval but can advise sponsors not to move forward, and often do. In other words, they cannot veto the decision to move forward but can recommend against it. Far too many important change initiatives are never integrated because change agents fail to gain support from technical analysts. On the other hand, technical advisers play an essential role in screening out ideas that really don't make sense and to identify unrealistic, costly, or ill-conceived change efforts.

Technical analysts examine the components of the change solution and look at the pieces of the puzzle and see if they fit. This enables them to determine if the solution can be integrated into the organization's culture and blended with its values and leadership philosophy.

Unfortunately, some change agents avoid or discount the role of analysts. Of course, this is a bad mistake because they have the "ear" of the sponsor and can negatively influence their decisions. Consequently, the most effective way of working with analysts is to understand their importance and address their concerns with quantifiable information.

### Coaches

In every change situation, self-appointed individuals serve as your coaches. These individuals act as guides during the interaction between sponsors, implementers, and technical analysts. Coaches are the individuals or groups who want to bring about change but lack the power and authority to achieve it. Coaches are typically individuals with informal networks of influence, long-time employees with deep knowledge of the organization, or serve to provide guidance as to how to work successfully within the organization. They provide and interpret information about the cast of characters involved in the change initiative, their expectations, the problem that will occur during implementation, and ways to proceed. Coaches are concerned about the success of a change and want the change initiative to succeed because it will improve the organization. Coaches ask one simple question: "How can we pull this off?" Their role becomes one of an ambassador serving the needs and wants of all involved.

Coaches can be found anywhere in the organization but must meet three criteria. They must have credibility with the cast of characters involved in the change initiative, want the solution being presented, and have credibility with the change agent. Since coaches have already interacted with sponsors, implementers, and technical analysts involved in the change process, they understand the various operating styles and interests. Therefore, they can better influence this group to provide leadership or the support required to foster change.

To facilitate change, you need to identify credible coaches and work closely with them. You should follow their advice unless it seriously violates your guiding principles, values, or ethics. Additionally, coaches are aware of how each one of the cast of characters will benefit from implementing a successful change initiative, which is invaluable information for you.

## Phase 3: Creating a Sense of Urgency

To facilitate change, change agents need to create a sense of urgency (Kotter, 1996). Without it, you may find it difficult to gain needed cooperation from employees, other managers, and organizational leaders. When complacency exists, change usually goes nowhere. Under this condition, it is extremely difficult to recruit people with enough power, credibility, and influence to create and communicate a change vision. It is equally difficult to energize employees to address problems within the organization. Without a sense of urgency, the momentum for change never materializes.

A period of complacency is sometimes referred to as "organizational equilibrium," which occurs when stress levels are low and productivity is adequate. However, this is the period when the organization can get too comfortable and fail to maintain its competitive edge. Disaster can result if this period lasts too long. Therefore, as a change agent you must be able to recognize when apathy has taken root and take the initiative to identify appropriate innovations and change to awaken the organization from its slumber.

There are a number of ways to raise the urgency level within an organization. Although each method may generate results, the first four are primarily considered negative attempts at raising the urgency level, and the last five are positive approaches. Change agents can:

1. Create a crisis by allowing a financial loss, exposing managers to major weaknesses vis-à-vis competitors or allowing errors to blow up instead of being corrected at the last minute.
2. Eliminate obvious examples of excess (e.g., company-owned country club facilities, multiple company planes, gourmet executive dining rooms).
3. Establish revenue, income, productivity, customer satisfaction, and cycle-time targets so high that they cannot be reached by conducting business as usual.
4. Stop measuring subunit performance based solely on narrow functional goals and insist that more people be held accountable for broader measures of business performance.
5. Make available more data about customer satisfaction and financial performance.

6. Insist that people interact regularly with dissatisfied customers, unhappy suppliers, and disgruntled shareholders.
7. Use various means to provide more relevant data and honest discussion at management meetings.
8. Promote honest discussions of problems in company newspapers and senior management speeches, and stop senior management "happy talk" about real, serious problems.
9. Provide employees with information on future opportunities, on the wonderful rewards for capitalizing on those opportunities, and on the organization's current inability to pursue those opportunities (Kotter, 1996).

## Phase 4: Developing a Change Vision

A change vision helps you create a picture of the future with some implicit or explicit commentary on why people should strive to create that future. It helps you direct the change effort and develop strategies for achieving that vision.

A change vision serves three important purposes. First, it clarifies the general direction for change. Second, vision motivates employees to take action in the right direction and helps overcome employees' natural reluctance to change. Third, a good vision coordinates the actions of different employees by aligning individuals in a remarkably efficient way. A good vision "acknowledges that sacrifices will be necessary but makes clear that these sacrifices will yield particular benefits and personal satisfactions that are far superior to those available today—or tomorrow—without attempting to change . . . is *imaginable* in that it conveys a picture of what the future will look like . . . *desirable* because it appeals to the long-term interests of employees, stakeholders, and others who have a stake in the enterprise . . . *feasible,* enabling organizations to develop realistic, attainable goals . . . *focused,* providing guidance in decisionmaking . . . is *flexible,* allowing individual initiative and alternative responses in light of changing conditions . . . is *communicable* in that it is easy to communicate" (Kotter, 1996, 72). Without a shared sense of direction, interdependent employees may constantly conflict, whereas a shared vision clarifies the direction of change and helps employees agree on the importance and value of change.

As a change agent, use every avenue possible to communicate your change vision and strategies, and rely on the collective cast of characters to model the behavior expected of employees. Creating a communications plan will help achieve these goals. An effective communication plan should be a simple, straightforward, jargon-free document that paints a picture of the outcomes of a change initiative. It relies on two-way communication; behavior on the part of change agents and organizational leaders must be consistent with the message being communicated.

## Phase 5: Charting the Course for Change

Recommending a viable option(s) tests the change agent's true mettle. This phase of the change process is like charting a course when you sail from one point to another. The captain must determine every step along the route to avoid danger and make certain that the ship reaches its desired destination.

Charting a course involves setting up clear and precise goals and identifying activities that have to take place to carry them out. It includes specific tasks, activities, and expected results. It also includes naming specific dates, times, and people who are responsible for producing results.

Charting a course is a prerequisite to control; no plan equals no control. Therefore, before you begin conducting a diagnosis or implementing a change initiative, assess alternatives and identify more than one way to achieve the desired results.

## Phase 6: Conducting a Diagnosis and Providing Feedback

One of the most important steps in the change process is conducting a diagnosis and providing feedback. By conducting a diagnosis, you identify which methods will be employed during discovery (personal interviews, questionnaires, observations, analysis of existing data). Who will be involved? What type of data is necessary and when will it be required? How will data be compiled and reported? These questions guide the change agent's diagnosis and decisions, leading to thorough understanding and appreciation of the employee's opportunities and encumbrances. Further, you identify employees' perceptions of a proposed change initiative. This process can help reveal willingness or resistance to change. In other words, it is used to identify the pain or opportunity for which a change initiative is disposed to address.

Change agents must delve deep beneath the surface to expose and appreciate the nuances and influences on any opportunity or challenging situation. Employees sometimes perceive this in-depth analysis as obtrusive; therefore, before participating in the change process, they should reflect on their own willingness to undergo such scrutiny and their commitment to change. Culture, for example, routinely affects whether an employee is able and *willing* to change and accept the ambiguities that are an inevitable part of the process.

One of the authors recently worked with a large financial institution intent on improving its customer service. In-depth analysis of the firm revealed that the cause of the poor service was insufficient training for newly hired employees. The organization, however, was unwilling to alter its training methodology and "the way we do things around here." Under such conditions, there is only so much that a change agent can do.

Following isolation of the genuine problem or opportunity, you identify and evaluate possible solutions. Often, past experience proves invaluable, offering options that have proved successful under similar circumstances. When unique and unfamiliar situations present themselves, your creativity and problem-solving abilities must surface.

What is the proper reporting form and forum? How should the information be presented? Change agents face many choices regarding dissemination of data and clarification and interpretation of findings. Some information is best shared one-on-one, privately, in an environment in which the employee feels safe and in control. Discussions regarding problems and their causes, for example, require careful planning. Individuals often resist feedback they perceive to be negative; thus, it is imperative that the interaction be planned and managed strategically. Extremely public declarations, such as before a large meeting of managers, often inspire controversy, defensiveness, and an unwillingness to "own" the problematic situation. In this instance, conversations with the individual employee or select managerial group are generally better received.

### Phase 7: Implementing the Change Initiative

Implementation is simply carrying out the above detailed plan. Simple? Not always. Remember the journey along the Yellow Brick Road—fraught with danger and unforeseen obstacles. If the process is so simple, why didn't the organization engage in it in the first place?

Implementing your recommendations challenges an organization's internal fortitude. From staffing and logistics issues to fear of change, implementation uncovers many barriers. Here, too, employees can benefit from your experience and exposure to similar circumstances as they are guided along previously unknown paths.

As a change agent, you help employees prepare adequately for impending change, a step often overlooked or underemphasized by organizations, even some change agents. Glenda the Good Witch neglected to prepare Dorothy for her impending journey—and look what happened. Unprepared for the obstacles that lay ahead, Dorothy and her newfound friends experienced confusion, fear, and setbacks that hindered their ability to behave proactively.

Implementation often begins with communication designed to educate and motivate employees regarding the implementation of change. Newsletter articles, company flyers, and "kick-off" sessions are common for large, organizationwide change. Smaller "localized" meetings and training sessions predominate for initiatives aimed at change in departments, units, or divisions. Typically, you are instrumental in the design and delivery of these meetings.

You need to be actively involved during the implementation of a change initiative. Your involvement will directly impact your success. Involvement, however, does not mean total independence or dictatorship. On the contrary, your aim is to encourage self-management on the part of your employees. Thus, you work *with* organizational leaders, other managers, and employees during implementation, coaching and training them along the way.

### Phase 8: Obtaining Sounding Along the Way

During the construction of the railway system in the western United States, it has been said that on more than one occasion crews tunneling from opposite sides of a mountain failed to meet in the middle because they did not take soundings along the way. Unless special care was taken to determine the exact location of the other work crew, they could easily pass each other. Whether this story is true or not is irrelevant, but it does point out the importance of obtaining feedback for employees, implementers, and organizational leaders to determine the impact of a change initiative as well as the quality of its installation. This is a very easy but critical step during the change process. Simply do it.

### Phase 9: Anchoring Change into the Culture

When a change initiative is incompatible with the organization's culture it will be attacked violently. Changes in work groups, a division, or an entire organization can unravel, even after years of effort, when new approaches haven't been anchored firmly in group norms and values. Organizational culture can sometimes be difficult to change because it is nearly imperceptible, which makes it hard to address directly. An organization's culture is powerful for three reasons: individuals are selected and indoctrinated so well, culture exerts itself through the actions of hundreds or thousands of people, and all of this happens without much conscious intent and, thus, is difficult to challenge or even discuss (Kotter, 1996). Therefore, you need to have a long-term plan for incorporating change into the culture. In other words, you will need to administer the equivalent of antirejection drugs to overcome the "immune system" that is present in every organization. This includes continually reminding affected parties of the purposes for change and its benefits as well as the cost of not changing.

### Phase 10: Evaluating the Change Initiative

In the evaluation phase, the change initiative's accomplishments are compared with its goals. Evaluating results reveals whether the assignment has been successful as planned or requires modification or termination.

Successful change initiatives require planning to ensure their long-term effects. Lasting change should not be assumed because organizations have the tendency to revert to their previous state without careful maintenance. The evaluation phase affords you a prime opportunity to meet employee needs by determining whether change was integrated or not.

### Phase 11: Terminating the Change Process

When the work is done and the employee's needs are met, it's time to celebrate. At some point you disengage from the assignment, having helped your employees develop the ability to sustain meaningful, positive, lasting change—and independence.

A change effort should lead to a mutually satisfying termination of the engagement, whether of an isolated initiative or the entire working relationship. Provisions for disengagement and closure should be discussed and specified during the first phase; thus, the change initiative should yield no surprises. Well-planned closure enriches both parties by encouraging feedback and allowing each to share and reflect upon the success of the initiative—as well as opportunities for future collaborations.

## Conclusion

Change is never easy. Therefore, you need to understand what change is, and its purposes. You also need to understand the interaction between ones' organizational culture and the change process. You need to be able to identify and isolate barriers to change. Further, you need to know the myths of organizational change and which strategies to employ to overcome them. Finally, you need to apply the eleven phases of the change process and identify your individual responsibilities during each phase.

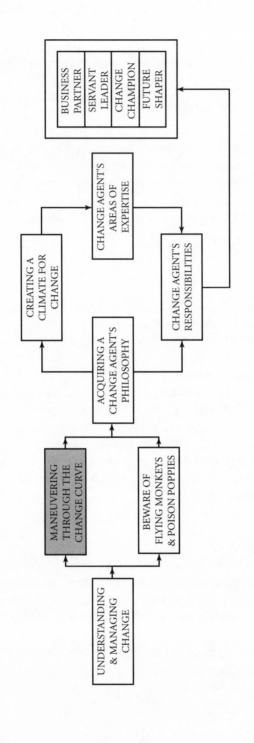

THE MANAGER AS CHANGE AGENT BLUEPRINT

# Maneuvering Through
# the Change Curve

As a change agent, accept the reality that you are going to cause some level of disruption (and potential pain) for those on the receiving end of change. Employees, who are most resistant to change, become the first individuals that you must manage through the change curve. Their resistance can range from subtle to downright nasty.

## The Change Curve

Your best defense is knowledge of the change curve. Observe the behaviors and emotions that indicate where individuals are located on the curve at any given time and employ strategies that will help them move forward toward exploration and commitment (Figure 3.1).

The change curve consists of four quadrants (Bibler, 1989). The upper left corner maps out denial, a period of time in which many employees feel enthusiastic—only because they believe that the change they been hearing about will have little, if any, impact upon them. When the change is perceived to be something that will happen to others, these nonimpacted employees feel comfortable, which is a typical symptom of denial. Based on their lack of knowledge related to the change, this quadrant is oftentimes called *uninformed enthusiasm*.

The lower left quadrant is where reality starts to sink in. Once employees start receiving specific information about the implementation effort, they begin to realize that they will be impacted in some way by the change. Consequently, many employees begin to actively resist change. As we discussed in

45

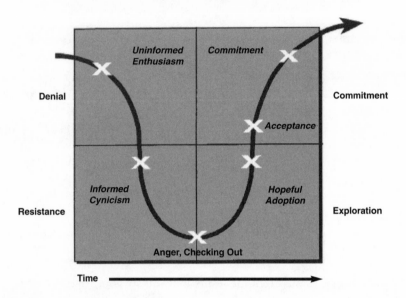

FIGURE 3.1    The Change Curve

Chapter 2, much of managing people through the change curve depends on providing them information as they are impacted by change. This is the irony of communication: When you first present information about a change effort, the very information employees seek will typically throw them, at least temporarily, into a state of *informed cynicism.* Don't let this throw you off course and tempt you to stop the flow of information. People need to go through this portion of the change curve before they can move toward accepting and supporting the change.

It should be noted that a critical point in the change curve is located at the very bottom of the curve, between resistance and exploration. This is typically where some employees choose to check out, emotionally and even physically, in a state of anger, frustration, and disappointment. As a leader of change, you obviously want to minimize the number of check-out situations. On the other hand, accept the reality that, in some cases, this is ultimately the best solution for everyone. What you cannot afford is to have employees "check out" mentally and emotionally but to physically remain in the organization.

The third quadrant, in the lower right corner, is where progress can be realized in the journey toward acceptance of change (exploration). In the state of exploration the realities of change are perceived more positively than negatively. Individuals enter a period of *hopeful adoption,* where they accept the reality of the change that is occurring and can start seeking positive outcomes.

The final stage, commitment, in the upper right quadrant, is where employees accept the change and are fully committed to the new way of doing things. This is where you can utilize collective energies and finally realize the full positive impact of your change initiative. Unfortunately, some organizations never reach this stage, simply because they fail to usher employees through the previous three stages.

During the first phase, sometimes referred as the "honeymoon," employees feel extremely positive about change, which produces naive enthusiasm based on insufficient data. The second phase occurs when employees begin to doubt the appropriateness of the change opportunity. Some employees even withdraw from the change engagement, "checking out" because they have serious reservations or a low tolerance for pessimism. Although informed cynicism is inevitable, checking out is not.

Cynicism doesn't suddenly disappear, but it lessens as employees move into *hopeful adoption*. This isn't a return to the *"everything is wonderful days"* of uninformed enthusiasm; it simply means that employees begin to understand the *positive possibilities* of change.

As more concerns are resolved, employees become increasingly confident and move into the stage that is characterized by the *acceptance* of change as a positive growth and development opportunity and a positive career decision. Further, employees demonstrate their *commitment* to the change initiative by supporting and managing its implementation. Once this stage is reached, employees enter a period of equilibrium and tranquillity.

As a change agent, you need to develop an environment for confronting conflict in a constructive way. By valuing the energy of dissent, you show everyone involved in the change process that honest conflict in a safe environment nourishes the seeds of rich solutions to organizational issues. When conflict surfaces, you need to move to the tension point, not away from it. Tension can be used creatively by capitalizing on the energy of dissent and leading people to reach solutions everyone can accept.

## Traveling Through the Change Curve

The speed with which employees move through the change curve and the severity of disruption in productivity stemming from change will vary, depending on:

- how significant the change is
- whether the person chooses the change
- what other changes are also going on in the person's life.

If you can help manage the timing of your change initiative so that it doesn't coincide with other major organizational changes, you will find your journey less complicated. If the timing is not up to your discretion, at least become aware of other significant changes that have preceded your efforts and, if possible, new initiatives that lie on the horizon.

Traveling through the change curve is not a one-way trip. Even Dorothy didn't get to see the Wizard on her first try. Depending on the day, the circumstances, and the individual situation, expect to see each employee move back and forth through the change curve several times during your implementation efforts. Some analysts refer to this process as the "swing." Just when people think they are making progress, they suddenly reexperience old feelings. A meeting, a message, a "bad day at work," a chance meeting with a former employee—such events can trigger a backward swing into the stages of denial and resistance. Moving forward oftentimes feels risky and thereby difficult for individuals. But with your encouragement and support others can go through the stages at a pace that meets their needs and in a way that helps them understand why they are reacting as they do.

Avoid the temptation to either force or rush employees immediately from denial or resistance to exploration of or commitment to the change. Ultimately, the change process can be prolonged if people are not allowed to experience and move through all four phases. By attempting to skip a stage or move too quickly through a stage, you don't necessarily change people's reactions. In fact, you may see increased resistance. Even worse, you run the risk of driving their reactions underground, leaving you to battle invisible but potentially destructive resistors.

## Danger: Change Curves Ahead

As individuals journey through this curve, watch for the following road signs that indicate which part of the curve your employees are navigating (Figure 3.2). By recognizing the telltale signs of denial or resistance as they surface, you can respond in a way that addresses the issues at hand directly and honestly and provides individuals with the support they need to continue moving forward. When you see signs of employees entering the exploration phase, take advantage of the opportunity to reinforce and encourage them to move to commitment.

The following information provides an overview of verbal communication signs to listen for, actions to observe, and potential steps you can take to support individuals on their change journey.

The sooner you recognize where employees are on the change curve, the better your chances of reducing the negative impacts that result from resis-

| Signs of | What your employees might say | What your employees might do | How you can help your employee move on |
|---|---|---|---|
| Denial | "I'll believe it when I see it." <br><br> "Others may have to change, but it won't affect me." <br><br> "I think this will be easy." | · Avoid the topic as much as possible <br> · Wait; don't take any initiative; appear unconcerned <br> · Act as if nothing is happening <br> · Only do routine work <br> · Focus on little details; ask picky questions <br> · Blame outside forces/others for difficulties <br> · Question decisions and processes | · Confront the employee's behavior <br> · Provide as much information as you can; communicate why the change is happening <br> · Help them realize what they are really feeling |
| Resistance | "They can't make me change." <br><br> "It'll never work." <br><br> "If we don't cooperate, they can't change." | · Get quiet/withdraw <br> · Show anger at you or the organization <br> · Feel overwhelmed and depressed <br> · Continue to do things the old way <br> · Bring up past failures <br> · Complain <br> · Say the task is impossible | · Listen to employee's concerns <br> · Listen to your own feelings <br> · Provide information freely <br> · Help them stay focused on what lies ahead, not what has gone before <br> · Be patient <br> · Provide ways for employees to say "goodbye" to the past |
| Exploration | "This isn't so bad." <br><br> "This could work." <br><br> "This change will give me the opportunity to…" | · Seek new ways <br> · Move to learn and discover possibilities <br> · Take risks and try new things <br> · Have trouble staying focused <br> · Generate lots of ideas <br> · Work together and seek help from each other | · Help employees focus their energy in positive ways, including brainstorming <br> · Identify possible opportunities and advantages in the new situation <br> · Deal with the many options and choices and avoid doing the first thing that comes to mind <br> · Help employees work together to take action, to learn, to plan, to develop responses to change |
| Commitment | "I can't remember how we used to do things." <br><br> "I like things better this way." <br><br> "I wonder what will change next?" | · Begin to look for the next challenge <br> · Feel in control <br> · Feel comfortable <br> · Work effectively | · Acknowledge employees' efforts & accomplishments <br> · Reflect on lessons the team has learned that will help them manage future changes |

FIGURE 3.2   Signs of Change

tance and denial. Because Dorothy's family knew how to recognize the warning signs of a tornado, they took shelter in the root cellar and were protected from harm and potential disaster. In the same way, you can use timely and time-tested ways to prevent negative impacts that will keep you and your project safe.

Don't wait for resistance to strike. If you already have some idea of who might resist and in what way, take appropriate steps to either circumvent the resistance strike altogether or at the very least try to minimize the potential damage resistors can cause.

### Your Journey on the Change Curve

Just because you are the change agent, don't assume that you won't travel through the change curve yourself. In fact, every time you encounter resistance, you may find yourself doubting your own abilities, plans, and strategies; you may want to give up. In essence, you will ride the change swing yourself. *You* need to be supportive of the change yourself before you can get others to accept the change. Double-check yourself to make sure you believe in what you are asking others to do. Until you can navigate yourself through the change curve into the areas of exploration and commitment, it will be difficult, if not impossible, to effectively lead others along that path. Your commitment or lack thereof will be obvious to others. They can and should expect their leader to model the correct positive behaviors. When you begin to doubt yourself, keep in mind the following strategies for managing your reactions to change or for helping others manage change (Figure 3.3).

## Understanding and Dealing with Resistance

When a race car driver receives a black flag, it is because a serious violation has occurred. If not corrected, the violation can cause racing officials to disqualify the race car and its driver. When attempting to implement organizational change, black flags exist that can prevent change agents from moving forward. Quite simply, you need to be aware of and account for the black flags of resistance during the change process. Otherwise, employees and organizational leaders will disqualify the change effort.

When critical information is missing, the first black flag is waved. Until this information is made available the change process will not move forward. The second black flag is waved when employees are uncertain about information, confused, or overwhelmed by the complexity of change. As a result, they resist making the decisions or commitments that moves change forward. Their uncertainty and confusion will delay decisions until their concerns are properly addressed. This can weaken the credibility of change agents because it gives the appearance that employees were not given enough information to make an adequate decision. When employees are uninformed, the third black flag is waved. This is particularly problematic. It allows employees to generate wild and crazy possibilities about the decisions being made regarding a change. The fourth

| Your Coping Skill | Your Coping Strategy |
|---|---|
| Face your limiting beliefs | Identify one limiting belief: How might you look at the belief differently?<br>· Question your assumptions. (What is driving you to fear this change? Reality? Perception?)<br>· Take a bigger picture view. (In the greater scheme of things…is this really that bad?)<br>· Look at experiences in which this belief didn't hold true.<br>· Think of one step you could take to move forward. |
| Focus on what you can control | · What actions can you take that you CAN control?<br>· What can you do to "let go" of things you cannot control? |
| Take risks | · List risks you have taken that have turned out well. Analyze what supported you to take these risks.<br>· How could you get similar support to take risks today?<br>· What specific risks could you take to support this change? |
| Seek assistance from others | · What do you need to learn? To know more about?<br>· Who can you get it from?<br>· When/how will you ask for help? |
| Provide assistance to others | · What can you provide to others for dealing with change?<br>· Who might need this?<br>· How will you discover what others need? |
| Accelerate your learning | · Identify and develop the new skills you need for the change.<br>· Identify your learning goal, and its future benefits to you and your business. List specific action steps and identify the resources you will need. Anticipate the barriers you may encounter along the way, and identify specific target completion dates and how you will measure the results. |

FIGURE 3.3   Coping Skills and Strategies

black flag is waved when the change agent relies on newly hired employees to make decisions about the organization's future. This is especially true when these individuals are senior managers and executives. Because new employees are an unknown commodity within the organization, they may lack credibility. Consequently, they may be reluctant to make critical decisions. Change agents should avoid relying on their support when implementing changes.

Resistance is predictable, natural, and a necessary part of the learning process (Block, 1999). It is a commonplace occurrence. Although resistance is inevitable, many change agents are shocked when it occurs and wish that it would never happen or would just go away. The only solution for dealing with resistance is to understand the underlying reasons behind it and learn to address them. In fact, when confronting resistance you get the opportunity to address employees' fears and vulnerabilities as well as to confirm support for your solution.

The question that change agents need to address is "what are employees resisting when they are resisting change?" In most situations, the employees' resistance can be traced to their difficulties in dealing with an unpleasant or difficult situation. These are not easy situations to deal with and addressing them may produce defensive behaviors. Why? It is natural for people to push back when they feel they are being pushed. One solution might be to present only alternatives that do not cause people to become defensive, but this is not realistic. Change agents are responsible for pointing out difficult realities. These cannot be avoided just because employees become defensive.

There are many reasons for resistance. The most common are:

- The purpose of the change is not made clear.
- Employees affected by the change are not involved in the planning.
- An appeal for change is based on personal reasons.
- The routine patterns of the work group are ignored.
- There is poor communication regarding the change.
- There is fear of failure.
- Excessive work pressure is involved.
- The cost is too high or the reward inadequate.
- There is a perceived loss of control.
- Anxiety over job security is not relieved.
- The vested interest of the employee or department of the organization is involved.
- There is a lack of respect and trust in the initiator.
- There is satisfaction with the status quo.
- Change is too rapid.
- Past experience with change is negative.
- There is an honest difference of opinion about whether change is needed or what results change might bring.
- There is a lack of management support for change (Gilley, 1998).

When change is proposed, whether learning a new skill or reorganizing a department, people feel uncomfortable. Typically, there is conflict over a number of things: resources, timing, recognition and rewards, organizational values, and the amount and type of commitment to change. Disagreement over these issues can produce resistance, which is expressed both directly and indirectly. Some employees may remain completely silent. Others say things like:

- The solution is impractical.
- We've done that before.
- We need more information before we can proceed.
- Your approach is wrong.
- I'm confused.
- The timing is off.

Many employees avoid embracing change by not directly confronting or openly expressing their real issues, opinions, or concerns.

The primary reason why employees resist change is fear (Block, 1999). They fear losing control over their lives. They fear losing the power and authority required to be effective on the job. They fear losing status in the workplace. Some even fear losing their position altogether. People also fear becoming vulnerable during the change process. However, most people will not admit it. Some often rationalize their behavior or blame others for creating the situation.

## Resistance Strategies

Most analysts agree that the best strategy to head off resistance before it strikes is through proactivity. Rumor and damage control are always much more difficult to manage than taking proactive steps to avoid or diminish the impact of resistance in the first place. But there are times that you simply cannot predict or plan for the attacks. The following tips and hints are intended to help identify steps and options for controlling damage when resistance strikes.

When you are in a reactive mode, you need to rely on your intelligence (brain), heart, courage, and vision (see Chapters 9, 10, 11, and 12). You need to employ the interplay of all these strengths to get yourself and the change initiative back on course.

*Monitor Your Own Behavior.* By now, you realize the importance of building and maintaining positive relationships with the employees and various stakeholders in the organization (Chapter 2). The temptation is to spend most of your time and attention on formal sources of power, the "influential" people, whom you perceive as the ones most beneficial to you and your cause.

Be cognizant, however, of how others—the "less important" people—the informal power sources, the general mass of employees, and even your team members—will perceive your association with the "influential" people. Be careful of what you say about your relationships with those individuals. Others may see it as name-dropping or perceive you to be on a power trip.

Find a way to assess your behavior and the reactions of others to you throughout the change process. If they observe a change in *you,* what are they observing? Why might they be responding to your behaviors in a negative way? Find out. Continually adjust your behavior so that you retain as much support from all of your stakeholders—not just the ones who have formal power. It's a delicate but critical balance that you must maintain.

*Avoid Anger.* When on the defensive, your most likely reaction will be to strike back in anger. Don't! Not all change-resistant behavior is a personal assault. Avoid making judgments until you know all the facts. Tally up the issues before you proceed. Choose your battles strategically, to avoid fighting battles on a daily basis that don't let you accomplish your actual goals. In most cases, attacks aren't intended as direct assaults on you as much as they are signs of resistance being lodged against the impending changes.

The essence of resistance is control. You can successfully counter it by following two rules:

1. Never resist resistance. Back off; take a second. Examine your stance, tone, and choice of words to see if you might be inadvertently fueling the resistance.
2. Name the issue and take the hit! Sometimes, simply stating in a low-key, nonconfrontational way how you see the situation—while assuming culpability—can drain the tension (Bell, 1996).

Know what you really want and what's important to get you there. Save your energy for the battles that count, keeping in mind that others will be observing your behavior and reactions. You have an opportunity, an obligation in fact, to demonstrate and model effective ways to deal with problems and criticism. Rather than assuming that criticism is an attack, see if you can treat it as useful feedback for improvement. Explain why you appreciate the criticism, even though it may be difficult to do. Accepting an employee's right to have a point of view does not mean you automatically agree. At the very least, do something to indicate that you're willing to listen by asking for information and ideas.

Don't burn bridges even when it would feel good to do so. Use your negotiation and communication skills to identify effective compromises. The energy you expend trying to salvage a relationship is energy well spent.

*Don't Play the Blame Game.* Take inventory of and responsibility for your actions. Take ownership of your reactions to other people. If you have made a mistake, admit it and do not try to shift blame to others. All relationships should function on a 50/50 basis. Thus, as a partner in any initiative, you need to accept 50 percent of the responsibilities. Even if you truly believe you do not deserve any blame for a particular situation, you may need to give more than your 50 percent for the sake of keeping everyone focused on the projected outcomes.

If you face a particularly difficult challenge with an individual or group, ask to meet with them personally. You may be tempted to meet the opposition on your turf, in your office or working space. Instead, muster up the courage to step outside this comfort zone and meet the opposition face-to-face on *their* turf. Ultimately, putting yourself in a less comfortable zone will keep you on your toes. It will also allow the other person to be in his or her comfort zone, which can reduce their discomfort and therefore makes them less defensive than if you asked them to meet in your space.

*The VIP Method.* A number of common communication techniques and models can help you repair damage caused by change resistance. Never forget that each employee's foremost need is to be heard. When evaluating a conflict, consider using the VIP model (Validate, Inform, and Participate):

- Validate: Agree that things are changing.
- Inform: Provide participants with as many details as you know; encourage them to seek information from others.
- Participate: Ask those involved in the change initiative to think of one or two single actions they can take right away. This will help them to move toward the exploration stage. At the same time, continue to remind them that the change *is* going to happen.


*Resistance Resolution Method.* When resistance develops, change agents should not take it personally and become defensive. They need to remember that resistance is simply the result of differing perspectives and the fear of losing the status quo. Change agents who maintain an objective viewpoint will be better able to deal with employee resistance to change. They can reduce resistance by presenting recommendations and information in a timely and orderly fashion.

Change agents can also address resistance by using the resistance resolution method. This can be thought of as a set of skills to govern conflict. The resistance resolution method is a constructive process for handling emotion-laden disagreements between change agents and employees. Its purpose is to bring to the surface underlying fears that cause resistance, so employees can understand and accept the proposed change (Gilley, 1998). This technique stresses assertive communication and sharing feelings. It does not permit the typical free-for-all attitude that blocks creative resolution. The resistance resolution method consists of acknowledging and clarifying resistance, problem solving, and confirming the solution (Gilley, 1998).

### Acknowledging Resistance

Acknowledging resistance is the first step in the resistance resolution method. This is critical because change agents and employees must be willing to agree that arguing and fighting over their differences of opinion will accomplish very little. Thus, acknowledging resistance helps with controlling emotions and feelings associated with differences of opinion.

Acknowledging resistance consists of two activities: listening and sharing. First, listen carefully to what an employee is saying. Remember, most emotion-laden statements made by employees are a way of verbalizing excessive tension or fear. However, the very process of converting tension into words serves to reduce the tension, even if the words themselves do not actually reveal its nature or the reason for it. Second, sharing is a form of support. Effective change agents demonstrate that they understand how the employees are feeling. When they are not surprised or upset by employees' negative statements, they can deal better with the tension of disagreement. They remain calm and neutral, not doing or saying anything to increase tension or fear.

Consider the following communications tactic when addressing resistance to change. Learn the other side's story. Listening to your employee can be not only a proactive technique for resistance management but also a way of diffusing resistance. As you listen, avoid the temptation to interrupt with clarifications and corrections. A colleague once suggested that asking the "why" question five times in a row is a way of truly driving an issue down to its root cause as well as a way of not jumping to conclusions too soon. If something is not clear, encourage employees to give you specific examples that illustrate their issues.

A simple yet effective communication technique is to acknowledge the pressures and concerns the employee is experiencing. If possible, share and reflect on similar situations you have encountered on your change journey. In many cases, what they are feeling today is very similar to what you experienced earlier in the project. By reflecting on the techniques that you used to overcome the same concerns and doubts, you gain credibility as a sensitive and caring change agent.

When you detect resistance, assess it from that employee's frame of reference. Perhaps your expectations are unclear. The individual may not yet understand the outcomes, either because the outcome is yet to be determined or the employee doubts the outcome's likely success. In some cases, the employee is right to expect some negative side effects, and you need to help them sort through their emotions to identify the potential positive impacts they might realize. Help them identify realistic alternatives for reacting to the change.

### Clarifying Resistance

Next, you clarify the employees' thinking so they are willing to receive new and logical information. Even when employees understand their true emotions, few are ready to reveal them. Employees learn to cover them up with plausible reasons, explanations, and justifications, all designed to prove that they are acting in a well-thought-out and logical manner. In a word, they *rationalize* their behavior.

When addressing negative statements, learning how to make the employee's words lose force without making him or her lose face is the real challenge you face. Asking nonthreatening questions can do this. Thus, you grasp a better understanding of your employees' negative statements. Ask them to give you examples that illustrate their point of view. Encourage them to discuss their perspectives in greater detail so they can figure out their meaning more clearly.

### Problem Solving

Once you have clarified a negative statement, you are ready to actually address the resistance by using critical information and evidence. Using problem-solving techniques, which include identifying the problem and solutions to the problem, analyzing them, and selecting one best does this.

### Confirming the Answer

The last step of the resistance resolution method consists of mutually working out solutions to employees' concerns. This includes implementing a solution and evaluating it. When resolution is reached, you must make certain your employees are committed to taking action to address the resistance, which can be accomplished by asking for an immediate commitment that reinforces the employees' willingness to accept the solution.

## Conclusion

You need to encourage employees to participate in decisions that encourage long-term change, at the same time discouraging activities that feed ravenous appetites for resistance. By understanding the change curve and its implications, you can dramatically affect the types of decisions that will be made during the change process. Additionally, an understanding of resistance strategies and the resistance resolution method can reduce stress, so common during change. Thus, you and your employees can experience change is a more positive and developmental way.

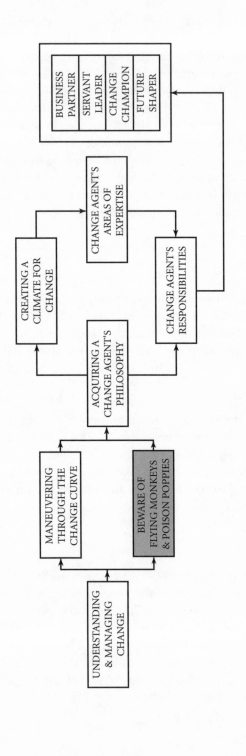

THE MANAGER AS CHANGE AGENT BLUEPRINT

Boxes in the diagram (read in flow order):

UNDERSTANDING & MANAGING CHANGE

MANEUVERING THROUGH THE CHANGE CURVE

BEWARE OF FLYING MONKEYS & POISON POPPIES

ACQUIRING A CHANGE AGENT'S PHILOSOPHY

CREATING A CLIMATE FOR CHANGE

CHANGE AGENT'S AREAS OF EXPERTISE

CHANGE AGENT'S RESPONSIBILITIES

BUSINESS PARTNER
SERVANT LEADER
CHANGE CHAMPION
FUTURE SHAPER

# Beware of Flying Monkeys and Poison Poppies

In *The Wizard of Oz,* Dorothy and her friends encountered a number of characters along the Yellow Brick Road that turned out to be much less frightening and dangerous than they first suspected (e.g., the crab apple trees in the forest). In fact, in many cases, those they feared turned out to be their friends (the Munchkins and the Good Witch Glinda). This was also the case with the flying monkeys, who were indeed a frightening force, but who, in the end, supported Dorothy. This chapter will address the issue of flying monkeys and the lure of the poison poppies, helping you not only to identify barriers to change but to manage them and protect yourself from them.

## What Are Flying Monkeys, Anyway?

Flying monkeys are those unexpected characters, events, and situations that jump out and attack you at the most untimely moments. Unlike perceived fears, flying monkeys are real . . . and they can make or break your success as a change agent. Flying monkeys can attack at any time. The attack can take place as early as the first meeting with your employees. Most often, flying monkeys attack during the implementation of a change initiative, usually just when you are thinking to yourself how well things are going. Perhaps the most frustrating flying monkey attacks take place after the change initiative has concluded, when you run the risk of seeing any positive outcomes from the change initiative destroyed, leaving your good reputation and that of your employees in shreds.

Flying monkeys aren't always people. They can show themselves in behaviors, unexpected and unanticipated situations, and attitudes. These attacks can be subtle, subliminal, or open, flagrant attempts to chastise or embarrass you in public.

In any change initiative, flying monkeys are inevitable and represent degrees and levels of resistance you should expect to encounter in any major change effort. Realistically, if you want to move any significant change in ideology or activity forward, you should expect resistance, differences of opinion, and diverse perspectives about how, when, and why to proceed. The sooner you find these flying monkeys and meet them head-on, the sooner you can make progress toward your desired goal.

The bottom line is that you had better be wary if you don't sense any resistance or problems and think that you're out of the woods and flying monkey-free. They're out there somewhere . . . hiding, lurking, just waiting to attack. Expect and assess the degrees of resistance you will encounter. You need to expose the resistance so you can manage and minimize the potential negative impacts.

But why not ignore the flying monkeys and pretend they don't exist? Why not play the waiting game and see if the flying monkeys give up? Because they won't go away! In most cases, the flying monkeys will only multiply and become more threatening and dangerous. These conflicts must be resolved or managed constructively so that individual, team, and organizational performance can be maintained. By not dealing directly with the flying monkeys in a timely and effective way, you run the risk of dramatically diminishing the respect others have for you, and that will have long-term ramifications for your ongoing success in an organization.

There are four broad strategies for dealing with flying monkeys—the same strategies that proved to be invaluable for Dorothy and her friends. These strategies will be discussed in great detail later in this book, but keep the book's central theme in mind as you embark on your journey of change. As a change agent, you will need:

- Brains (the knowledge and skills to be a legitimate business partner, Chapter 9)
- Heart (the sensitivity and sensibility to be a caring and personable leader, Chapter 10)
- Courage (the strength to lead change as you know it should be led, Chapter 11)
- Vision (the wisdom, visualization, and passion to help build a new and better future, Chapter 12)

Just as the Tin Man carried his oilcan as a survival tool, so should you pack essential survival strategies in your tool kit (think of this as your oversize monkey wrench), for use in fighting the flying monkeys that inevitably can block or alter achievement of your vision.

## Types of Flying Monkeys

Flying monkeys come in all shapes, sorts, and sizes. They can be people, events, activities, and attitudes. The rest of this chapter discusses types of flying monkeys, their identifying features, and how to recognize them.

### The Cultural Flying Monkey

Perhaps the most important potential flying monkey for you to be aware of is the cultural flying monkey. As discussed previously, culture is defined as the underlying beliefs, values, and assumptions held by members of an organization and the practices and behaviors that exemplify and reinforce them. In other words, "the way we do things around here." Some aspects of organizational culture are easy to observe. Other aspects, such as assumptions, values, and core beliefs, are harder to observe. There are seven indicators of organizational culture that include relevant constructs, facts, practices, vocabulary, metaphors, stories, and rites and rituals (Deal and Kennedy, 2000).

Since organizational culture tugs at the very heartstrings of employees, it is oftentimes the most difficult barrier to overcome when leading a change effort. All too frequently the official culture, as reflected in glossy brochures, framed mission statements, and official employee handbooks, is far different from what is actually practiced by employees or perceived by external employees. It is critical, therefore, to conduct a "culture check" to compare and validate the official culture of an organization against the perceptions of the culture that are held by those within and outside the organization. Recognize that much of the true culture may be hidden beneath the surface, invisible to the occasional visitor. Subcultures can be as subtle as the way people dress or the vocabulary they use. If you're observant, you should be able to identify employee behavior and actions that give you the look and feel of the organization. You can then compare and contrast what you see, hear, and observe with what you have been officially told through printed documents and official corporate wordspeak.

When first investigating a change opportunity, your initial mission is to learn as much as you can about the workforce (employees) with whom you will be working. Your task is to attain a clear sense of the organization's history, growth, economic challenges, current mission and purpose, and goals and objectives for the fiscal year. You will also want to make certain that you have a knowledge of your organization's current and future products and services.

Try to get some sense of the group's history from its beginning to where it has been in the past year. How smooth or turbulent has this history been? How has the group succeeded or failed in previous attempts at large implementation efforts that involved change? Always remember: Future implementation success is directly related to previous implementation results. As you assess the implementation history, ask what could have been done differently with unsuccessful and successful attempts? What contributed to successful implementations?

Get some historical perspective on how this group of employees has previously worked with other managers, both successfully and unsuccessfully. Analyze what contributed to those successes and failures. More important, do a "reality check" on that history: How much of what you hear about the working relationship with other managers is hearsay versus reality? If there is any history of previous problems or dissatisfaction with managers, what were the symptoms and the probable causes? Can you identify whether the employees approached previous managers from the perspective of employees working together, or did the employees enter the arrangement with an adversarial stance?

Keep in mind that if employees perceive they have been victimized in the past, they will no doubt hesitate the next time. Have they developed a negative perspective based on one bad incident or unacceptable situation? Did they enter into the previous arrangement with unrealistic expectations? What extenuating circumstances might have created problems for the employee, the manager, or both?

By doing some background analysis of this situation, you should have a better idea of the employees' hot buttons. Try to gain some advance sense of the employees' tolerance level. You obviously don't want to repeat the mistakes of those who have walked the Yellow Brick Road before you. If, based upon your cultural analysis, you believe the employees were responsible for the majority of the problems encountered in previous change situations, you at least have some idea of what to look for and what to avoid as you begin your relationship with these employees.

### The Organizational Leader Flying Monkey

Once you have some sense of the overall culture and climate of the organization, you should then focus on examining the personality of the organization's leaders. What roles does the leader envision for you as a change agent? Is the leader looking for a subordinate type of relationship, where you, the change agent, will be viewed as a lesser being—an outsider here to complete a mission, then move on? Or does the leader desire a partner/associate type of relationship, whereby you work on a peer-to-peer basis and where the relationship may extend well into the future?

In many cases, the organizational leader will clearly identify the need for a team approach. But be sure that they are not just saying what you want to hear versus what the reality will be. Try to get the leader to clearly define what a "team" is. Can the leader give you some examples of previous successes they have had that exemplify good teamwork? How closely does the employees' description of teamwork match what you expect of a team—a group of people committed to achieving a common purpose that requires each member's individual contribution and mutual cooperation?

Chances are that the first person with whom you will visit is the "official" sponsor (see Chapter 2), the one who holds the license for formal power. It might be the great-and-all-powerful Wizard in the Land of Oz (who, in reality, wasn't really that powerful!). But don't assume that the actual power begins and ends with this singular "important" person.

Identify others in the group who currently exercise formal powers (Chapter 2). Who are they? What are their titles and roles? What are the specific areas for which they are held accountable and for which they have decisionmaking power? What are the expectations for involvement through this change initiative—both from the perspective of the formal leader as well as these individuals?

You want to align with the person(s) who already holds sufficient formal power in the organization to be able to fight successfully for your proposals (coaches, see Chapter 2). Who is going to own and champion this change initiative, to clear obstacles from your path? Who will help ensure implementation of your recommendations?

Also look for leaders who can help you in times of crisis and who can provide you with an effective and delicate balance of guidance, direction, and freedom. When seeking your Good Witch Glinda, look for leaders who hold enough power to help you achieve your goals without getting in your way, typically a sponsor and champion.

## The Organizational Flying Monkey

The organizational flying monkey refers to any of the need-to-know groups or individuals whose importance doesn't necessarily jump out on an official organizational chart. You are looking beyond the name or names of the few official leader-managers just discussed. Organizational flying monkeys are the people who hold informal power, who, in actuality, may be *more* powerful than those who hold the official titles (such as technical analysts, see Chapter 2). To identify them, you need to conduct a subtle investigation and background check. Such individuals frequently have significant impact on the way an organization is run day to day. Who are they? What is their history? How did they get this informal power? Of what significance is this informal power in the overall operation of the organization?

*Who's Who?*  First, figure out how far down the organizational ladder power is exercised in making decisions, negotiating details, and approving changes in plans. In some organizations, albeit not the ideal majority we would like to see, formal leaders give their employees a great amount of autonomy and freedom to make decisions that are in the best interest of the organization, avoiding a long chain of bureaucratic power struggles. In other organizations, once you've identified the formal leader or management team that's where the buck (and the power) stop. At this stage, you are trying to identify all the individuals who have legitimate credibility throughout the organization or at least among major clusters of employees.

Take every opportunity to identify and meet as many individuals within the organization as may be involved with your change initiative or who have some vested interest in the change initiative's outcome. Identify their names, official (and unofficial) roles, and relationships to others within the organization. Then consider applying the following rating scale, based on your initial research and meetings, to determine how critical each individual will be to your overall success in the change initiative. This effort should not take a lot of time; there is nothing scientific at this point. It serves as your initial attempt to assess just how strong (or weak) the support and alignment are on the part of those with whom you will be working. For all the individuals you meet, rate them using the following scale:

5 = critical to your success
4 = necessary to your success
3 = important to your success
2 = helpful to your success
1 = minimal impact on your success

Once identified, you can rank the individuals' importance from the most critical to the least.

*Who Does What?*  As you examine the different types of power that exist within your organization, you may be surprised at how much "power" is actually exercised at various levels and among various roles within your organization that fall outside the "official" list provided to you by the leader.

The four primary types of power that typically exist and should be examined are

- Position power: legitimate authority
- Personal power: influences the behavior of others
- Resource power: controls resources—time, money, people, information
- Relationship power: networks with and knows others

Keep in mind that as you identify the various players and roles, you are trying to build a complementary relationship versus a takeover or replacement. Be very careful to establish this premise with everyone you meet, to avoid individuals perceiving you as a threat. Every time you are introduced to another individual within your organization, ask yourself, "How can this person I am meeting with help me be more productive, effective, or efficient?" At the same time, ask yourself, "What information, resource, support, or help can I reciprocate with that will benefit the person I've just met?" This will make the relationship mutually beneficial.

*Who's Destined to Be a Rising Star?* Once you've familiarized yourself with the various power brokers within the organization, take a moment to also identify the up-and-comers—*the rising stars*. A rising star is a person whose experience is limited, although you have complete confidence in their "potential abilities." Under this condition, you work closely with the employee by training him or her and assigning tasks to be completed, providing positive and constructive feedback about performance. Developing a mentor-mentee relationship is most appropriate when working with this type of employee. Further, get a sense for who is aligned with whom. Who seems to have the most immediate and frequent access to those with formal power? Who seems to be playing the role of "understudy"—individuals ready to seize the opportunity to leap on stage at a moment's notice?

You will need to be familiar with the organizational chart so that you can meet as many of the future influencers within the employee's organization as you possibly can. Make a shortlist of the five or six most influential people in the part of the organization with which you will be working. Again, these people may not necessarily be part of the official change initiative team. They may not serve any formal roles. They may not even be considered an "official" sponsor, technical analyst, or applier, in the traditional sense of those words.

However, these individuals may very well serve in any of these respective roles someday and you may need their support at that time. Think about the possibility of inviting these individuals to occasional informal lunch meetings. Keep them updated on the progress of the change initiative team. Perhaps you can send a complimentary copy of your reports to these key people. When appropriate, consider asking them for their advice or feedback. In fact, rising stars may very well be able to keep you apprised of the pulse of the overall employee base, the overall mood of the Munchkins, so to speak. This is something that is all too frequently overlooked once you are deep in the heart of a change initiative. More in-depth details and ideas about ways to keep this group aligned as your allies will help you achieve your vision and objectives.

*What's What?* As a part of your organizational analysis, you will want to get a sense of the work climate and environment in which you will be working. The first time you walk through the offices and cubes, take note of and remember the general atmosphere within the work environment. Is it eerily quiet? Do you hear occasional friendly banter over cubicle walls? If you encounter employees in the halls, do they acknowledge your presence with a smile or greeting or do they look so deep in thought (or stress) that you step aside to let them pass?

Just like formal and informal power, every workplace has behavioral guidelines that are both written and unwritten. These guidelines identify the acceptable and unacceptable behaviors that dictate the way employees, and eventually you, are expected to conduct your business. First, examine your written policies and guidelines. These can include departmental procedures for day-to-day operations, including arrival and departure times, and the degree of freedom allowed employees in determining their daily schedules. How are problems handled? What if there are interruptions to the daily, routine work?

But what about the unwritten guidelines? How do you ever get a "copy" of them? You will learn about these as a result of watching and listening closely to your employees as they go about their daily tasks. You will quickly get a sense of how they operate as a team and what they deem as appropriate behavior for interpersonal relationships. Is humor common within this work environment? Compare and contrast actual behavior to the official, written guidelines. How closely do they match? How closely are individuals monitored and held accountable for operating within these guidelines? What goes on, officially and unofficially, regarding such things as time tracking, lunch and coffee break schedules, informal gatherings, and the way meetings are conducted?

You will also want to identify the key functions within the organization and who officially manages these functions. Who is held accountable for the success of these functions? How formal or informal are the rules, procedures, and guidelines for calling meetings, for obtaining office supplies, for taking time off? Unfamiliarity with the written and unwritten rules of organizational conduct invites attack by "flying monkeys," such as those who are just looking for an excuse to criticize you or to find fault.

*Technologically Speaking.* A critical area to observe today is the role that technology plays within your organization. Technology can become a flying monkey when you attempt to use it in ways that run counter to the "norm" within the organization. How tied to technology are the functions and roles of individuals in the organization? Is e-mail considered the official and preferred way to communicate internally? How much is e-mail used as simply a way to CYA (cover your assets) versus a legitimate way to record and track change initiative details? How up-to-date are the technology assets (both hardware and software) within this part of the organization? Are the employees using technology to effectively manage the details of their work, or is it simply an awkward stumbling block that is used just because it exists?

What are the official rules and guidelines related to the use of technology, as compared with the actual behaviors and practices of the employees? Does the organization encourage the use of the Internet, for instance, as a business tool, or does it view its use as just another way to divert employee time and attention from doing "real work"? How much do employees use e-mail and the Internet for personal use during company time? How does this compare and contrast with any official guidelines for use of technology?

By doing some subtle undercover investigations as well as simple observations, you can identify how closely aligned the actual behaviors, practices, and attitudes of employees are with the official change initiatives image that is provided to you by organizational leaders. Just as you will uncover informal leaders within the organization who can have significant impact in your success or failure, so also will you begin to realize how important it is to know the formal and informal, the written and unwritten practices and behavior that will play a critical part in your journey down the Yellow Brick Road.

## Behavior and Attitude Flying Monkeys

Some of the more irritating flying monkeys you might encounter during the change initiative may come from individuals who don't necessarily hold a great deal of either formal or informal power. But these seemingly harmless creatures, through their behaviors and attitudes, can have a persuasive and negative impact on the rest of the change initiative team, or on you and your reputation as a change leader.

Like the proverbial wolf in sheep's clothing, flying monkeys oftentimes cleverly disguise themselves, so be prepared for the flying monkeys that don't immediately look like flying monkeys. For example, someone may be particularly silent at your team meetings, never asking questions or offering suggestions. Don't assume their silence is agreement and support. This individual could be the first to criticize you when among peers as soon as your back is turned. Consider "inviting" this individual into a dialogue or conversation. Ask him what he thinks about the decision that was just made at the meeting. You won't necessarily encounter or identify them in any of your initial analysis or introductory meetings. Most times, they will appear once you have engaged in the change initiative and are already well under way.

At all times, carefully examine the nature of these flying monkeys when you first encounter them. How dangerous is the behavior and attitude flying monkey in reality? In some cases, you may perceive more danger than actually exists. In *The Wizard of Oz,* the crabapple trees in the forest seemed perfectly harmless. In fact, it was only after Dorothy and her cohorts picked an apple from a tree that they realized that the trees would protest with threats. Rather than panic and run or give up on the journey, the scarecrow, with a bit of ingenuity and some carefully spoken words, cajoled the trees into freely tossing their apples to Dorothy and her team—which was all they wanted in the first place. Likewise, who would have thought that a simple snowfall would cause the Tin Man to rust? By being careful not to panic, Dorothy remembered that she already had the appropriate defense, the oilcan, to get the team back on course.

The moral of these tales is to be aware that a number of negative characters, attitudes, and behaviors can, and most likely will, pop up during the change journey. Review the following classifications of flying monkeys and the potential danger they can inflict on your efforts. In many of these cases, you can't do anything in advance to ward off these attacks. Moreover, by remaining calm and thinking before you become defensive or panic, you can take simple steps that offset the potential damage that flying monkeys may inflict.

Always remember that there are real flying monkeys that pose significant threats to your success. And there are the more invisible flying monkeys that may simply require some clever thinking and actions (Figure 4.1). Keep your emotions and behavior in balance at all times, choosing to "fight" the big battles . . . and to adjust to the less significant issues.

| The flying monkey | Characteristics | The danger |
|---|---|---|
| Clueless | Doesn't have a clue for what to do. | When completely at a loss, most likely unable to properly specify what he/she needs or expects in terms of deliverables. This makes it more difficult for you to effectively "meet the expectations" of your employee. |
| Rubber Stamper | In search of affirmation and validation; already "knows" the answer or what he wants the answer to be. Tell me what I already know; back me up on this; help me build consensus among those who just don't get it yet! | The affirmation you're being asked to provide may very well NOT be for best or correct approach. You run the risk of doing considerable harm to your reputation if you align with a strategy that is not ultimately in the best interest of the organization. |
| Nitpicker | Continually dwells on minute details and issues that frequently have little, if any, impact on the overall success of a change initiative. Frequently is positioned in the resistance portion of the change curve, using nitpicking details as a way to delay or offset the change. | By allowing them to delay the progress of the change initiative or a discussion, you may lose the interest and support of other team members. You will want to build in a place for them to change or contribute without damaging your plan/proposal. |
| Blamer | Wants someone else to do the dirty work for them, allowing someone else to be the "fall guy." May be someone who sees you as the source for figuring out how they got into this mess in the first place, to help them identify someone to "blame" versus help them identify and actually fix the problem. | Spending time with a blamer, trying to identify a source for blame, is counterproductive, unless you take the next step, which is to identify a solution. |
| Challenger/Tester | Gives you an unbelievable (and perhaps unachievable) task or goal with no apparent purpose, just to see how you cope. Frequently plays the game of psyching out. | These individuals feel the need to "test " you before you win their respect and support. Can be very supportive of you if you do successfully pass their test. You may need to engage in their game playing at first, but will also need to know when it's time to call their bluff. |
| The guru | Believes he or she already knows the answers before you have even identified the problem. | Increases the risk of setting off power struggles. This person may continually try to convince others that you add no value to the change initiative, that you are bringing nothing to the table that he/she doesn't already know. |
| Quick fixer | "Dismisses" the manager too soon; think they know what they need to know before they really do. Sees detailed analysis as a waste of time, energy, and money. | In looking for quick, cheap, and easy answers, they attempt to apply a bandage when you are recommending major surgery. |
| Procrastinator | Avoids making decisions. Continually delays critical steps in achieving progress, many times out of fear of the unknown or fear to make commitments. May require excessive documentation and record keeping that is more time consuming than it is valuable. | Can evolve into analysis paralysis. |
| Hired hand/grunt | Doesn't look for a partner to help determine a strategy and solution as much as simply another body to get the job done. | If you allow yourself to become the hired hand, you will lose credibility as someone who can provide solutions and be a partner in achieving success. |
| Techno-nerd | Sees technology as the solution for every problem. Rarely values any analysis of the problem, but prefers to immediately identify a solution that includes purchase and implementation of a technology-based solution. | Can result in solutions that are totally inappropriate or excessive. |

FIGURE 4.1  Miscellaneous Flying Monkeys

## Flying Monkey Business

So far, the flying monkeys we've discussed have been people, ranging from people in positions of formal to informal authority, as well as the behaviors and attitudes found within organizations. Actually, it may be easier to fight flying monkeys in the form of people, simply because they are real, visible bodies with whom we can associate behavior and attitudes. For many, the next set of flying monkeys presents a greater challenge, since they are not necessarily tangible and concrete people or things. In any given change initiative, there is a strong likelihood that at least one or more of the following will attack: unanticipated events, changes in change initiative scope, and changes in resources.

### Unanticipated Events

Given the rate of change in today's organization, chances are that the circumstances surrounding the initiation of a change initiative will not remain stable throughout its life. Unanticipated events can include anything from a change in people assigned to the change initiative to changes in the business need that initially prompted the change initiative.

You can count on at least one change in the staffing, for instance, which can occur at the leadership level or among the members of the actual team. Any change in leadership will impact the degree of active support you receive, at least in the short term. It is critical, therefore, that you conduct another stakeholder analysis to help you reevaluate your overall strategies and approaches (see Chapter 2). If the change occurs in the leadership ranks, immediately identify what role this leader (or leaders) played in your overall strategy. Was that leader considered to be your primary sponsor or advocate? If so, what's your fallback plan? If the parting leader was truly fulfilling an active sponsorship role, that individual should be willing to help you identify a replacement sponsor. Use this leader to help you realign the roles and responsibilities to ensure a smooth transition.

If the change occurs among the change initiative team membership, assess the impact that the absence of this individual will have on your overall change initiative. Also assess the impact that will be felt among the rest of the team. Is this perceived as a "good" or a "bad" thing? What roles and responsibilities did this individual hold? Who else might be able to take on some of those roles? A change in only one member of a team can change the dynamics and relationships of the entire team.

In the best of all possible worlds, at the very beginning of the change initiative you would already have identified the few critical areas where you cannot afford to lose certain talents, skills, and knowledge. In this ideal situation, you would already have in place an appropriate back-up plan with understudies already in place, so that minimal disruption would occur. But because of limited and already-stressed resources, in the more frequent scenario you will be forced to use a more reactive than proactive approach.

In this case, identify the realignments or changes in others' assignments that need to occur to minimize disruption to the change initiative. Perhaps one of the best ways to assess this impact and to make adjustments is to involve the rest of the team in identifying the next steps. Team members will frequently and willingly step forward to take on additional tasks and roles, in the interest of the change initiative, but perhaps also for their own self-promotion and development. In many cases, what first appears as potential trouble and disaster can turn into genuine growth opportunities for the rest of the team. The critical link in all this is you and the positive leadership and direction you provide to implement any necessary changes in assignments, strategy, or approach.

Another event that is certainly out of your control is the structural changes and reorganization that take place as a results of mergers and acquisitions. Once again, your role as change agent is to quickly assess the situation and its short- and long-term impact on your employees and to work closely with your sources of power and support to keep the change initiative on target, as much as is possible given the circumstances.

This is a case where, if you have effectively built an internal "grapevine" among the formal and informal leaders, you may have advance warning of the flying monkey attacks. The more connected you are to sources of valid information, the more proactively you can make adjustments in a timely manner. Your ability to stay well connected and linked within the formal and informal power structures of an organization can only enhance the image others will have of you. As a result, they will see you as someone who is able to either avoid crisis situations, or, at the very least, as a person who has the ability to address related issues calmly and effectively, with little loss of time and energy.

### Adjustments in Change Initiative Scope

There is probably no one who has escaped the flying monkey of scope creep, where the magnitude of change initiative deliverables increases with no additional provision of resources. Unfortunately, most scope creep is subtle. It slithers, almost invisibly, into the final list of change initiative expectations and is rarely clearly identified and stated. In many cases, scope creep is not necessarily an outward attempt to try to get more freebies out of you. It is more the result of the employees becoming excited about the prospects of the change initiative once they begin to see the positive impacts it might have on their business. You don't want to stifle that enthusiasm, but you certainly want to prepare your employees for potential negative impacts.

Once again, given the perfect change initiative scenario, you would have already prepared and delivered a document that identifies specific deliverables, time lines, and resource plans. The appropriate power sources would have signed off on the document. Any change in change initiative scope would then require a review and rewriting of the overall change initiative plan. Be prepared to present at least a couple of alternative scenarios, with the emphasis on your willingness to provide leadership in making this a win-win situation for everyone.

One alternative may be to reprioritize the deliverables. If you are being asked to add more to the overall deliverables, what is the possibility that some of the initial deliverables are no longer important or at least could be delayed? This is certainly a situation where your negotiation skills will come in handy.

## Changes in Resources

Resources are defined as the people, money, tools, time, and deliverables associated with completion of a change initiative. Rarely will you have the luxury of completing a change initiative in which there is not some adjustment in resources. Even more rarely will that change in resources take the form of *additional* people, time, and money dedicated to the change initiative. In other words, this flying monkey attacks by taking away one or more of the critical resources you originally projected as necessary to the completion of a successful change initiative.

Use the logic of the resource triangle to help you manage the discussion around changes in resources. For instance, if you are told that you will be expected to complete the change initiative sooner than anticipated, the "time" line shortens on the triangle. To maintain a triangle, you then need to increase the cost line (increase the number of people assigned to the change initiative or perhaps purchase an off-the-shelf solution that can be implemented faster), reduce the quality (reduce the quantity of deliverable), or both.

If you are told that the overall resources will be reduced, for example, the number of people assigned to the change initiative will be reduced, you then need to discuss the need for additional time to complete the change initiative, a reduction in quality and deliverables, or both. In all cases, your discussions

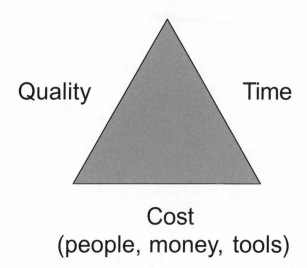

Quality Time

Cost
(people, money, tools)

FIGURE 4.2    Elements of Any Change Initiative

will focus on the concept that one side of the triangle cannot be changed without appropriate adjustments being made to the remaining sides.

### Flying Monkeys Can Be a Good Thing... Really!

We've spent considerable time warning you about flying monkeys, offering ways to prevent their attacks or to lesson the damage done when they strike. We've warned you against becoming defensive and employing aggressive, get-even tactics. Now we ask you to think about flying monkey attacks as something with potentially positive consequences. Such attacks are not necessarily a direct route to disaster and trouble.

Identifying and dealing with flying monkeys can actually help you reap benefits, including the following:

- You may gain more and better ideas, simply from listening to the flying monkeys and reflecting on the attacks to gather "lessons learned."
- A flying monkey attack can prompt you to search for alternative approaches, which many times may help you reap better results than the original plan envisioned.
- It is possible that you may be the first person within a group that actually addresses the issues of change and encourages individuals to clearly state their resistance. As a result, you may discover that other,

older issues and problems might surface and can actually be resolved in the process.

- Encouraging others to become involved in the change process frequently results in improved creativity and innovation within an organization. Once they've been encouraged to come forth and participate in the change process, people who were previously silent frequently can achieve surprising results. Certainly you will see a greater involvement in problem solving, ownership, and commitment to solutions once you've successfully involved others.
- Every time you fight a flying monkey, you have an opportunity to clarify personal interests, values, and expectations. You may find yourself continually refining the vision statement to the point where everyone has a better understanding of the value and impact of the change.
- The entire process of managing flying monkeys can enhance your personal development and growth in areas like problem resolution, communication, interpersonal relationships, and change leadership. Certainly, that can lead to increased respect from your colleagues and superiors, but even more important, increased self-respect.

By managing resistance, dealing directly with flying monkey attacks, and affecting more win-win resolutions, you have ample opportunities to build stronger relationships throughout an organization. Think about the flying monkeys in the story of Oz. They went from attacking and fighting Dorothy and her friends to actually thanking her in the end, when the witch was dead. Their strains of "Hail to Dorothy" acknowledged a newfound partnership and positive relationship. Your flying monkeys can become your future allies.

## Flying Monkey Management

So you can now recognize flying monkeys and you see them flying toward you . . . *now what do you do?* You have several immediate options for short-term protection from the flying monkeys of resistance.

You can ignore them, but probably not for long. The reality is that you can pretend only for a very short time that there are no negative reactions to your change initiatives. The reality of any significant change is resistance. The sooner you accept this fact and face the resistance, the sooner you can get people focused on helping you achieve positive outcomes. "Accept [resistance] as unresolved tension that needs to be understood and to be channeled in a positive direction" (Bell, 1996).

You can fight back by scolding and lecturing those who resist, by telling people to get over it, by telling them how inappropriate their behavior and words are. This is not a good out-of-the-gate approach to deal with resistance. In fact, you run the risk of reinforcing negative feelings and driving them underground, which only prolongs the resistance to your vision.

Whatever you do, do *not* react to significant signs of resistance. Some leaders wait for permission to move forward and address the issues. Rarely do real change leaders "think first and foremost about what they can and cannot do, who they can and cannot call, or how they can or cannot propose an idea" (Katzenbach, 1995, 41). Instead, first identify the right thing to do and who you should involve to accomplish it.

## Models and Techniques for Managing Flying Monkeys

Consider the following two models as simple yet effective tools that will help you collect constructive feedback from those affected by and involved in the change initiative.

Model 1.

- State the change initiative management objectives clearly and up-front
- What went well (and should be repeated)?
- What could have been done differently?
- From the target's frame of reference, was this change initiative a success?
- How do we know?
- Were the original change initiative objectives met, both technical and human?
- What type of formal reporting or closure is needed?
- What rewards or celebrations are required?

Model 2. A very simple model employs three words: Start, Stop, and Continue. Ask your stakeholders to identify any specifics that fall into each of these categories:

If we were to engage in another change initiative of this type,

1. What would you recommend we *start* to do?
2. What would you recommend we *stop* doing?
3. What would you recommend we *continue* to do?

The answers to these questions can provide a wealth of practical information and ideas that will help you assess the success of your initiative and provide you with useful information for your next change venture.

Finally, some common courtesies will help control flying monkeys and prevent their attacks:

- Return phone calls and respond to e-mail messages as quickly as possible.
- Arrive to meetings on time.
- Answer correspondence as soon as you can.
- Carbon copy significant others as a courtesy.
- Tell the truth.
- Deliver on promises.
- Maintain a sense of humor (take charge of your morale and attitude).
- Maintain an upbeat and enthusiastic attitude.
- Balance flexibility with firmness.

### Reflection and Self-Assessment

Any time you have surfaced and fought flying monkeys, take the time to engage in evaluation, seeking input and feedback from your employees and stakeholders. Too often, we simply end a change initiative and begin the next, never taking the time to reflect on our lessons learned. As a result, we lose valuable opportunities to grow personally and professionally and risk becoming burnt out and bitter. At the conclusion of a change initiative, ask yourself and others the following questions:

- What do I need to know or be able to do differently or better?
- How will I benefit from what I learn?
- How will my learning benefit my team or my organization?
- What actions do I need to take?
- What do I need to learn?
- What resources do I need?
- What might interfere (time, resources, individuals, change initiatives)?
- What time line and target dates will I set for my self-improvement activities?
- How will I measure my progress?

# The Lure of the Poison Poppies

As Dorothy, the Tin Man, the Cowardly Lion, and the Scarecrow were on their way along the Yellow Brick Road, they came upon a fragrant and beautiful field of scarlet poppies. Their path distinctly led around the field of poppies, but they could already see their destination, the Emerald City, on the far side of the field. They wondered, "Why go all the way around, when it looked so much faster and more pleasant to run through the poppy field?" What could possibly go wrong? They believed that the faster they got to their destination the quicker their personal needs could be gratified. Readers who remember this classic tale know that something did go wrong. Being seduced by the promise of a quick fix, Dorothy and her friends left the Yellow Brick Road and ran rapidly across the field of scarlet poppies. They soon fell prey to the poison poppies lying in wait for their next victim, which is so typical of a shortcut to one's destination. Luckily for the Oz characters, the Good Witch Glinda was watching over them and she lifted the spell of the poppies. Unfortunately, as a change agent, you can't count on anyone else to bail you out of the poor decisions that you make.

## Quick Fixes

Everyone loves quick fixes. Change agents, employees, organizational leaders, and senior managers alike enjoy the idea of an easy, quick solution to their problems. They save time and money. They make everyone look good. Or do they? What is a quick fix? A quick fix is a rapidly applied solution to an easily identifiable and politically visible problem. It does not take a committee or a team of people to study the problem. The solution is easy to determine.

Throughout the change initiative process, there will be opportunities for shortcuts, quick fixes, and temporary, Band-Aid, solutions that appear to be every wizard's magic answers. The allure of these quick fixes will be quite tempting. They are often easily sold to and accepted by employees and the organization. After all, everyone likes the home-run solution, the one thing that will fix everything quickly and without much effort, pain, or cost. For example, many organizations identify communications as a serious problem because it prevents them from achieving their strategic business goals. As a way of correcting this dilemma, many organizations elect to provide training for their employees to improve their interpersonal skills. This is a typical quick fix because it ignores other complex systems that interfere with communications, such as the organizational structure, culture, mission and strategy, job design, managerial practices, and work climate and the performance management, compensation, and learning systems. Unless these systems are examined and correction made to improve their interaction and integration, communications will never improve.

Beware! Although these easy answers look inviting, most will weaken your overall effectiveness as a change agent, and some can ultimately damage your credibility with your employees and organizational leaders. You must make every effort to develop and implement a well-thought-out plan to which both you and your employees commit to and adhere. Do not be lured into taking the shortcut and running through the beautiful, fragrant poppy field when you see the desired goal just on the other side. The poison in those poppies can interfere with, slow down, or even end your progress toward the goal.

## The Legitimate Quick Fix

There are occasions when a legitimate quick fix is appropriate. In fact, you can greatly enhance your credibility and increase the comfort level of your employees by applying a quick fix as soon as possible in the beginning stages of your change process (see Chapter 2).

How do you determine when a quick fix is legitimate? Any time you are in the initial stages of a change initiative certain hot issues will surface. Some will be major obstacles and cannot be solved with a quick solution. Others will be problems that can be easily fixed but are so insignificant or so limited in their scope that a solution would either go unnoticed or be of little importance to most people. What you need to identify is a problem that affects a large number of people and one in which a quick solution is viable and will be visible to most of the group with which you are working.

For example, at a mid-size insurance company, a list of barriers to efficient work flow was discussed early in the change process and a quick fix was identified. A very hot topic for some time had been the lack of communication between the insurance employees and the computer programmers; they did not speak each other's language. The programmers did not know or understand the insurance terms and the underwriters and adjusters did not know the computer language. Yet these groups had constant need to work together and communicate with each other. Each group had determined that it was the other group's responsibility to solve the problem and had left it at that.

In this particular example, the insurance operations people responsible for entering policy information into the computer received a daily report from the programmers listing the data entry errors for the day. The errors were listed in the report as computer programming codes. The insurance operations people had no idea what the codes meant. The programmers could not interpret the list for them because they did not know the insurance terms for the errors. Both groups had become very frustrated with the process. Through two very brief discussions with the heads of these two groups the manager (change agent) was able to identify the problem. The vice president of computer operations knew that one of his employees had held a previous position in insurance operations. She was the link that was needed to enable the two groups to communicate. She was given the task of developing a list of data entry errors and translating them into terms the insurance people could understand. Thus, the problem was quickly solved to everyone's satisfaction in a relatively short period of time. Because of the high political visibility of the problem, the ultimate solution gained credibility for the manager and opened a positive pathway for future problem solving.

As a change agent, you are likely to hear many suggestions for quick fixes from your employees and other organizational members. Some will be legitimate solutions. For example, a training director for a small but highly automated reinsurance company was struggling with a plan to increase employee usage of the company training resource center. Her department had spent valuable time and money upgrading the center. The obsolete books were purged and new ones ordered. Supplemental CDs and videotapes had been added as study resources. She had advertised the new revisions and held an open house for all employees. Still, employees were not taking advantage of the training resources available. Finally, during a monthly staff meeting, the department's training coordinator suggested a possible quick fix. The company had a highly developed intranet as well as a culture that encouraged the use of automation. Employees would have easier, more convenient access to training materials if the resource center was made available to them through the company intranet. The programming involved to develop this automated version of the center was minimal. Once the resource center was available on the intranet, employees' use of the materials was significantly increased. In this case, the change agent was able to identify the problem and find a workable solution very quickly with little expense to the company.

Before you can decide whether a solution is a viable quick fix you must take several precautionary steps. You may find yourself alone in resistance to run through the poppy field. You may not be popular with stakeholders at this point. However, you will be far less popular if you lead them into the poison of a dangerous quick fix. Take time to analyze the solution. Ask, and be able to answer, the following questions:

- Do you need time for buy-in of the stakeholders?
- Is the solution a fad?
- How does this solution affect the big picture?

### Stakeholders' Buy-In

Often the answer to a particular problem is obvious to you because you see how the operation works at the macro level and have access to information needed to solve identified problems. In this case, an instant solution used to address the problem seems like an appropriate quick fix. However, there will be situations when extra time is necessary to identify the problem more closely, isolate the root cause, and generate an acceptable solution.

Here's an example. Facilitating a meeting with a group of customer service employees, a change agent identified several barriers to work flow. A serious problem affected several work groups including the mailroom and the programming and billing departments. The result of this work flow barrier was a delay in customer billings. The change agent shared this information with the division vice president, who immediately arrived at a quick-fix solution. As the change agent and the vice president discussed the solution and its implementation, they realized that this quick fix was not appropriate.

The VP was familiar with employees in the areas affected by the impending change, many of whom were suspicious of corporate mandates and would resist change without having been involved in the decision. He also knew that getting buy-in from those who had to implement the change would not be easy.

It was decided to invest some time initially in order to save time later. The change agent formed a team comprised of employees from each department affected by the problem. This team explored the problem and after four meetings reached the same solution that had been proposed by the VP. Since employees solved the problem themselves there was immediate buy-in from others within the affected departments. This is because *people support what they create.* Management did not have to sell the benefits of change or explain the decisionmaking process. The team members took care of that themselves. The change was immediately implemented and was successful in correcting the problem.

Allowing time for stakeholder buy-in is not always a necessary ingredient for change. It is, however, usually worthy of consideration. Sometimes, as in this case, it is well worth the time spent.

### Change Solution or Fad?

Several change fads have caused considerable damage to the credibility of change initiative over the last forty years. Some of the more popular fads have been management by objectives, quality circles, one-minute manager, reengineering, and so forth. Fads typically work for a while, but are usually replaced by the next, latest, and hottest trend. Most fads are considered quick fixes, such as downsizing or other overhead-slashing schemes. Change agents who rely on fads to solve their employees' problems are the equivalent of the alchemist who tried to turn lead into gold. To move an organization forward, leaders and change agents must deal with these fads, see them for what they really are, and realize the price paid for using them.

### How Does the Solution Affect the Big Picture?

Deciding whether a proposed solution is an appropriate quick fix or even a viable option at all requires looking outside the narrow scope of the immediate stakeholder group. How will it affect the organization as a whole? What is good for one department may be detrimental to another. Many a change effort has been implemented with initial success only to backfire later when the results spread through other areas of the organization.

Anticipated changes in technology, market competition, resource availability, and so forth must also be considered when looking at a possible quick fix. Will this problem go away on its own with an anticipated improvement in technology? Is the marketplace in flux, making this change unnecessary or no longer effective?

All problems and their possible solutions exist within a political environment. Thus, it is important to consider the views and perspectives of organizational leadership. Change of any kind can be threatening. Hence, it is wise to consider management's concerns, company culture, and stakeholders' tolerance of change prior to taking action.

## Conclusion

The sooner you recognize the types of flying monkeys and poison poppies described in this chapter, the better equipped you will be to manage them in a way that works to your advantage, or at the very least, to minimize the damage they can do. Just as doctors preach the merits of preventive measures to avoid health problems, this chapter supports the value of taking preventive, proactive steps that may prevent flying monkeys from attacking in the first place. But for those inevitable times when the flying monkeys get the best of you or when you are tempted to adopt a quick fix, we have presented strategies for minimizing the damage, enabling you to continue moving forward down your change path.

# Part B

## Philosophy, Practice, and Responsibilities of a Change Agent

As a change agent, you need to adopt a new philosophy that reflects your developmental orientation and commitment to motivational strategies. Additionally, you will need to create a work climate free of fear. Finally, you need to demonstrate five areas of expertise that will enable you to meet your responsibilities as a change agent. These topics will be covered in the following chapters.

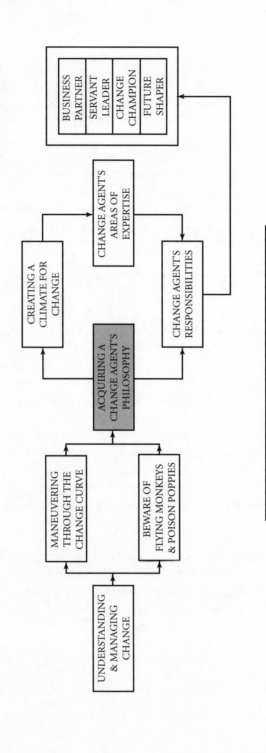

THE MANAGER AS CHANGE AGENT BLUEPRINT

# Change Agent's Philosophy: Embracing Employee Development and Motivation

If you are serious about becoming a change agent, you will need to adopt a new philosophy that embraces employee development and motivation. Such a philosophy allows employees to build on their strengths and manage their weaknesses. In this way, employees are encouraged to engage in work-related activities and assignments that they are passionate about. As a result, they develop expertise that is useful in helping the organization achieve its strategic business goals and objectives. You will also need to embrace a motivation philosophy that helps you to adopt motivational principles and strategies. When adopted, they encourage employees to participate in change initiatives that alter them personally and professionally.

## Development: Whose Responsibility Is It, Anyway?

Every organization is faced with the difficult question of *who should really be responsible for developing employees?* Some contend that training professionals should be responsible for this process because they possess the theoretical expertise and the instructional skills needed for the job. Training professionals are experts in the design, development, and presentation of training programs. Most possess excellent communications and facilitation skills and relate well to others. They also have the ability to engage people for long periods of time and have a solid foundation in adult learning, theory, and practice.

Although most trainers are dedicated to employee well-being and are highly talented professionals, they often have a limited impact on improving organizational performance or facilitating change. One reason is that most training professionals are not held accountable for employee performance and change implementation. Moreover, they are not responsible for conducting the performance appraisals used to determine whether employees are applying learning on the job. Furthermore, they are not in a situation to provide performance feedback and reinforcement so critical to learning transfer.

Since training professionals are not responsible for improving employee performance through learning or implementing change, why, then, are they responsible for learning and development within the organization? Part of the reason is that during World War II many organizations created separate operational departments responsible for training and development through formal learning activities. Commonly known as the training department, it originally appeared to be effective (i.e., during World War II), but it systematically deprived managers of their developmental responsibilities. Furthermore, some less competent managers (certainly not change agents) become coconspirators by failing to accept these development responsibilities. Such individuals love to wash their hands of this responsibility and pass it on to the training department. In effect, such managers have someone else to blame when employees don't improve their performance.

The other explanation is based on the myth that the learning process requires specialized talent that most managers lack. Some argue that managers can't be held responsible for training because they don't have the interpersonal and communications skills necessary to do an adequate job. However, the primary skill sets required by managers to secure results through people are, quite simply, interpersonal and communications skills. If managers don't possess such skills, we question whether they should be allowed to be managers at all. In fact, allowing them to continue as managers only exacerbates an organization's inability to improve its performance and implement needed change.

We contend that organizations should hold the individuals who conduct employee performance appraisals, confront poor performance, account for employee performance and productivity, answer for employee productivity declines, or account for organizational failures to be responsible for implementing the learning process. Since managers are responsible and accountable for these actions, they should be primarily responsible for the growth and development of employees through the application of the learning process. In short, managers should facilitate learning and change, since they are on the front lines of performance improvement.

## Acquiring a Developmental Philosophy

As a manager that aspires to be a change agent, you combine job knowledge and experience to help employees apply new information on the job. Enthusiasm combined with knowledge fuels an employee's interest and curiosity, and can be quite contagious. Well-prepared, component, and passionate change agents inspire others. As a result, you present information in a logical order, from simple to complex, so employees are better able to grasp difficult concepts. You need to be able to relate to employees, illustrating new ideas in terms of common experiences that provide them with familiar references, thus awakening your employees' desire to learn, grow, and develop.

Indifferent managers lack the motivation to share their knowledge and experience with employees. They demonstrate a lack of respect for them and are ineffective as learning agents. Furthermore, many managers lack or fail to adequately develop competency as change agents. They mistakenly believe that employees are solely responsible for their own growth and development and they have no role in their employees' learning success. Such managers are ill prepared to train employees. Poor planning skills further hinder employee learning and development.

You should generate excitement and mobilize commitment for learning and change, alter systems and structures to better support learning and change initiatives, oversee progress, and encourage actions that make change last. This requires you to understand how to link learning and change to other human resource systems such as appraisals, compensation and rewards, communication, and so forth. Being a learning and change catalyst requires you to build coalitions of support for learning and to recognize others who are committed to the same beliefs. You also need to enlist support from key individuals in the organization. Furthermore, facilitating learning and change initiatives requires you to measure success, identify results, and recognize benchmarks of progress. Finally, as a successful change agent, you must have a plan for adapting learning and change over time.

During the past few decades, most organizations have provided organized, formal training and development activities used to enhance employee performance capacity. Such programs are based on the assumption that training and development activities are used to "fix" employees so that they can perform at a more efficient and productive level rather than discover things that they do well, enjoy doing, and are passionate about. Consequently, most training and development activities are designed to *fix weaknesses* instead of capitalize on employees' strengths (Clifton and Nelson, 1992). This approach is based on the prevailing myth that fixing employees' weaknesses improves their performance and enhances the organization's effectiveness. Although this is a common practice, it can have a negative impact on organizational performance because it assumes that something must be wrong with employees.

To further complicate the problem, some organizations rely on a diagnostic approach to identify performance problems and recommend strategies for their improvement. In other words, they adopt the *medical model* to examine situations in search of a solution. The operating assumption that underlines· the medical model is to return people to their "normal" state. Such an approach is expensive, time consuming, and may result in solutions that don't correlate with symptoms. This approach implies that it is important to fix employee weaknesses in order to return employees to a normal or average performance level, rather than an outstanding level. Moreover, employees often attend training and development activities with a negative or defensive attitude, which introduces unnecessary barriers to the development process. Additionally, some managers believe that employee weaknesses will take care of themselves (via time, experience, or luck). As a result, weaknesses often worsen and lead to more complications in the future. In reality, weaknesses don't "disappear," they must be identified, addressed, and managed.

As a change agent, you need to consider a fundamental shift in your developmental philosophy and practice. In essence, you need to move from a reactive diagnostic-oriented performance improvement approach to a proactive, preventive approach that focuses on identifying what employees do well and creating growth and development plans that maximize their contributions. This approach suggests that *excellence* is the result of building on employee strengths while managing their weaknesses, not by their elimination (Clifton and Nelson, 1992; Buckingham and Coffman, 1999). Thus, employees build expertise via continual practice and reinforcement; therefore, effective developmental activities improve existing competencies rather than fix deficiencies. Quite simply, you need to adopt an approach that allows employees the opportunity to *build on strengths while they manage weaknesses.*

## Identifying Strengths

Identifying strengths challenges you to examine your employees' behaviors and successes. Five behaviors are indicative of employees' strengths: ambition, enthusiasm, rapid learning, curiosity, and performance zones.

*Ambition.* Ambition is an intensified desire to engage in specific activities or focus on selected subjects. It is a strong indicator of a potential strength. Your internal drive promotes such desire and fuels the initiative to try new things, creating an attraction to or curiosity about a subject or activity. Unfortunately, desire alone does not necessarily indicate strength. You need look no further than the thousands of would-be artists, singers, professional athletes, and even managers. Motive is sometimes suspected as well. For example, many salespersons want to become sales managers for reasons other than the improvement of organizational outcomes such as personal need for power, control, or career advancement. In many situations, some would-be sales managers demonstrate little concern for the development of people—the primary purpose of management. Such *internal dishonesty* can derail an organization's ability to identify employees' true strengths and opportunities for mastery.

*Enthusiasm.* A high level of enthusiasm when completing a task or activity is often indicative of strength. The sheer pleasure derived from a task well done becomes a motivator in itself and encourages employees to participate in similar activities in the future. However, employees might be very good or even excel at performing a particular activity, but dislike doing it. Consequently, they may not be enthusiastic about the activity, and thus not excited about performing it. Competence and satisfaction are not always related. For example, an individual may dislike close interaction with people even though he or she is good at securing adequate results from employees as a supervisor. Such an individual appears to possess the abilities required to be a supervisor but may lack crucial interpersonal skills necessary to build and maintain employee relationships. As a result, he or she may lack the ability to be a successful supervisor over the long term, in spite of their ability to produce short-term business results. Over time, an individual may become dissatisfied or may burn out because of lack of fulfillment on the job.

*Rapid Learning.* Something attained easily or learned very quickly is indicative of strength. Employees who maintain sufficient innate abilities often build proficiencies that eventually become strengths.

For example, a political science professor at Iowa State University discovered that he grasped statistical concepts and principles rapidly. Although he was never professionally trained in statistics, he engaged in self-development activities and over time has become one of the university's most qualified statistics instructors. For him, discovery is part of the learning process, and making errors or mistakes accelerates his learning curve. Learning occurs via interactions and experiences. Buckingham and Coffman (1999) refer to this phenomenon as *rapid learning*—when employees catch on quickly and it is not uncommon for them to be good at performing tasks the first time they tried.

*Curiosity.*　Another indication of strength is the curiosity for knowledge and the desire to learn as much as possible about a subject, jobs, or task. If allowed to flourish over time, curiosity leads to heightened interest that forms genuine interest. In this situation, learning is a delight, not a chore. Learning rates, of course, differ from employee to employee. For this reason, you need to isolate activities that employees perform well and design jobs and create work environments that allow them to flourish.

*Performance Zones.*　When employees or teams perform without conscious awareness of the steps involved, they experience a *performance zone* (Gilley, 1998). These employees and teams unconsciously rely on their strengths to achieve extraordinary outcomes. In the performance zone employees enjoy supreme satisfaction, which is the ultimate demonstrator of strength. They often feel invincible and powerful, wanting to repeat the performance over and over again. Repetition brings improvement, which leads to expertise and mastery. Organizations need to employ such cycles to enhance renewal and improve performance capacity. Additionally, these experiences enhance employees' self-esteem and shape their confidence. When in a performance zone, tasks are completed with ease and quality is outstanding, often exceeding employees' expectations.

## Identifying Weaknesses

Identifying weaknesses is the first step in managing them. Sadly, one's weaknesses are often easier to identify than strengths. It is easy to identify weaknesses when others have been pointing them out for years. As a result of negative criticism, some people have difficulty recognizing good things about themselves, which affects their willingness to accept constructive criticism or embrace change.

Certain behavioral clues, however, are instrumental indicators of weakness. *Slow learning* is the first indication of a weakness. Another indication of weakness is the lack of growth or improvement after several repetitions of a task or activity. This is particularly true if such a pattern persists after several months of performance. To complicate matters, most employees feel inferior when they fail to live up to performance standards, which causes them to be defensive about their performance.

Some employees attempt to master their weaknesses by working excessive hours on tasks or activities that they cannot perform adequately. Such a pattern of behavior can lead to obsessive performance that can become destructive. As a change agent, you need to address this performance pattern by acting quickly when it is observed so as not to risk losing the employee altogether.

## Strategies for Building on Strengths and Managing Weakness

Every employee needs opportunities to develop critical competencies, participate in important activities, and generate meaningful deliverables, including acquiring new skills or knowledge, participating in creative endeavors, being granted new and exciting responsibilities, participating in visible, important projects, or providing opinions and insights regarding the organization's direction. The purpose of such activities is to enhance the self-esteem of an employee.

Although identifying strengths and weaknesses is an important first step, their management makes the difference. As a change agent, you should consider several strategies to help employees minimize their weaknesses while building on strengths. This allows them to focus on the things that they do extremely well.

*Develop a Master List of Employee Strengths.* A way to improve strengths is to help employees develop personal master lists of strengths. When completing this task, you can use the five behaviors (ambition, enthusiasm, rapid learning, curiosity, and performance zone) previously discussed as a guide. First, employees need to identify all of their strengths. This should be a brainstorming activity free of bias, judgments, and criticisms. After compiling the personal master list, ask them to isolate a single strength and work on developing it for a month. Employees should select a strength they will have an opportunity to employ on a regular basis and record how it is used and the outcomes that result (Clifton and Nelson, 1992). This process should be repeated until all strengths have been fully developed. Once your employees have identified the strength that they want to improve, you need to provide regular, timely feedback regarding performance.

Developing personal master lists of strengths emphasizes employees' special skills and abilities, providing a foundation upon which they may rely in the future. The purpose of this exercise is to improve performance, job satisfaction, work relationships, and employee confidence as well as to further develop employees' strengths. Furthermore, employees will realize that they enjoy improving their performance when encouraged to build on strengths rather than on "fixing" weaknesses.

*Visualizing.* Visualizing is another way employees can build on strengths. Visualizing is the process of mentally rehearsing a successful event. It allows employees to relive the steps that were followed in creating a positive outcome as well as the emotions and satisfactions of the moment. As a result, employees manufacture inspiration to further develop their strengths. Both employees and the organizations are strongest when successes are clearly pictured in their minds.

*Journeying.* Writing about successful activities is another way to capture the essence of achievement. Employees should be encouraged to keep a journal that provides descriptions and characterizations of strengths. Entries should include feelings of success, location, pinnacles of achievement, dialogue, and so forth to allow employees to creatively yet realistically review and relive accomplishments. Once written, employees can reread the entry as a way of solidifying the event in their minds, as though they were experiencing it anew, which powerfully inspires employees to further develop their strengths. Reliving success permits employees to enjoy the moment over and over again. The more past successes are relived, the more future success is encouraged.

*Dialoguing.* Some employees need to talk about how they have successfully used their strengths, which allows them to recount their proudest moments and discuss how their strengths helped them achieve extraordinary outcomes. You should encourage employees to discuss their exemplary skills and abilities, which encourages other employees to emulate them. Heroes inspire employees to develop their personal best.

*Design Jobs Based on Strengths.* When designing jobs based on strengths it is important to make certain that three independent but interrelated steps, performance outputs, activities, and standards, are clearly identified and linked to strengths (Rummler and Brache, 1995). First, you identify the performance outputs that every job generates. Performance outputs are the deliverables that employees are paid to produce, whereas performance activities are the steps that employees engage in to create performance outputs. They may represent the number of sales calls made by telemarketing representatives, sales made per month by sales personnel, service claims handled by customer service representatives, the number of packages delivered per day by postal workers, and so on. Hence, outputs represent the hourly, daily, weekly, monthly, quarterly, or yearly expectations of employees in a specific job classification. Additionally, performance outputs are also the internal deliverables used as inputs by other employees in the execution of their jobs. On the other hand, external deliverables are the products and services produced for customers outside the organization. They are the tangible outcomes of employee performance that defines one's contribution within the organization.

Every employee engages in performance activities to create performance output. Each performance activity consists of microtasks, which collectively form the components of an employee's job. In job design, you examine performance activities to determine possible breakdowns. If a problem is identified, a growth and development intervention should be designed to help employees demonstrate acceptable performance.

The relationship between performance output and activities can be expressed through *job descriptions*. They should be written to achieve three goals. First, job descriptions should be written to clearly identify performance output for each job. Second, they should identify the performance activities required by employees to produce these deliverables. Third, they should demonstrate the relationship between activities and output. In other words, a job description is simply a written document that describes an employee's performance activities and deliverables.

Once performance output and activities have been identified, you can begin to develop appropriate performance standards for each. Performance standards represent excellence criteria used to measure product and service quality and worker efficiency. They provide measures against which employees compare their efforts and outputs to determine whether they are performing at acceptable levels. Quite simply, performance standards represent the targets used to measure the quality of employee output and the efficiency of their performance activities.

Performance standards allow employees to monitor and correct their performance because they can determine for themselves how well they are performing and whether they are producing satisfactory performance output. They allow employees to regulate the quality of their performance output and activities, avoid needless mistakes, and maintain consistency. Performance standards encourage employees to continue to produce at an acceptable level. Consequently, they will do their jobs and know when they are doing them well.

Performance standards help you determine acceptable performance and measure the quality of performance output. Without performance standards, neither you nor your employees will be able to ascertain whether they have created performance output or executed performance activities acceptable to internal and external stakeholders. However, when performance standards are present you and your employees will be able to determine when performance output and activities have been generated at an acceptable level, which leads to better organizational results.

Once performance output, standards, and activities are identified, you can identify the competencies employees need to accomplish them. Sometime referred to as *competency maps,* they represent the culmination of the knowledge, skills, behavior, and attitudes an employee possesses to complete job tasks that comprise performance activities. Competency maps are useful in *recruiting and selecting* employees for given job classifications. They are also helpful when determining the *growth and development activities* in which employees must participate to master performance and for revealing employee strengths and weaknesses, thereby guiding formulation of career development activities as well as performance growth and development plans.

Examination of each of these three steps and determining their dependencies allows you to identify efficiencies that enable your organization to be more profitable and competitive. In fact, it could be said that an organization is only as efficient and effective as its job design activities.

*Delegating Based on Strengths.* Typically, delegation is viewed as an approach that allows more experienced employees to delegate tasks and responsibilities to less experienced employees, giving them the opportunity to acquire new knowledge, skills, and competency. In theory, the delegation cycle should enhance an individual's performance capacity to such a point that they are able to take on even more difficult tasks and responsibilities. As the cycle continues, employees grow and develop, gradually becoming more important assets within the organization. Thus, delegation is quintessentially a growth and development strategy.

Delegation is an everyday event in most organizations, but some managers fear delegating work to employees, often contending that it takes twice as long to explain how to do a task than to do it themselves. Such managers believe that employees will not perform the task as well as they can. The excuse prevents employees from growing, developing, and maximizing their strengths. These managers need to be reminded that their job is to secure results through people. Therefore, they are obligated to delegate tasks and responsibilities, and grant appropriate levels of authority to achieve desired organizational results.

Rarely, however, is delegation viewed as appropriate for employees who have strengths in a given area. Consequently, organizations miss many opportunities to maximize performance growth and development, as well as opportunities to assign tasks, activities, and responsibilities to individuals that can perform them at an excellent level. Furthermore, organizations miss opportunities to have the most qualified and talented individuals performing assignments that they excel at, which can result in diminished business results.

*Contrasting Performance Appraisal with Developmental Evaluation.* One of the most important activities that you and your employees engage in is conducting regular performance appraisals. Sometimes called performance reviews, performance appraisals give you the opportunity to judge the adequacy and quality of employees' performance and create growth and development plans that improve their performance.

The most important component of every performance appraisal is feedback. Think of performance appraisals and coaching as very similar activities. The fundamental difference between the two is that coaching is an ongoing, minute-by-minute, day-by-day feedback, whereas performance appraisal is designed to be formal, summative evaluations. In some respects, both coaching and performance appraisal are designed to achieve the same end: to provide employees with information regarding their performance and contribution and to create growth and development plans in order to improve their performance. Consequently, performance appraisal must be specific and timely for employees to improve and produce the desired results.

If employees lack the feedback, they will make mistakes that may cause disastrous results. Without feedback employees do not know where they are, how they're doing, or whether they're producing satisfactory results. Unless you tell them, employees don't know if they're producing results on time, at the correct level of quality, or in the correct form. In the final analysis, performance appraisal gives you the opportunity to share your perspectives of their performance and discuss means of improvement. In this way, performance appraisals serve a vital function within the organization.

In theory, performance appraisal is an effective developmental activity that rewards past performance, improves future performance, and encourages career development. In reality, nothing could be further from the truth. Unfortunately, the term *performance appraisal* restricts your ability to work collaboratively with employees in their development. To overcome this problem, we suggest referring to performance appraisals as developmental evaluations.

Developmental evaluation provides employees with feedback on their performance and change aptitude and readiness, helps them recognize their strengths and achievements over a specific period of time, and identifies areas where they can continue to grow and develop. They define performance goals for a short period of time, and review the fit between the organization's expectations and those of the employee. In essence, developmental evaluations help organizations make decisions regarding employee performance and aid in the creation of developmental and career planning activities that enhance their work.

Since many employees fail to perform adequately because of genuine barriers, developmental evaluations are valuable in isolating these obstacles and formulating strategies for overcoming them. Developmental evaluations:

- provide employees the opportunity to participate in discussions that improve the work environment and general conditions under which they are asked to perform.
- help employees analyze their personal job design and assist in identification of improvements and efficiencies in the execution of job tasks.
- enable you to assess employees' strengths and weaknesses, determine whether employees are producing adequate performance outputs, and executing performance activities that meet or exceed performance standards.
- provide you with opportunities to analyze your employees' knowledge, skills, and attitudes, and determine those areas of excellence that can be further developed.
- enable you to determine areas of weakness so that strategies can be created for their management.
- help you determine whether internal and external stakeholders are satisfied with performance outputs produced by employees.
- present opportunities for you and your employees to discuss current and future developmental goals and objectives, and how employees plan to achieve them.
- are a vehicle for discussion of future growth and development activities that will enhance employees' strengths and advance their careers.
- are effective tools in confronting employee performance and making recommendations for building on strengths and managing weaknesses.

## Adopting a Motivation Philosophy, Principles, and Strategies that Encourage Change

Far too many managers believe that as long as employees receive a paycheck they should be motivated to perform adequately and to embrace change. These managers create work environments where employees are treated as units of production that are easily replaced. Mistrust, tension, and resentment characterize such work climates. Typically, productivity, quality, and employee morale and loyalty are low.

If you want to become a change agent, you need to recognize that employees have reasons for everything they do. You realize that employees elect to perform the way they do because of some internal or external motivation. Employees choose to change what they perceive is good for them. In other words, employees choose to change their performance behavior if they see an immediate or long-term payoff. Employees participate when the goal they have chosen to pursue is attainable and they are rewarded accordingly. To ensure greater participation, you must understand this simple motivation principle.

The purpose of any organization is to secure results, from increasing market share or sales revenue to improving quality or profitability. Improving organizational performance, productivity, and effectiveness remains a difficult undertaking that requires the cooperation of the organization, its managers, and employees. As change agents, you are instrumental in adopting effective motivational principles, philosophies, and strategies and aligning each of them with the guiding principles and values of the organization.

## Developing an Appropriate Motivational Philosophy

A motivational philosophy should be based on rewarding people for the "right" performance. In this way, organizations demonstrate their understanding that "the things that get rewarded get done" (LeBoeuf, 1985). When this approach is adopted, it assures that the organization will secure its desired results. On the other hand, failure to reward the right behavior or performance leads to unsatisfactory results.

A motivational philosophy should be flexible enough to take into account the dynamic nature of the organization's change initiatives and other important organizationwide activities. When this occurs, the motivational program remains fluid, subject to review, alteration, or redesign. This is an approach that guarantees continuous compensation improvement. Such a philosophy reflects the organization's culture, values, guiding principles, and strategic business goals and objectives. Moreover, an effective motivational philosophy defines who participates in motivational decisions, whether decisionmaking should be centralized in the human resources department or decentralized within departments that managers can influence. It also determines how you will be held accountable for your respective decisions and contributions to the motivational program (Flannery, Hofrichter, and Platten, 1996).

The motivational philosophy should also take into account each step of the organization's performance management process. In this way, a motivational approach is developed that allows organizations to identify stakeholder needs and expectations; design jobs that produce maximum results; encourage you to build synergistic relationships with employees; encourage you to make the transformation to performance coach; require you to conduct formal developmental evaluations with employees; and collaboratively create performance growth and development plans designed to enhance performance capacity.

## Adopting Motivational Principles

Motivating employees to embrace change requires a well-conceived, designed, implemented, and monitored plan. There are several principles that can help you in this effort (Flannery, Hofrichter, and Platten, 1996, 247–250).

1. *Align your motivation program with your organization's culture, values, and strategic business goals.* Compensation and rewards should be integrated with all aspects of the business.
2. *Link compensation to other changes.* Compensation and rewards should support and reinforce organizational change initiatives.
3. *Time your motivation program to best support your other change initiatives.* Timing is everything. Compensation and rewards should not force change or lag behind the change process.
4. *Integrate the motivation program with other people processes.* Compensation and rewards are not a substitute for developing relationships with employees.
5. *Democratize the compensation and reward process.* Incorporate employee opinions and decisions in motivational strategies.
6. *Demystify compensation and reward programs.* Explain the compensation model of your organization to your employees.
7. *Measure results.* Performance can and should be measured with fairness and consistency.
8. *Refine the motivation program.* Continually improve the compensation and reward program—analyze and revise. Keep up with the times.

## Motivational Strategies

Employee motivation can be greatly enhanced when you understand several assumptions that underlie change behavior (Carlisle and Murphy, 1996). First, employees are motivated to change their behavior when given clear, sharply focused objectives. Second, employees need to thoroughly understand how to perform their jobs correctly. Third, they are more likely to change their performance behavior when they are given opportunities to participate in problem-solving and decisionmaking activities that directly affect them. Fourth, change requires personal commitment for action, which obligates you to secure employee buy-in prior to the creation of growth and development plans. Fifth, clearly communicate positive and negative rewards that are linked directly to performance improvement. Sixth, demonstrate patient, persistent follow-through when providing positive feedback and reinforcement. Seventh, you should be realistic regarding the types of rewards offered, while acting within their discretion and authority.

Motivational programs should be designed to help organizations achieve specific outcomes. Historically, motivational programs have been based on performance alone, giving little consideration to desired attributes that contribute to achieving results. It is very important to reward people for their entrepreneurship, involvement, performance growth and development, teamwork and cooperation, creativity, and commitment and loyalty.

*Rewarding Entrepreneurship.* When organizations reward entrepreneurship, they encourage employees to take intelligent risks, which should lead to better business results. Employees should be rewarded for taking risks and decisive actions that improve organizational efficiency and effectiveness and for discovering ways to improve business processes and performance activities. Employees should also be rewarded for acting on their convictions and beliefs and be supported by their managers when such decisions are made. When these behaviors are rewarded, employees will actively, even aggressively, produce more positive results. Consequently, organizations should establish motivational programs that reward entrepreneurial behavior.

Employees who operate as entrepreneurs can and do energize others, creating an atmosphere of positive dynamism. This is how to recognize an entrepreuneur. Entrepreneurs have ten personal characteristics (Meyer and Allen, 1994, 34). Entrepreneurs are persistent, refusing to abandon a project, activity, or initiative until it is complete. Entrepreneurs are creative in that they are willing to try something unconventional in search of new ways to solve problems. They are responsible for their conduct and actions. They are inquisitive; they constantly ask questions and search for answers. Entrepreneurs are goal oriented and want to establish and accomplish priorities and formulate a plan to make it happen. They are independent, autonomous, and self-reliant, which is demonstrated through their decisive and directive actions. Entrepreneurs are demanding: They are unwilling to settle for mediocrity and constantly seek to improve themselves and their environment. They are confident and have faith in themselves and their decisions. Entrepreneurs are risk takers who are not afraid of adversity, putting themselves on the line for their beliefs, or tackling the unknown. Finally, they are restless, which is demonstrated by their dissatisfaction with the status quo and constant search for challenge and improvement.

Another aspect of rewarding entrepreneurship involves encouraging employees to apply new skills and knowledge on the job, in spite of the potential risk of their failure to produce the outcomes desired. We believe that failure is one of the best learning experiences an employee can have. When employees are allowed to discover new ways to achieve results, they develop an ownership attitude that enhances their commitment and involvement.

*Rewarding Involvement.* Many employees are comfortable as followers rather than as active problem solvers. These employees are content to let others make decisions about the direction of the organization or implement actions that steer the organization accordingly. Moreover, many talented employees lack an opportunity to exhibit their competencies on the job. This prevents talented, qualified employees from making contributions that improve the overall effectiveness of the organization. Too many inflexible organizations fail to tap into the wealth of talent available within their walls, content to pool power and authority among a select few.

Although many organizations encourage involvement, they seldom reward it. Consequently, an involvement vacuum often exists in many of today's organizations. To overcome this condition, organizations must reward employees who take risks, offer opinions, and make suggestions to better the organization. Unfortunately, some managers discourage this practice because they fear that others will supersede their power and authority within the organization. They operate as though others' opinions and ideas are less important in value than their own. Organizations need to avoid appointing such individuals as managers because they only serve to diminish employee involvement and commitment. They further suggest that organizations encourage managerial malpractice when these individuals have the opportunity to restrict opinions and ideas. Thus, organizations need to integrate involvement attributes into job descriptions, provide opportunities for expression and development, and assign mentors to help develop involvement potential among future managers.

You can reward several involvement roles that you can reward within the organization (Flannery, Hofrichter, and Platten, 1996, 169–170). One such role is that of team leader, a person formally appointed as team guide who is often pulled from the ranks. Another role is that of innovator and creator whose expertise and knowledge is valued within the organization. A third involvement role is that of the translator. Such an individual is responsible for translating the organization's ideas (particularly those of innovators and creators) into marketable concepts. Producer and orchestrator is a fourth involvement role. These individuals often temporarily spearhead new projects for which their particular involvement skills are most valuable.

*Rewarding Employee Performance Growth and Development.* Employees are the organization's greatest assets; therefore, you must develop long-term motivational strategies that encourage employees to participate in performance growth and development activities that foster continuous learning and skill acquisition. Historically, motivational programs have been performance based, with little consideration given to rewarding employees for continually enhancing their skills or competencies. However, motivational programs can be used to increase employee development as opposed to mere performance achievement. Of course, the intent is not to mitigate the importance of performance, but to clarify that performance improvement without employee growth and development will lead to stagnation or even decline overtime. Shifting motivational programs to encourage employee growth and development ensures that employees' skills and competencies continue to evolve.

The shift from rewarding performance to growth and development involves a remarkable transformation. Successful evolution includes rewarding employees for applying what they have learned on the job and rewarding supervisors who create environments conducive to learning transfer. By rewarding performance growth and development, you create environments that enhance continuous improvement and quality. It also enhances an organization's readiness to reinforce and encourage employees who show the initiative to achieve performance results. By encouraging growth and development, production efficiencies become an operational reality rather than mere slogans or diatribes.

First, you need to work collaboratively with your employees in identifying performance growth and development goals. It is important that such goals enable employees to contribute to one or more of the organizations strategic business goals and objectives. Next, you need to determine whether proposed employees' performance growth and development goals match the organization's motivational strategy. If these two elements are incompatible, adjustments must be made in the organization's strategy, employees' performance growth and development goals, or both. This step helps determine whether the organization's long-term reward strategy is compatible with employee development activities.

Moreover, you must make certain that employees' performance growth and development goals are specific, measurable, agreed upon, realistic, and time bound (SMART). If for some reason these goals fail to meet such criteria, they should be reevaluated, reclarified, and rewritten to ensure clarity and specificity.

Fourth, rewards must be substantial enough to motivate employees to continue professional development activities. Therefore, you must ascertain whether rewards indeed motivate employees to participate in performance growth and development activities. Those that fail to motivate employee participation in professional development activities should be reevaluated, clarified, or both. This can be accomplished through a variety of evaluation techniques including focus groups, personal interviews, questionnaires, or small group discussions.

Once results have been achieved, you need to conduct developmental evaluations. Once conducted, you should evaluate the entire process to determine whether the organization's motivational program encourages employees to enhance their performance growth and development. Additionally, you should examine whether employees' performance growth and development goals have been rewarded appropriately and whether the performance enhancements desired have been achieved.

*Rewarding Teamwork and Cooperation.* Many organizations desire teamwork and cooperation, advocating its importance and value in helping the organization achieve better business results. However, most employees are confused because their organizations continue to compensate and reward individual efforts and contributions rather than group efforts brought about through teamwork and cooperation. If organizations desire teamwork and cooperation, they must reward people for helping each other rather than continuing to foster a competitive, counterproductive environment that reduces employees' self-esteem. Remember that teams win together and lose together, play together and struggle together. Therefore, they should be rewarded together. When this occurs, employees must be willing to give up the attitude of "what's in it for me?" and adopt a "we attitude" characteristic of cooperation and esprit de corps.

*Rewarding Creativity.* Many managers wonder why experienced and talented employees fail to share their ideas and opinions. They are confused because some employees are comfortable with the status quo, content to merely perform on the job day after day. When facing this situation, some managers blame employees for their lack of participation and information sharing, discounting their intellectual creative abilities. These individuals seldom look inward to discover whether they have established policies and procedures that prevent sharing creative ideas. Fortunately, these managers are beginning to discover the importance of encouraging and rewarding employees who share their innovations. Their eleventh commandment has become *Thou Shalt Not Kill a New Product Idea*, which motivates employees to share their creative insights.

Regrettably, some managers quickly reject new, creative, innovative ideas by declaring them infeasible or impractical. Further, employees are rarely rewarded when a new idea is accepted. Organizations need to develop work climates that encourage new ideas and make innovation part of every employee's job to avoid creating a "creativity wasteland." Several major ingredients are necessary to establish an innovative climate, such as tolerance for failure, a relaxed, informal work environment, rewards for successful innovations and ideas, and an environment of friendly, supportive competition. Others include supporting fantasy and unorthodox ideas, soliciting employee involvement and participation, and teaching employees the basics of creative thinking and idea generation.

*Rewarding Employee Commitment and Loyalty.*  Business success is a journey that all organizational members take together. Therefore, you need to understand one important principle in order to adopt appropriate reward strategies—the principle of reciprocity. Simply stated, it means that employees will reciprocate like behavior (Thorndike, 1931). When employees are treated with respect they in turn treat others with respect. For example, loyalty begets loyalty, commitment begets commitments, involvement begets involvement, and so on.

Although many managers expect, even demand, loyalty and commitment, they rarely examine their motivational programs to determine whether they are practicing hypocrisy. In other words, they must reward loyalty and commitment in order to get it. Thus, they must determine whether providing job security, appropriate work environments, promotion and growth opportunities, and a fair, livable wage are essential in enhancing employee commitment and loyalty. When you are willing to invest in and reward employee commitment and loyalty, you are recognizing their importance to the execution of the business plan. Consequently, most if not all employees will respond by being loyal and committed to the betterment of the organization as a whole. It's that simple.

Unfortunately, some managers are guilty of the unpardonable sin of hiring new employees to perform identical jobs and paying them significantly more than current employees. When the primary employees discover this, they feel disenfranchised, demoralized, discouraged, and violated. Quite simply, these managers have violated employee trust and further complicate the situation by providing insignificant rationales for its decisions. As a result of this practice, employee loyalty and commitment are low and many talented employees leave the organization.

## Conclusion

Becoming a change agent proves a difficult undertaking requiring a shift in your developmental philosophy. As we discussed previously, capitalizing on strengths makes sense; asking employees to perform outside their areas of expertise wastes valuable talent. Why, then, do organizations spend millions of dollars every year on career development "fix-it strategies" unrelated to employee strengths? Often, organizations fail to define and focus on their strengths and the strengths of their employees. Consequently, you need to change your developmental philosophy to embrace the importance of building on strengths and managing weaknesses. These change initiatives will enable employees to develop proficiencies that will improve their performance and generate organizational renewal.

Becoming a change agent requires you to adopt a motivational philosophy, principles, and strategies that encourage and foster change. Each of these provides you with tools useful in building better manager-employee relationships, enhancing employee growth and development, improving employee performance, and ultimately enhancing change.

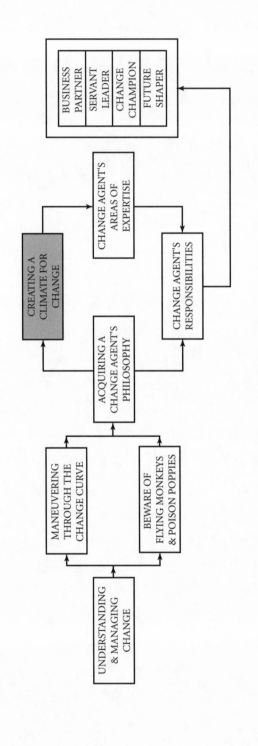

THE MANAGER AS CHANGE AGENT BLUEPRINT

BUSINESS PARTNER
SERVANT LEADER
CHANGE CHAMPION
FUTURE SHAPER

CHANGE AGENT'S AREAS OF EXPERTISE

CREATING A CLIMATE FOR CHANGE

CHANGE AGENT'S RESPONSIBILITIES

ACQUIRING A CHANGE AGENT'S PHILOSOPHY

MANEUVERING THROUGH THE CHANGE CURVE

BEWARE OF FLYING MONKEYS & POISON POPPIES

UNDERSTANDING & MANAGING CHANGE

# Creating a Climate for Change 6

Work environments that are full of fear are very unpleasant, tension ridden, and anxiety prone. Under such conditions, it is impossible for employees to implement change. However, some managers don't think they have done a good job unless all of their employees fear them. This is simply wrong—another classic example of managerial malpractice.

The only way to achieve organizational change is for managers to create a climate that fosters transformation. By doing so, employees feel good about their contributions, involvement, and accomplishments and the organization becomes an empathetic entity that focuses its energies on building relationships and fulfilling the developmental needs of every employee.

Creating a climate for change requires you to create work environments free of fear, demonstrate respect, apply the principles for creating climate for change, demonstrate relationship skills, and develop communication skills (Figure 6.1).

## Creating a Work Environment Free of Fear

Fear is one of the primary reasons that employees do not successfully implement change. Moreover, fear destroys employee morale, confidence, damages lives, destroys relationships, stifles growth, and limits entrepreneurial spirit. To eliminate fear, change agents treat employees with respect instead of treating them with a cavalier, dismissive attitude.

To create work environments free of fear, you must break down the wall of autocratic persecution by championing change. To achieve this end, you must encourage a free exchange of ideas and feelings. Employees need a safe and comfortable environment in which to implement change. How employees define "safe" and "comfortable" may be quite different from one organization

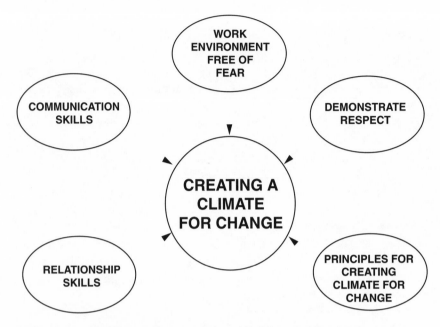

FIGURE 6.1    Activities Used in Creating a Climate for Change

or situation to another. For example, "safe" may mean that employees do not feel threatened with physical or mental harm during change or in the environment surrounding it. Or "safe" may mean they may be able to implement change without fear of the consequences. Regardless, employees who feel safe will be more likely to express ideas, opinions, or concerns more freely.

To create healthy and fear-free environments, change agents must take the time to provide personal interactions that are devoid of fear. This may require some managers to think outside the box by behaving differently from the norm. This includes allowing employees to take risks without fear of reprisal. Many managers operate as though belittling, embarrassing, or humiliating their employees' efforts will motivate them to change. In reality, the opposite is true. What managers should try to create is a work environment that stimulates positive action in employees, that drive and challenge them to take responsibility for what they do. Such environments encourage a sense of accomplishment, hope, and inclusion.

Another way for you to create a work environment free from fear is to follow several practical steps helpful in implementing and encouraging change. First, ask thought-provoking questions to excite employee interest in change, such as: "What do you think is the best way of implementing . . . ?" "What problems are we going to experience?" "Who will or will not be supportive?"

"How would you proceed?" Next, you should develop empathy for your employees by trying to understand what they are experiencing when implementing change. Further, allow employees enough time to implement change in order to gain insight and understanding. Learning new procedures or developing new skills takes time. Employees must first unlearn the steps that they have used in the past before they can integrate new knowledge. Additionally, employees are reluctant to give up habits, behaviors, processes, or approaches that have brought them success. Many employees would rather do it the "old way" rather than adopt more efficient methods. This is because the old way serves as a feedback mechanism that provides positive reinforcement regarding performance, which is very relevant when managers fail to provide such information. It is as though employees create their own feedback loop when it is not provided for them by their managers. Under this condition, change represents giving up the way employees validate their efforts. Further, encourage employees to ask questions when they are confused or do not understand and surpress your desire to tell them all you know about implementing change.

A work environment free of fear is fostered when you are open to ideas, encourage risk taking and creativity, and allow employees to gain ownership of problems and their solutions. Moreover, you should support your employees' efforts and contributions and facilitate their creativity, independence, and diversity. Additionally, you should unleash the collective minds of your employees by relinquishing power and authority. For example, an employee of a major management consulting firm wanted to develop a better understanding of the business development process used to enhance revenues. Rather than being a gatekeeper of such knowledge, her manager encouraged her to accompany him on client calls. He encouraged her to observe the selling process and identify techniques used during the selling process. Once she had gained an understanding of the process, the manager encouraged her to join him during client meetings as an equal. Next, he arranged for her to be the lead during several future client interactions. Finally, he assigned her several clients and delegated her the responsibility of developing a business relationship.

Fear-free environments can be created by demonstrating "personal openness." By personal openness, we mean approachability. Approachability is demonstrated by your willingness to be available to interact with your employees and let them get to know what you think and feel. Employees are encouraged to be candid and honest about decisions, assignments, and responsibilities. Openness, however, does not mean a total exposure of your every thought and feeling. Sharing too much information or becoming too familiar with your employees can have a negative impact.

One of the best ways to create work environments free of fear is to demonstrate personal changeability. This illustrates your personal reaction to change. Your employees will closely observe your reaction to such event. If you demonstrate a willingness to accept and incorporate change, employees will be encouraged to reciprocate.

Next, winning the battle only to lose the war is not a smart way to create positive work environments. Let's illustrate. Because of deadlines, work stress, and competing priorities, managers sometimes become overly confrontive, critical, harsh, and condescending. They justify their behavior with flimsy excuses like: "I don't have time to be diplomatic, we have a deadline to meet." "I don't care what other projects you're working on, I need this done by the end of the day." Such managers further justify their position by asserting that they "believe conflict is a positive thing because it opens the line of communications and as a result better ideas emerge." Although they may win today's battle, it is at the expense of losing the "war" of positive relationships. This is because every conflict leaves interpersonal scars that will impact future interactions. Over time, negative conflicts add up, creating resentment, anger, and ultimately hostility (open or passive). Regardless, conflict that damages relationships will ultimately be counterproductive. Thus, an open, honest, and positive work environment will never be developed, preventing effective employee performance and the realization of business goals.

## Demonstrating Respect

All employees feel a deep-seated need to be *respected as persons of worth*. In the workplace, this need is met through interactions with coworkers, managers, and organizational leaders. Unfortunately, this basic need is rarely met. Moreover, some managers treat employees with little respect and demand that they perform at ever higher levels. To become a change agent, you need to realize that this basic need must be met to achieve organizational harmony and efficiency.

Thorndike (1931) suggested that people tend to treat others the way they are treated. Quite simply, creating a climate for change begins with treating employees with dignity and respect so that they reciprocate in kind. Several years ago, we witnessed this firsthand. A longtime employee of a southern high school had the reputation of being difficult, even hateful, to students, teachers, and staff members. At first it was hard to interact with her because she was so critical. But we believed that she could be won over, so we kept treating her in a respectful manner but not letting her impede our objectives or progress. We were careful to honor her way of getting things done and let her meet her responsibilities her way. We presented ourselves in a friendly manner, always having time to talk to her, treating her as a person of importance. Whenever possible, we solicited her opinions and suggestions. On several occasions we implemented her recommendations and suggestions. We thanked her for her efforts and publicly recognized her contributions. After about six months, she started to participate in staff meetings, discussing plans for improving her area. We were overwhelmed by the transformation. She was no longer a cynic, critical of management actions, student behavior, or teachers' work performance but was an open, contributing member of the organization. She was helpful and supportive and made several unsolicited contributions to our success. Why the turnaround? She later confessed that much of her negativity was her way of forcing us "big shots" to treat her as an equal and not to take advantage of her. Her behavior was also her way of making certain that her needs and expectations were met. In the past, other managers got into a battle over who was going to "blink first" and she found that quite amusing. She also confessed that we surprised her by being "nice" rather than trying to force her to comply or show her who was the boss. Additionally, she was surprised by our willingness to embrace her and solicit her opinions, considering her unpleasant disposition.

There are several things that you as a change agent can do to demonstrate respect and thus establish a climate for change. First, employees need to know why change is important. Regardless of whether the change requires developing new skills, learning additional techniques, acquiring new information, or participating in a major reorganization effort, employees want purpose, combined with thorough, thoughtful explanations as to why the proposed change is necessary. They also want to know how the change will benefit them. Second, employees desire control over their actions and the ability to influence outcomes. This is especially true of more senior employees who believe that they deserve respect because of their tenure with the organization. Third, most employees possess a wealth of personal and professional experience that can be an invaluable resource through the change process. Additionally, employees benefit by sharing these experiences when interacting with each other.

## Principles for Creating Climates for Change

When implementing change, there are several principles that you can apply. Each of these principles is a proven method for meeting the needs and expectations of adults as learners (Zemke and Zemke, 1995). They can guide your action with employees and help keep you focused on real, practical solutions to complex problems.

*Employees tend to be problem-centered in their outlook.* Employees are pragmatic, desiring change that helps them cope with real-life situations or that helps them achieve tasks or solve problems. As a result, employees will embrace change when it helps them perform tasks or deal with problems they confront in their lives.

Employees will embrace change when it addresses their immediate personal and professional problems. As a change agent, you should identify the problems that employees presently face and together determine the best course of action to resolve them. For example, employees fail to support change in their compensation and reward system unless they believe that they are being fairly treated. When working for a large retail electronic company, we were asked to redesign its compensation program for commission salespersons to improve both profitability and retention. Instead of conducting an audit of competitors in the industry to determine the fairness and competitiveness of our compensation program, we assembled a team of salespersons ranging in seniority from six months to ten years. Each of these members were successful salespersons but varied from average to superior performers. We asked them to design a compensation program and outlined the organization's objectives. They met three times a week for six weeks. At the conclusion, they had designed a compensation program that improved profitability but provided incentatives for continuous knowledge and skill acquisition. The program included a bonus program for all salespersons based on both revenue goals and profitability measures. It also included a provision whereby salespersons could track their compensation daily. Finally, the saving that was realized as a result of the program (increased revenues and profit margin) was placed into a bonus program for the top performers at the end of each fiscal year. The task force presented their program to senior management and they unanimously supported the proposal.

*Personal growth, development, and advancement motivate employees.* Employees are motivated by a desire to improve their lives or future job prospects. Therefore, employees are interested in change opportunities that benefit them personally and professionally (see Chapter 7). Since appeals to self-interest will often work, employees should be questioned about their interests and desires for personal gain.

*Motivation for change can be increased.* A majority of employees are very responsive to external motivators such as promotions, advancements, increased compensation, recognition, and other rewards. However, the most influential motivators are intrinsic, strategies that enable employees to increase their job satisfaction, self-esteem, and quality of life while acting on and demonstrating their values and beliefs. When establishing appropriate recognition and rewards, you need to identify those that encourage employees to embrace change (Chapter 5). Further, employees respond favorably to positive reinforcement, embracing honest and constructive feedback designed to improve their skills, abilities, and competencies.

You can enhance employees' motivation to change by helping them understand how a change opportunity will benefit them. Important questions to consider include:

- What are the employees' present levels of motivation for change?
- How obvious are the benefits to employees?
- What can be done to increase employee motivation?

*Feedback and recognition should be planned.* Employees should be provided with ample opportunity to receive feedback on their efforts to implement change (see Chapter 11). As a result, you will need to know your employees well. In particular, you should provide the type and frequency of feedback and recognition most likely to be successful with each employee.

*Employees incorporate and implement change in different ways.* Thus, you should identify your employees' learning styles, account for differences, and incorporate them into the change process. Interpersonal and learning style assessment may include surveys, questionnaires, or one-on-one discussions.

*Change initiatives should accommodate employees' continued growth and changing values.* Employees' interests and needs change throughout their lives. Effective change initiatives adapt to these changes. Discovering employees' values, including what they want and why (values clarification) allows you to isolate issues associated with those values that will correspond with employees' needs (see Chapter 10).

When facilitating change it is important to remember that employees have a great deal of firsthand experience, a past that can positively or negatively influence change opportunities. They have established strong habits and attitudes that are difficult to alter but possess the ability to change. Employees have very tangible things (for example, reputations, job security, status, influence, relationships) to lose during change. Thus, they demonstrate a considerable amount of pride that should be accounted for accordingly. Each potential loss should be accounted for during the change process to enhance the likelihood of a successful engagement change. Finally, an employee's personal and professional experiences, relationships, assumptions, beliefs, and values can either accelerate or impede the change process. When past experiences pose a negative predisposition to change, you will need to isolate the problem and provide corrective action, which will alter their assumptions and maximize change opportunities.

## Relationship Skills

Relationship skills allow you to enhance your relationships with employees. They help you build a positive, comfortable, and nonthreatening change climate with employees—one that encourages employees to discuss performance problems, career alternatives and options, and organizational development ideas openly and honestly, without fear of reprisal. Such an environment establishes conditions that will expedite building positive, collaborative work relationships. A closer examination reveals that certain key elements and skills are needed for the proper climate for change to be developed.

### Elements of Positive Relationships

Elements essential to success include *understanding, acceptance,* and *involvement.*

*Understanding.*   When change agents demonstrate understanding, they are able to recognize and correctly interpret the feelings, thoughts, and behavior of their employees. Although it may be impossible to completely understand every employee, understanding is essentially the process of interpreting employees' experiences, perspectives, and personal and professional histories. Understanding can take two forms. By internal understanding, we mean the ability to step into the perceptual world of your employees, which includes identifying with their fears, successes, and failures. By external understanding, we mean the ability to be aware of your employees' actions and behaviors.

One of the best ways to develop an understanding of your employees is to use personality measuring instruments such as Meyers-Briggs, DiSC, the Birkman, and Social Styles Profile. Each of these tools can give you tremendous information about the way employees interact with one other, make decisions, express their emotions, achieve tasks, express ideas and opinions, generate information, and organize work activities. These instruments will help you to identify differences among employees in such a way as to celebrate their differences. In other words, they bring attention to the strengths of individual differences and how they contribute to the diversity and complexity of your organization.

Understanding is not a difficult process but it does require you to listen carefully to what employees are saying, interpret their expressions, and attempt to comprehend their feelings. At the most fundamental level, understanding is the recognition of your employees' behavior, personality, interests, and desires. This can be achieved through simple observation activities or having conversations with each employee. A second level involves attempting to step into the perceptual world of your employees whereby you are able to identify their deepest convictions, fears, anxieties, and passions. In this way, you are able to discover the real person behind the mask of being an employee. This requires you to identify the values that are important to each of your employees (Chapter 11). Additionally, you will need to determine when your values and beliefs interfere with your employees' values and beliefs and determine whether the differences are critical to achieving business results. The highest level of understanding is achieved when employees feel safe in their work environment and, more important, comfortable with you as a person as well as an authority. When this is achieved, employees are free of hidden agendas and communications are open, honest, and candid. It could be said that you and your employees have reached a level of trust and honesty.

*Acceptance.* Acceptance is the basic attitude change agents must hold toward employees. By acceptance, we mean a "warm regard for a person of unconditional self worth . . . an acceptance of and a regard for his/her attitudes, behaviors, and thoughts no matter how negative or positive"(Gilley, Boughton, and Maycunich, 1999, 34). It implies that each employee is a unique individual with differing characteristics, life experiences, and professional paths. This belief maintains that effectiveness lies in individual differences and it is your responsibility to challenge employees to capitalize on their unique gifts.

Acceptance is an attitude that demonstrates a synergistic approach. Synergy can be defined as the interaction between individuals whose combined efforts are more effective than if they were to work alone. Synergistic relationships, therefore, are the interdependence of individuals working toward a common goal, which simultaneously provides for growth and development opportunities for both participants as well as the organization. To achieve synergy, spend time getting to know each employee and discovering how their personalities differ as well as guarding against the bias that all people are the same and should be treated the same.

Acceptance is demonstrated by allowing individuals to differ from one another in the way they interact, perform work tasks, and solve problems. Acceptance is a direct outcome of your ability to be nonjudgmental. Acceptance is also communicated through your verbal and nonverbal behavior. Furthermore, acceptance and understanding of yourself is essential before you can be accepting of your employees.

Another way of demonstrating acceptance is for you to focus on results, not activities. In other words, you need to direct your attention on the outcomes produced by your employees instead of how they go about producing them. By doing so, you will be less tempted to judge your employees' behaviors and efforts but to evaluate the things that they achieve. To achieve this end, you will also need to control your biases by realizing that there are several ways to achieve outcomes and regardless of your preferred approach, results are what count.

Finally, perfection is not reality. It is important to strive for it but seldom does it ever really happen. Acceptance is demonstrated when you embrace differences and allow others to be included regardless of these unique differences.

Acceptance leads to personal involvement that enhances trust, honesty, and mutual self-esteem. Additionally, acceptance is demonstrated when employees believe that they are unconditionally understood, liked, and respected.

*Involvement.* A change agent's willingness to care and feel responsible for employees is called involvement. Acceptance and understanding are passive, but involvement implies action; it means active participation in the employee's problems and needs. Only through activity and involvement can you demonstrate the skills of a change agent. This requires face-to-face contact with employees. The outcome will enhance the relationship between you and your employees.

Acceptance is a prerequisite to involvement. Without it, you will never be able to develop a climate that facilitates organizational change. Involvement does not mean that you must become personally entwined with employees, but instead requires engaging in conversations that enable you and your employees to create a positive, collaborative working relationship. This may require you to open up and share some information about yourself, revealing yourself as a real human being with feelings and emotions. Another way you can create involvement is through observation. For example, any work station provides clues as to what is important to your employees, including pictures of family and pets, outdoor activities with friends, awards, books, objects of affection, and so forth. You can discover a wealth of information with little effort.

Another technique is *relationship analysis*, which is used to identify an employee's socialization pattern and how this pattern is used in the workplace.

The purpose of relationship analysis is to obtain a better understanding of your employees. It involves watching and observing employees interact with other employees on a daily basis. The aggregate of these observations reveals a great deal about employees' values and beliefs because people seldom spend time with those they feel uncomfortable with. Regardless of what you discover, don't judge or evaluate the social pattern; simply observe and attempt to understand it. The primary benefits of relationship analysis help you identify employees who want to work together on future job assignments and discover who employees feel comfortable with on the job.

Third, you can ask questions that help you discover unique and interesting things about your employees. Most employees like to talk about themselves, so let them. Moreover, employees like it when others take a personal interest in them as human beings instead of as employees. Therefore, you should take every opportunity to discover important events that occur in your employees' lives as well as things that hold personal meaning to them.

To successfully establish a climate for change, you need to interact with employees on a regular basis. You must also take time getting to know employees as people. This requires face-to-face interaction. Interaction also implies a personal engagement with employees. As a change agent, take the time to discuss issues and problems with employees. In fact, spending time with employees helps managers build credibility.

Unfortunately, some managers spend very little time interacting with employees. But increased contact time (interaction quantity) with employees is just the beginning. Interaction quality remains equally important. To improve a change agent's quality of interaction, several techniques referred to as relationship and communication skills prove helpful.

## Skills Required to Build Positive Relationships

Relationship skills include *attentiveness, empathy,* and *genuineness.*

*Attentiveness.* Attentiveness is the effort made by a change agent to hear the message conveyed by an employee. This can be achieved by demonstrating that you are interested in your employees' problems, points of view, thoughts, and ideas. As a result, you come to know and understand the thoughts and feelings of your employees.

Attentiveness requires active listening skills and the ability to resist interrupting employees when they are speaking. It implies that you are not dividing your attention between the employee's message and other competing activities. For example, what happens when you and an employee are engaged in conversation and the telephone rings? Many managers simply pick up the phone and begin a conversation with an unknown person. Although technology (such as caller ID) can help identify the unknown party, the point is that answering that call implies that the caller is more important than the person sitting in one's office.

*Empathy.*  The word *empathy* comes to us as a translation of a word used by German psychologists, *Einfuhlung,* which literally means "feeling into." It is the ability to understand another person pretty much as he or she understands himself or herself. Empathic change agents are able to crawl into another's skin and see the world through his or her eyes. They communicate in a nonjudgmental way. Becoming empathic is key to overcoming personal criticism of employees. Empathetic understanding is the change agent's ability to recognize, sense, and understand the feelings that employees communicate through their behavioral and verbal expressions, and to accurately communicate this understanding to employees.

Another word that demonstrates empathic understanding is sensitivity. In other words, change agents are able to comprehend the internal conflicts that employees experience when facing a change opportunity. They convey this understanding by letting the employee know that they too would have similar feelings if they were confronted with the same situation.

Demonstrating empathy does not mean to imitate or mirror your employee's feeling or make useless statements like "I understand how you feel . . . ," or "I feel your pain . . . ," or "What I hear you saying." These expressions demonstrate that you lack sincerity because they are trite and overused nonconnective fillers. Be honest; you may have used these statement in the past. Empathetic understanding is a transposing process where you truly place yourself in another person's world. For example, 200 years ago, John Woolman walked barefoot from Baltimore to Philadelphia. He did it to better understand the pain black slaves suffered when they were forced to walk barefoot over long distances. By putting himself in the slaves' place, he better understood what slavery meant to the slaves.

*Genuineness.*  Genuineness refers to your ability to be yourself in all work situations rather than playing a part or role. It occurs when you know who you are and what is important to you, and act on this knowledge accordingly. Furthermore, genuineness implies being honest and candid with employees while serving as a change agent. To demonstrate genuineness you sometimes have to disclose your feelings and deepest thoughts, but it does not necessitate a total unveiling of one's personal or professional life.

Genuineness is also the ability to recognize your own feelings, accept them, live them, and express them. This enables you to be who you are, not what people want you to be. In other words, genuineness requires authenticity and transparency.

## Communication Skills

The next step in creating a climate for change is for you to become more of a participant. Unfortunately, it is one of the most difficult things for managers to master because it requires them to have the courage to relinquish control and dominance over their employees. A participatory approach requires a gentle shift away from authoritarian control to allow employees to participate in the implementation of change. In this way change becomes less threatening to employees.

The participatory approach requires you to develop an understanding of the importance of having a positive working relationship with employees and to realize that employees bring a great deal of experience to a situation, which is an invaluable asset to be acknowledged, tapped, and used. However, some managers fail to understand that this asset can provide a wealth of information that would be beneficial in a working relationship. Such recognition is indeed difficult but is essential when creating a climate for change.

Communication skills are helpful in enabling you to become participatory. They are also useful when discovering the thoughts and ideas of employees. In order to accomplish this, you should allow employees to do most of the talking. There are several skills that you can use to better follow your employees during one-on-one conversations. They are *active listening, encouraging, questioning, "I" messages, silence, nonverbal techniques, clarifying, repetition,* and *summarizing.*

### Active Listening

Most managers spend as much as 70 percent of their time communicating. Over half of this time involves listening. Improving your listening skills will help you reduce disagreements with employees, improves data gathering, and enhances understanding of employees' points of view. Therefore, active listening is one of the most important skills that you can develop.

Active listening requires command of several techniques. As an active listener, you concentrate all your physical and mental energy on listening to the messages conveyed by your employees. You avoid interrupting them as well as demonstrating interest and alertness when interacting. Additionally, you seek areas of agreement with the employee to maintain a positive conversational tone. Moreover, you demonstrate patience and ask questions designed to understand your employee's point of view. Avoid getting hung up on specific words and phrases and provide clear and unambiguous feedback to employees. Repress the tendency to respond emotionally to what is said and withhold evaluation of the message until the employee is finished and understanding of the message is mutual.

## Encouraging

Encouraging is a technique that allows employees to expand or elaborate on how they feel. Encouraging tells employees that what they are saying is important and they should continue until they are comfortable with your understanding. Encouraging is a technique in which you attempt to solicit more information from your employees or to extend their ideas as well as draw implications from their statements to check comprehension. Common encouraging techniques include "I understand," "tell me more," "how so?" "I hear you," and nods of the head, which serve to strengthen employees' responses and their efforts to continue speaking.

## Questioning

One of the most overused techniques is questioning. It is one of the most effective methods when used properly, but if used too often employees feel as though they are being interrogated. Questioning is an excellent way to guide and direct conversations with employees. It helps create structure during an interaction. Furthermore, it is a critical technique for improving understanding and gathering data but should be used carefully to avoid abuse. The most common type of questions are open-ended and close-ended. Open-ended questions allow employees to expand the conversation in several different directions and generally require more than a few words to answer. An open-ended question differs from a close-ended question in that it is designed to solicit extended conversation from the speaker and not specific information. Examples of open-ended questions are "How did you feel about the work we did for you on your benefits communication?" "What's your current understanding of pay-for-performance systems?"

By contrast, close-ended questions can be answered specifically, in relatively few words. Although an open-ended question is designed to solicit more information from your employees, close-ended questions are designed to solicit specific information. The answer to a close-ended question should be, for example, a "yes" or "no," a specific number or name, an amount of time, and so on. Examples of close-ended questions include "By what date do you need that information?" "How long has this system been in effect?" "When would you like us to convert the system?"

## "I" Messages

In many cases, we hesitate to say how we actually feel when we respond to others. We say, "That's not funny," instead of saying, "I don't like to be laughed at." This tends to give the impression that everyone would agree and to distance you, personally, from the statement. It is much more precise and honest to use *"I" messages* and own up to feelings as your own.

An "I" message is any statement that has a first-person pronoun in it such as "I," "my," "me," "mine," or "myself." In the example given above the "I" message version is: "I don't like to be laughed at." This is direct and honest and does not imply that the collective universe is on your side against the speaker. Some other examples: "Nobody uses that performance appraisal system anymore!" versus "I don't use that performance appraisal anymore." Another example would be "Everybody knows you don't run a good meeting without an agenda." versus "I've found that using an agenda makes my meetings run more efficiently." A well-phrased "I" statement is not possible to refute since it is simply a statement of your own feelings and opinions—which you have a right to express.

## Silence

Silence is a very difficult technique to master because it can make you and your employees uncomfortable during an interaction. However, silence helps employees think through what has transpired and provides additional information or explanations when appropriately used. You should use silence in combination with other techniques, such as active listening and encouraging. This will allow employees the opportunity to freely express themselves. When silence is overused it may communicate a lack of interest on your part. Consequently, it should not be used extensively as a way to encourage employee involvement.

## Nonverbal Techniques

One of the best ways to demonstrate an interest in and acceptance of employees is to use nonverbal techniques. These are also important to establish a positive communications climate. Effective eye contact, nods of the head, and forward engaging posture are the most common type of body language.

### Clarifying

Questions asked of your employees for clarification often take the form of a statement such as "What I understand you to mean by that is . . ." This is also known as a checking-back technique. It is a good idea to ask such questions during an interaction because of the ambiguous nature of language. Otherwise, you may falsely assume that both of you are engaging in the same topic of conversation. It is just this type of assumption that prompts the anonymous quote: "I know you believe you understand what you think I said, but I am not sure you realize what you heard is not what I mean."

### Repetition

A common method of interviewing during change initiatives is to repeat the speaker's words, phrased as a question. This is done to encourage the speaker to continue speaking and add more information. For example, the speaker says, "I've been having a problem with our executive compensation." A repetition response designed to encourage further elaboration might be, "So you say you've been having a problem with executive compensation. . . . "

### Summarizing

Another form of repetition is to repeat your interpretation of what your employee has said to check the accuracy of your understanding. A summary might take the form of a statement like "As I understand it, you've been very busy with retirement issues, but the executive compensation problem is something you feel is very important to deal with right now."

A summary statement provides an opportunity to check your employees' attitudes and values around their comments by adding these values into your summary, something a repetition does not provide.

## Outcomes of a Positive Change Climate

There are several outcomes of establishing a positive change climate. They include rapport, trust, honesty, and self-esteem.

## Rapport

If change agents are able to demonstrate understanding, acceptance, and involvement, as well as use effective relationship and communication skills, they will be able to develop unconditional positive regard with their employees, which we refer to as rapport. Rapport is a deep concern for the well-being of employees, not simply a superficial relationship. It can be demonstrated when you are as interested in your employees as you are in the results they produce. Rapport is established through your sincere interest in and acceptance of employees.

Rapport demonstrates that an appropriate working relationship has been established and maintained between you and your employees. It is through rapport that employees feel free to express their opinions, ideas, beliefs, and attitudes. Once rapport has been established, employees can rid themselves of their fears and conflicts and achieve a better understanding of themselves and connection to others.

## Trust and Honesty

Another outcome of creating a climate for change is improved trust between change agents and their employees. Let's face it, establishing trust is hard work. When trust is earned, it is because you have established a working relationship free of fear, listened attentively and communicated with employees, engaged in conversations that encourage interaction, accepted employees as unique individuals, and accepted invitations to become personally involved with employees. In other words, trust is granted because you have successfully accomplished each of the previous steps, used both communication and relationship skills, and addressed the barriers to communication.

Trust is not granted to you because of your pedigree or title or because you have power or authority over employees—it is earned. Trust is based on truth, which requires open, honest, and direct communication. Consequently, hidden agendas should be avoided and discouraged.

To maintain a positive climate for change, you should avoid several behaviors that will destroy trust between you and your employees:

- Criticizing—making unwarranted negative comments about employees' performance, attitudes, and decisions.
- Diagnosing—playing amateur psychiatrist by analyzing employees' motives and behaviors.

- Advising—giving employees "the solution" to their problems without asking for their input.
- Ordering—coercing and forcing employees to do things management's way.
- Threatening—controlling employees' actions with intimidating, negative consequences.
- Avoiding—resisting logical or reasonable requests because managers disagree with employees or simply want to be difficult.
- Questioning—the "Sergeant Friday routine," questioning every decision, idea, recommendation, or suggestion (Gilley and Boughton, 1996).

Does honesty come before or after trust? When creating a climate for change, we have found that trust leads to honesty. As you demonstrate understanding, acceptance, and involvement you begin to establish trust with employees. As a result, employees begin sharing more information with you and the level of professional intimacy increases.

## Self-Esteeming

Another outcome of building positive change climates is enhanced working relationships with employees—sometimes referred to as self-esteeming. Self-esteeming can be defined as mutual and reciprocal respect and confidence when two parties work collaboratively to achieve desired results (Gilley and Boughton, 1996). It is based on collegial partnerships between you and your employees and relies on two-way communication, trust, honesty, and interaction, and should be nonjudgmental, free of fear, personal, and professional.

Because the process is reciprocal, both you and your employees benefit by working and interacting together. How can both individuals increase their self-esteem at the same time? It's easy. As a result of developing an understanding of your employees, accepting them as unique individuals, and becoming personally involved with them as professionals, you have created a higher level of trust and honesty, which in turn increases employee confidence. As confidence increases, employees are more willing to try things that they were previously afraid to do. Thus, employees are able to demonstrate successes on the job as well as learn new and exciting ways of performing their jobs. Such successes will in turn increase their self-esteem. Additionally, you have developed an understanding of your employees on a personal level; therefore, you know what is important to them and they select motivational strategies that challenge and stimulate them. You benefit by working closely with your employees, observing their growth, development, and the results that they achieve, which increases your confidence in your coaching and change management skills, thus increasing your self-esteem. Moreover, you benefit by increasing your involvement with employees, which can energize you, motivating and challenging you to become the best change agent possible. Further, improving your self-esteem encourages you to take on increasingly difficult assignments that initiate change within an organization.

## Conclusion

Creating a climate for change is an ongoing, active, and participatory process that requires a great deal of time, energy, and effort. Improved change agent–employee relationships leads to greater trust, honesty, commitment, and productivity—yielding emotional and financial rewards for participants and the organization.

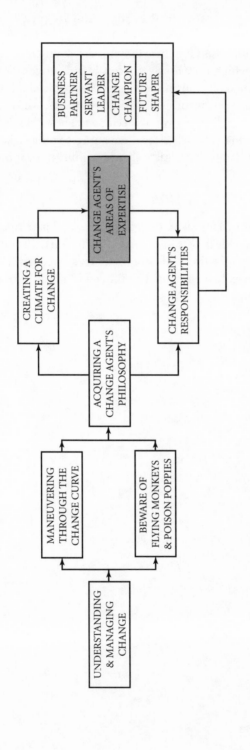

THE MANAGER AS CHANGE AGENT BLUEPRINT

# Change Agent's Areas of Expertise

Traditionally, managers have been asked to select, develop, appraise, and reward employees for their performance, but the challenge facing today's organizations requires them to understand and manage change. Therefore, they need to develop areas of expertise that are useful during the change process. Moreover, the role of change agent allows managers to exercise the greatest organizational impact and influence through their knowledge of the organization and the application of change practices and processes. It is as a result of this role that true organizational change occurs.

The primary goal of a change agent is to help an organization improve its effectiveness performance, renewal capacity, and competitive readiness. As a change agent, you help employees develop diagnostic skills used to analyze performance problems and address what gets done rather than what tasks are performed. Change agents examine the organizational structure, job design, work flow, performance appraisal and review process, employees' attitudes, performance criteria and standards, quality improvement processes, and so forth.

When implementing change, you rely on employees for technical advice and support, guide interactions between employees, or provide insight on all aspects. You work at all levels of the organization and with all types of people. Remember that certain employees have the informal power to make decisions, influence others, and provide resources needed to implement and support change, whereas others are capable of derailing a change initiative before its execution.

Change agents need to develop six areas of expertise to respond to unforeseen contingencies and provide solutions to complex, sensitive issues. The

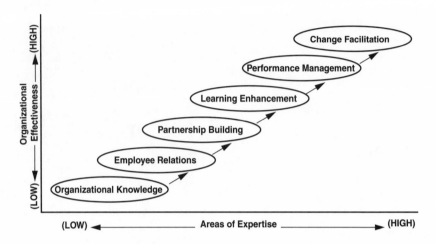

FIGURE 7.1    Change Agent's Areas of Expertise and Organizational Effectiveness

change agent areas of expertise consist of organizational knowledge, employee relations, partnership building, learning enhancement, performance management, and change facilitation (Figure 7.1). Each of these areas of expertise helps you achieve the goals previously identified, but some can have a more lasting impact. Actually, you need to combine all the areas of expertise for maximum impact. For example, your organizational knowledge and employee relations expertise can help you maneuver through the organization and bring about positive results, but your ability to build partnerships, enhance learning, conduct performance management, and facilitate change can have a transforming effect on the organization. Therefore, the latter four areas of expertise can and do have a bigger impact on organizational effectiveness.

## Organizational Knowledge

Organizational knowledge permits you to be a serious contributor responsible for its improvement (Figure 7.1). By understanding organizational operations, change agents encourage initiatives that improve an organizational effectiveness. Effective change agents demonstrate organizational knowledge by revealing an understanding of employees' needs and expectations. Thus, they adapt their practices, procedures, and initiatives to better serve their employees.

Change agents also add value to the organization by understanding business operations, thus allowing employees to adapt their practices and activities to changing business conditions. This requires strategic thinking skills, which is the ability to direct your attention to the organization's future. It includes the ability to anticipate business trends and processes and break them down into manageable units for others to understand and implement. By dismantling business trends and processes into manageable components, you generate a variety of solutions that narrow the gap between what is needed and what is delivered, making the necessary adjustments to ensure organizational success.

By demonstrating your operational insight and organizational knowledge, you improve your organizational impact and influence. This includes knowledge of organizational fundamentals, systems theory, and organizational culture. Acute insight and operational understanding will maximize your knowledge and ability to improve the organization's performance. Change agents also possess financial and organizational understanding to generate pertinent, practical solutions for their employees. Moreover, you demonstrate an understanding of the organization's philosophy that guides its action. Consequently, it is critical for change agents to think like their employees, understand how things get done inside the organization, and how and why decisions are made.

Three subroles demonstrate your organizational knowledge: scout, strategic partner, and systems linker (Gilley and Maycunich, 1998). As *scouts,* you operate as a visionary within your organization. You maneuver through the trees, avoiding obvious obstacles and guiding groups through uncharted territory in the quest for change. In short, you lead the organization into areas it has not gone before. As such you generate innovative solutions to complex problems, set priorities, synthesize employees' input, translate ideas into action plans, and direct the organization toward achieving its goals.

As *strategic partners,* you are able to understand the critical factors affecting organizational competitiveness. Strategic partners possess a thorough understanding of financial fundamentals, core processes, operations, and procedures of organizations. You therefore have the ability to communicate the benefits that change strategies can provide the organization.

Most organizations are comprised of myriad divisions, departments, units, and/or business functions, which should work in harmony to achieve efficient and effective financial results. As a *systems linker,* you unify these groups through aligning a common set of guiding principles that define the organization's direction, purpose, and focus. System linkers are able to establish connections within the organization by communicating the value and importance of teamwork. When achieved, affected parts of the organization work together in harmony.

# Employee Relations

Change agents are in a unique position to serve as employee relation experts (Figure 7.1). This area of expertise requires change agents to have the ability to build collaborative relationships with their employees, allocate resources used to improve performance, and make job assignments based on the knowledge, skills, and abilities of employees. Developing employee relationships was discussed in Chapter 6.

One of the keys to this area of expertise of change agents is to allocate resources in an efficient and effective manner. This requires change agents to maintain the correct balance between work demands and resources allocation, identifying legitimate demands on employees, and helping them focus by setting priorities. Employee relation expertise enables change agents to identify creative ways of leveraging resources so employees do not feel overwhelmed by what is expected of them.

There are several ways to assess whether you respond to demanding situations appropriately (Ulrich, 1997, 135). First, do employees control key decisionmaking processes that determine how work is done? Do employees have a vision and direction that commits them to working hard? Are employees given challenging work assignments that provide opportunities to learn new skills? Do employees work in teams or collaboratively to accomplish goals? Does the work environment and culture provide opportunities for celebration, fun, excitement, and openness? Are employees compensated and rewarded for work accomplishments? Do employees enjoy open, candid, and frequent communication with managers and supervisors? Are employees treated with dignity and are differences openly shared and respected? Do employees have access to and use of technology that makes their work easier? Do employees have the competencies (skills and knowledge) necessary to do their work well?

Positive answers to these questions enable you to determine the adequacy of employees' control, involvement, and commitment to the organization. They determine the type of challenging work provided to employees, the degree to which collaboration and teamwork are employed, and the adequacy of organizational culture. Positive answers also identify the quality of the compensation and reward systems used, quality and quantity of organizational communications, concern for due process, adequacy of technology, and employee competence.

Employee relation expertise enables you to devote most of your time guaranteeing that the organization is able to positively answer to each of the above ten questions. By doing so, you are able to enhance your organizational impact and influence. Additionally, you are able to develop relationship skills such as listening, reflecting, questioning, and summarizing. Such skills build mutual acceptance and positive regard with your employees (see Chapter 6). They also promote rapport and enhance your credibility so employees will be willing to accept your recommendations.

Developing employee relation expertise enables you to function as relationship builder, collaborator, and communicator (Gilley and Maycunich, 1998). Turning assertions into questions, giving employees options, making meetings and reports meaningful, helping employees implement solutions and interventions, being accessible, and always adding value are a few of the activities of a competent relationship builder.

Change agents establish credibility and gain employees' confidence to implement change by becoming collaborators. In this activity, you adapt your communications to your audience, listen and ask appropriate questions, present ideas clearly and concisely through well-organized written and interpersonal communications, engage in informal communications that build support, and identify common ground among employees to determine shared interests.

Developing employee relation expertise enables you to become a communicator. This activity requires developing active listening skills, using silence, demonstrating understanding, establishing rapport, communicating empathy, clarifying statements, providing timely feedback, and appropriately employing summarization techniques (see Chapter 6).

## Partnership Building

Becoming a change agent requires you to develop expertise in building partnership (Figure 7.1). A partnership helps you decide which change initiatives provide the highest value and have the greatest impact on the organization. They also promote establishment of working relationships based on shared values, aligned purpose and vision, and mutual support. Furthermore, partnerships are based on the business and performance needs of employees, not a change agent's career aspiration or professional success. Better management of limited financial and human resources is another reason for creating partnerships.

Unfortunately, some managers are not successful in developing partnerships with employees. As a result, they lack credibility with their employees, which creates an environment of mistrust and cynicism. As a result, these managers never make the transition to the role of change agent. To guarantee that this does not happen, you must develop partnerships that enhance your credibility and influence within the organization.

There are two primary elements of a partnership: purpose and partnering (Bellman, 1998). Purpose defines "why" a partnership is needed. Purpose, in essence, brings us together and provides a focus and direction for the partnership. In other words, purpose helps describe "what you intend to achieve as a result of a partnership."

Partnering exemplifies the observable dynamics between you and your employees and incorporates the common values, beliefs, assumptions, and expectations of all parties in a partnership. Managers and employees who attend to purposes but neglect partnering often fail in their work effectively altogether.

Creating partnerships helps break down walls between you and your employees. As a result, lasting commitments are developed and all parties make investments in change. You become immersed in employees' problems, needs, concerns, and expectations. Consequently, your organizational influence increases, which in turn improves your overall organizational impact.

Partnerships allow you to develop a responsive attitude, which is necessary to enable you to become customer service oriented. They enable you to develop trust and honesty with employees, allowing for the sharing of ideas, perspectives, and vision for the organization's future. Change agents engage in six interdependent activities to develop the partnership building area of expertise. Each activity enhances your credibility and acceptance within the organization and helps the organization achieve its strategic goals and objectives. As a partner, you promote an employee-oriented approach committed to helping every employee achieve performance goals and objectives. You create a positive work environment enabling change to be adopted and supported by organizational leaders, other managers, and employees. You examine the organization's efforts to determine their respective values and benefits, allowing decision makers to make critical choices about the actions that most positively impact the organization. You help the organization make positive career management decisions that help to shape the organization's direction and ensure future viability. You help employees make positive developmental decisions that help improve their long-term career expertise. You identify why employees participate in some change initiative and not others, which enables the organization to understand employees' motives and how to adjust accordingly.

By design, partnerships are long-term, synergistic engagements that focus on mutually beneficial relationships used in helping the organization successfully achieve its goals and objectives. These relationships assist you to acquire the responsive attitude necessary for you to become more customer service oriented, and better understand and anticipate employees needs.

Three types of partnerships help change agents enhance their credibility: performance, strategic, and change partnerships.

## Performance Partnerships

As a change agent, you must work closely with employees to create an environment that fosters performance improvement. To do so, change agents need to establish performance partnerships enabling employees to acquire critical skills and competencies to improve their performance and career development opportunities. This mutually beneficial partnership allows employees to acquire critical skills and competencies that enhance their performance and career development opportunities. At the same time, you enjoy better business results. Performance partnerships permit you to motivate your employees, create self-esteem in the work environment, delegate tasks and responsibilities, build on employee strengths while managing their weaknesses, and design learning acquisition and transfer plans.

Performance partnership is based on seven requirements (Burke, 1992). First, employees must want to change their performance behavior. Second, performance growth and development activities must be linked to employees' performance improvement needs as defined mutually by you and your employees. Third, change agents must identify the barriers and cultural issues that prevent learning acquisition and transfer. Fourth, change agents must identify conflicting job tasks and activities that reduce employee motivation for learning and change. Fifth, change agents must provide performance feedback, reinforcement, encouragement, and support to improve employee performance and productivity. Sixth, employees must accept the responsibility for acquiring new knowledge and skills and transferring them to the job. Seventh, change agents must recognize and reward employees for their participation in growth and development activities.

When these seven requirements for behavioral change are achieved, most employees will participate in growth and development activities. Over time, employee performance and productivity will improve, helping organizations to achieve better business results, improve their readiness for competition, and enhance their organizational renewal.

## Strategic Partnerships

Strategic business partnerships are intraorganizational alliances formed to ensure successful completion of the company's overall strategic plan. They permit change agents to align themselves with organizational leaders, senior managers, and employees for the purpose of helping the organization achieve internal alignment and long-term results.

Strategic partnerships are important for many reasons, including:

- Helping develop mutually beneficial, empathic relationships with employees, resulting in employees satisfaction and achievement of objectives.
- Breaking down walls between yourself and your employees, resulting in lasting commitments, investments in growth and development, and innovations that permeate their organizations.
- Encouraging your employees' contributions to change.
- Enabling the development of personal relationships that foster trust and honesty.
- Allowing discovery of your employees' unique qualities and to learn from them.
- Allowing you to direct their efforts at satisfying your stakeholders.
- Helping you establish credibility within the organization (Gilley and Maycunich, 2000b).

As a way of achieving strategic partnerships, you design and develop change initiatives in accordance with your employees' expressed interests as well as provide organizationwide change interventions that improve organizational effectiveness, responsiveness, and profitability.

## Change Partnerships

Because of ever-changing economic conditions and market competitiveness, organizations are forced to adjust to constantly mobile marketplaces. Consequently, change partnerships are formed to improve your organization's responsiveness and competitiveness. Change partnerships are not part of a "fix-it" strategy but rather a continual way of managing organizational change that, in time, becomes a way of organizational life. This type of partnership requires the involvement of all employees. Change partnerships are planned, data-based approaches to change involving goal setting, action planning, monitoring, feedback, and evaluating results.

Change partnerships are oriented to the long term and involve a systems approach that closely links employees to technology, organizational processes, and change. They are formed to meet employees' demands for better work environments and participation in decisionmaking. Change partnerships rely on collaborative involvement of employees and enable them to be treated as human beings instead of resources in the productivity process. These partnerships develop employees' full potential and help enhance the organization's full potential. These partnerships provide employees with opportunities for challenging work and ways to influence the manner in which they relate to work, the work environment, and the organization.

*Partnership Building Activities.* You must become skilled at performing the subroles of influencer, strategist, and problem solver in order to build lasting partnerships (Gilley and Maycunich, 1998). As influencers, change agents are directive in their attempt to influence employees thinking, initiate change, or provide specific recommendations that address complex organizational problems. To be successful as an influencer, you need to guard against your personal biases and strong opinions and remain receptive to others' views, ideas, and recommendations. You encourage the organization to take risks to achieve goals and objectives.

As *strategists,* you are competent in assessing organizational needs using quantitative and qualitative methodologies. Strategists incorporate the ideas of others into directive action plans and develop and execute financial initiatives. You also evaluate the effectiveness of change initiatives on overall organizational effectiveness.

As *problem solvers,* you strive to assess which perceived problems are critical to the organization. You take an active role in the decisionmaking and change management process. You spend a majority of your time helping employees make decisions that are beneficial to achieving desired results as well as advancing their careers.

## Learning Enhancement

For learning to be translated into value for the organization it must be successfully applied to the job. Unfortunately, many employees are "on their own" after a learning event because managers fail to support learning and fail to provide reinforcement on the job. Therefore, learning does not become a reality in the workplace. Consequently, some employees revert to their old habits as opposed to struggling with new skills and knowledge. Others neglect to transfer learning because they fear change, lack confidence, or perceive no payoff for trying new skills or knowledge. Still others fail to learn because they delay application of new knowledge or skill. Failing to execute skills properly or apply knowledge correctly will lead to the lack of learning.

Additionally, some employees fail to transfer learning to the job because managers neglect to assist them in integrating learning, skills, or knowledge, causing confusion and frustration on both sides. As a result, much of the learning is lost. Some managers fail to be positive role models, establish adequate performance standards, or create work environments conducive to learning.

Organizations contribute to the failure to transfer learning by establishing policies, procedures, work environments, and managerial practices that interfere with the integration and application of learning on the job. Moreover, some organizational leaders believe that employees are easily replaced, which encourages employees to think of learning as a waste of time. Finally, training and development practitioners present their own barriers to learning when they fail to realize that the learning process is the responsibility of everyone within the organization, or fail to link learning activities to strategic business goals and objectives.

To develop this area of expertise, you must improve your understanding of the learning process and your responsibilities before, during, and after learning acquisition.

## Learning Process

The learning process consists of both the dissemination of information and the facilitation of learning. As a result, you are responsible for providing employees with new information, ideas, content, or practice. At other times, you are responsible for encouraging them to initiate self-directed learning activities to deepen their experiences and understandings. The former refers to *infilling* (the process of disseminating information through traditional teaching activities) whereas the latter refers to *drawing out* (the process of facilitation of learning).

The desired outcome of infilling is to increase employees' knowledge, whereby you present ideas, facts, concepts, theories, and data during formal classroom activities. Typically there is little interaction between you and your employees. Drawing out emphasizes the application of ideas, facts, concepts, theories, and data based on employees' experiences and background. This process encourages interaction between you and your employees via the use of activities, application, discussion, and trial and error. Quite simply, learning facilitation requires you to provide employees information (knowledge, skills, and techniques) that they are responsible for applying on the job (see Chapter 8).

To improve learning transfer, change agents adopt several strategies before, during, and after learning acquisition.

## Responsibilities Before Learning Acquisition

Effective change agents embrace their responsibilities prior to a learning event. To do so, they focus on the learning readiness of their employees.

*Learning Readiness.* There are several reasons why employees neglect to acquire and transfer knowledge and skills to the job. The most egregious is their employees' failure to adequately prepare for the exchange of new information and content. Employees must be willing and able to learn before they can hope to acquire new knowledge and skills. If organizations fail to assess employee readiness, subsequent facilitation and developmental activities will fall short of achieving the desired results.

Possessing an attitude receptive of learning allows employees to acquire the skills and knowledge necessary to improve performance on the job. Many employees seek learning experiences to cope with specific performance requirements, which leads to promotional opportunities and improved job performance. They contend that the more practical the learning process is the easier it is to participate.

To enhance learning readiness, you need to help your employees become self-directed learners. As self-directed learners, employees need to adopt controls and techniques useful in teaching themselves about a particular subject. This is referred to as self-teaching. Next, employees need to develop personal autonomy. This is achieved by taking control of the goals and purposes of learning, and assuring ownership of learning—leading to an internal change of consciousness in which the learner views knowledge as contextual and fully questions what is learned (Knowles, Holton, and Swanson, 1998, 135). By combining these two principles, employees should be prepared to engage in learning activities that enable them to demonstrate personal autonomy and the competencies necessary to effectively participate in self-taught activities.

Moreover, employees must develop the ability to relate to peers collaboratively. They must see themselves as resources for diagnosing needs, planning learning activities, providing feedback or constructive criticism when necessary, and diagnosing their own learning needs realistically with the assistance of peers and other resources. Employees must translate learning needs into performance objectives through activities that ensure their accomplishment. They need to relate to you as a facilitator and helper and identify human and material resources appropriate for different types of learning. Employees need to identify and select effective strategies for making use of learning resources and implement these tactics skillfully and with initiative. Finally, employees need to collect and validate evidence that demonstrates accomplishment of their performance objectives.

## Strategies During Learning

Effective change agents embrace their responsibilities as trainers during a learning event. To do so, they focus on communication and language used during training, instruction, enlightenment, practice, and review.

*Communications and Language.* Learning will be incomplete unless the language used is plain and clear, language that the employee understands. Language functions as the instrument of thought. Thus, words are tools by which change agents shape employees' understanding of complex issues and ideas. Because ideas become inculcated in words, they take the form of language and stand ready to be studied and known, marshaled into the mechanism of intelligible thought. Thus, like surgeons use their instruments to save lives, change agents use language to bring about comprehension and enlightenment.

Many learning interventions require highly technical information that is a language unto itself. Thus, you need to frequently test employees' understanding of words to guarantee their correct usage. Moreover, study of employee language reveals the words and symbols they use along with their meanings. If the learner fails to comprehend, the idea or thought should be repeated in different language or an analogy should be presented as an example. Certainly, using the simplest and fewest words possible to express meaning decreases confusion or misunderstandings.

*Instruction.* The primary purpose of the learning process is to acquire information or content that is used to develop new skills, competency, or approaches to generating performance outcomes. The responsibility for learning falls primarily on employees; change agents are the conduit used in the transportation of information.

The instruction process is most effective when a problem-centered approach is used. This allows meaningful, practical information to be emphasized—the more practical the better. Information should be arranged so that each step leads easily and naturally to the next. Present one idea or concept at a time, allowing employees ample opportunity to integrate it with their existing knowledge. Further, information should be presented in a manner permitting mastery (exemplary performance).

Although employees maintain the ability to learn throughout their lives, special consideration should be given to individuals who do not have the ability to obtain or retain information as quickly as others. Using illustrations, examples, and stories and encouraging employees to share experiences with their peers provides a common framework on which to base learning activities.

*Enlightenment.* When learning moves from a theoretical to a practical act, employees obtain new awareness and insights. John Milton Gregory, in his 1884 classic *Seven Laws of Teaching,* pointed out that "learning is not memorization and repetition of words and ideas of the instructor . . . contrary to common understanding this is much more the work of the learner than the instructor . . . learning comes by progressions of interpretation which may be easy and rapid . . . no real learning is wholly a repetition of the thoughts of another" (106–107). In other words, learning is the process of internalizing knowledge and applying it. The learning process is not complete until this last stage has been reached. To ensure that this occurs, change agents help employees form a clear idea of the work to be done and ask employees to express in their own words or in writing the meaning of the information or content as they understand it. You should question learners in a nonthreatening manner, encouraging them to share their point of view. You help employees become self-directed, independent investigators responsible for their own learning, growth, and development. Finally, you challenge your employees' understanding of information so that they can reproduce it in a correct, acceptable form.

*Practice.* Practice is a very important step in the change process because prior knowledge interferes with new knowledge. Therefore, practice should continue until employees overcome prior learning or are able to replicate skills, techniques, or behaviors in a safe environment.

Practice can be differentiated from application in a simple way. Practice is the repetition of tasks or the demonstration of skills during formal learning activities conducted in safe environments where failure is common and expected. Application is the execution of new skills or knowledge under real life conditions. Although practice should be as realistic as possible, failures will not endanger others, diminish self-esteem, or result in loss of productivity. Practice need not be a concluding action during the learning process but it should occur throughout learning activities as new tasks and steps are introduced. It could be said that practice is a prerequisite step to actual application.

*Review.* In our haste to complete the learning process, review is often over-looked or not emphasized enough. Quite simply, review is a process of re-thinking, reviewing, reproducing, or practicing the material, information, content, or skills that have been communicated during instruction. As change agents, you should use feedback and summarize frequently to enhance reten-tion and recall. Failure to incorporate feedback and review into learning ac-tivities could result in the incorrect application of material or failure to apply it altogether.

Review, however, is more than repetition. A machine completes a process, but only intelligent human beings review and assess it. Review implies rethink-ing a task, skill, or competency to deepen one's understanding of how to per-form it correctly, including making new associations and conceptualizations.

Review should not be a separate act attached to an instructional event, but rather an important part of the process itself. Therefore, neglecting the re-view phase leaves work unfinished. Certainly, any exercise or activity using previously presented information or content is considered a review. Effective reviews provide employees with opportunities to apply new skills or compe-tencies accordingly. These controlled situations are safer and more secure than actual job situations, allowing for mistakes to be made in a relatively cost-free environment, both financially and personally.

## Strategies After Learning

Effective change agents embrace their responsibilities after a learning event. To do so, they focus on application, reinforcement and feedback, reflection, expectation, application, and inspection, and recognition and reward.

*Application.* Change agents greatly enhance learning by adhering to one simple principle—people learn best by doing. Learning by doing is simply a process of applying knowledge and skill on the job. Research has shown that the most effective learning results when application on the job immediately follows initial training.

New knowledge and skills may interfere with current employee perfor-mance. Consequently, it is critical for you to analyze the long-term effects of such conflict to determine the effects on overall productivity, which is re-ferred to as failure analysis. Failure analysis allows you and employees to identify possible conflicts to help integrate learning in the future.

One of the best ways to improve learning is to allow employees to fail in safe environments such as work simulations and case studies (see Chapter 5). Employees who are allowed to fail in comfortable, supportive settings will learn a great deal about which skill levels will or will not work on the job. The same approach should be applied when employees attempt to apply new skills and knowledge on the job.

*Reinforcement and Feedback.* Employees are more likely to repeat activities when positive reinforcement and feedback occur. Additionally, reinforcement and feedback provide rich incentives for learning by enhancing employee self-esteem and encouraging positive performance patterns. One of your best reinforcement tools is the performance review, which allows you the opportunity to measure employee application of new skills and knowledge on the job. Incorporating evaluation of learning into the performance review and appraisal process communicates to employees the value and importance of learning. If new skills and knowledge are being evaluated, they must be worth obtaining.

As a change agent, you follow several guidelines when providing reinforcement and feedback to employees, including being specific so employees know what they did correctly, being sincere so employees accept feedback without manipulation, and delivering feedback clearly and concisely, and immediately after employees perform tasks correctly.

*Reflection.* Reflection proves one of the most powerful activities in which employees engage to enhance transfer of new knowledge and skills. The goal of reflection is to solidify one's insight and to guarantee that mistakes and successes just learned are remembered, to identify themes and patterns of performance, to challenge one's assumptions, to ensure one learns appropriately, and to remain open to new change opportunities. Employees should reflect on major events such as crises, completion of big assignments, or major milestones in a project. They should conduct reflection activities periodically as a way of summarizing their progress. Further, employees should have ample opportunity to examine the application and results of new skills, knowledge, or behavior on the job.

Reflection enables employees to learn from their mistakes, understand their own thoughts and feelings, cope with barriers within the organization, and plot strategies for future use and application of skills and knowledge. Reflection enables employees to consider their next opportunities to apply new knowledge and skills. Moreover, reflection allows employees to consider different situations where their learning may be applied, as well as what they might do differently under similar circumstances. Finally, employees consider what performance components can be improved the next time they are able to apply the skills and knowledge being reflected upon.

*Expectation, Application, and Inspection.* Developmentally oriented change agents often discuss their expectations with employees prior to engaging in learning activities. This also provides employees with the opportunity to discuss the integration of new learning on the job. Furthermore, they assess whether the subsequent learning caused performance improvement. This three-way technique, known as expectation, application, and inspection, ensures you that your expectations are in alignment with the application of learning through inspection activities. This technique also guarantees that employees are held accountable for the application of learning on the job. When it is used, employees know what and how they are expected to perform as a result of new learning, including the quantity and quality of their performance outcomes.

Expectation, application, and inspection require scrutiny of employee performance to determine whether established performance standards have been met. It also helps determine whether learning activities facilitate performance improvement. In this way, expectations are linked with accountability, which ultimately enhances learning. In other words, learning will only take place when you link expectation and inspection together. Therefore, employees know what they are being asked to do and how they will be held accountable.

*Recognition and Reward.* Establishing a connection between integrating learning and organizational rewards is the single greatest factor in improving individual achievements. It could be said that *the things that get rewarded get done* (see Chapter 4). Learning, therefore, must be rewarded to ensure its success. Certainly, most employees want to be rewarded and recognized for integrating learning. When this does not occur, employees often feel that their application of learning is a waste of time and effort. Similarly, failing to reward learning that improves performance will extinguish learning.

Prior to beginning the learning process, you should identify how you will celebrate employees' new learning, increased skills, or improved attitudes. Active participation in celebration on your part reinforces the importance of learning.

### Questions Used to Improve Learning

The following questions assist you in improving employees' learning:

1. How are knowledge, skills, and attitudes being used on the job?
2. What barriers prevent learning from being transferred?

3. What roles do change agents and supervisors play in transferring and reinforcing learning on the job?
4. What should be done before, during, and after implementing the learning process to enhance it?
5. What role do employees play in learning?
6. What role does the organization play in learning?
7. What activities should be used to improve learning?
8. What can be done to increase learning effectiveness and efficiency?

## Performance Management

In today's competitive marketplace, you are rewarded for performance. Period. In fact, performance management, as a subdiscipline within the larger field of human resource management, has essentially been developed over the last five to seven years in response to this shift to a performance philosophy in employee evaluation, career development, and compensation. Performance management, put simply, is an attempt to integrate organizational needs for efficiency and effectiveness with employee needs for professional growth and rewarding work. This integration is long overdue and is the essence of true performance management.

Many organizations fail to achieve business results because they can talk the talk but can't walk the walk. Typically, these organizations have well-written, meaningful mission statements and strategic plans, but are ineffective in bringing about business results that are needed to remain vibrant and competitive. Although they boast that their employees are their greatest asset and most valuable resource, their actions express a different reality.

Such organizations fail to maintain a comprehensive performance management process that would be instrumental in bringing about needed performance improvements to secure desired business results. Consequently, their strategic business goals and objectives are often unrealized. To compound the problem, such organizations often believe that their employees are easily replaced, so policies and procedures demonstrate a *revolving-door philosophy* toward human resources. Additionally, they exhibit an attitude of corporate indifference whereby they *wash their hands of any responsibility for their actions and decisions regarding employee performance, and are quickly willing to blame scapegoats for their own failings.* The problem facing today's organizations is their ignorance regarding how to manage performance, develop people, or create systems and techniques that enhance organizational effectiveness. In short, organizations must transform employees into high performers who are their greatest asset. As a result, developing expertise in the design and development of performance management systems is essential.

The first step in improving and managing performance is to define the term *performance*. To *perform* means "to begin and carry through to completion; to take action in accordance with the requirements of; fulfill. *Performance* means something performed; an accomplishment" (Rothwell 1996b, 26). Thus, performance is synonymous with outcomes, results, or accomplishments.

Performance should not be confused with other terms like behavior, work activities, duties, responsibilities, or competencies. A *behavior* is an observable action taken to achieve results, whereas a *work activity* is a task or series of tasks taken to achieve results. Therefore, a work activity has a definite beginning, middle, and end. A *duty* is a moral obligation to perform, a *responsibility* is an action or a result for which one is accountable, and a *competency* is an area of knowledge or skill that is critical for producing key outputs that employees bring to their jobs.

To enhance organizational performance, you should engage in several activities:

- Sponsoring performance management systems
- Establishing appropriate goals
- Improving job design
- Conducting developmental evaluations
- Creating growth and development plans
- Linking compensation and rewards to employee growth and development

### Sponsoring Performance Management Systems

Successful implementation of performance management systems mandates significant change in organizational philosophy, operations, and strategy. This monumental effort requires organizational players—*managers, acting as change agents*—to sponsor change, since they are the frontline *doers* responsible for incremental performance improvement.

Sponsoring performance management systems requires you to generate excitement and mobilize commitment for performance improvement through change. To achieve this end, you eliminate systems and structures that interfere with change initiatives. Change initiatives that are linked to critical performance management components such as training, employee appraisals, coaching, and compensation and rewards will bring about the business results desired by an organization. Additionally, you supervise the performance management progress and encourage organizational leaders' and senior managers' actions that make change last. You build coalitions of support for performance management systems and to recognize others who must be committed to this effort (Ulrich, 1997, 160). Moreover, you enlist support from key individuals in the organization and build a responsibility matrix to bring about performance improvement through change. Furthermore, you measure the success of performance management systems, identify its results, and recognize benchmarks of progress. Finally, you have a plan for adapting performance management systems over time.

## Establishing Appropriate Goals

Every job within an organization has one or more goals to be accomplished. Goals define outcomes in terms of end products or services, act as continual points of reference for settling disputes and misunderstandings about the project, and keep all objectives and associated work on track (Weiss and Wysocki, 1992). It is a global statement of purpose and direction toward which all objectives, activities, and tasks will point. Work goals enable employees to stay focused on desired results and promote agreement and commitment regarding performance outcomes. Goal statements help you and your employees know a successful outcome has been achieved, thus they reveal to everyone involved what the end will look like (Randolph and Posner, 1992). Effectively written performance goals, those that are the result of collaboration between managers and employees, are specific, measurable, attainable, realistic, and time-based (SMART). Performance goals that meet this SMART criteria are more easily measured and allow employees greater understanding of what is in it for them.

## Improving Job Design

Organizations achieve their strategic business goals and objectives though the execution of myriad jobs. Therefore, it could be said that the heart of job design is the organization's strategic business goals and objectives that focus employees' efforts. Thus, these two components are dependent on each other. However, they differ in purpose and order. Strategic business goals and objectives represent the criteria used to measure the entire organization's success. The most common examples of strategic business goals and objectives are increasing sales revenue, market share, quality, and profits. Thus, they serve as targets for the organization. On the other hand, job design (that is, jobs) is the means by which strategic goals and objectives are achieved.

Jobs that fail to support organizational achievement of its strategic goals and objectives cease to be valuable. Thus it is critical to link job analysis to these outcomes. Accordingly, an organization must first identify its strategic business goals and objectives prior to participating in the job design process (see Chapter 5).

Every job is housed within a department, division, or work unit. At this level important business processes (for example, financial analysis, selling, record keeping, claims processing, and customer service) can be identified (Rummler and Brache, 1995). Therefore, part of the job design process involves identifying interfaces between differing business processes to eliminate breakdowns or isolate areas of improvement that ultimately impact organizational performance capacity. For example, an insurance claim passes through several business processes (departments and people) before a check is finally written and sent to a customer. In this example, a simple customer request passes through six different departments and several different people before the customer's needs are satisfied. Each of these interfaces can introduce errors, inefficiencies, and communication breakdowns. These include:

- The insurance agent or representative taking the claim (sales department—sales agent's representative)
- The claims department that processes the claim internally (claims department—claims agent)
- The claims adjuster that reviews the damage and submits a report to the claims department (adjustment department—claims adjuster)
- The supervisor of the claims department that approves the claim (claims department—supervisor)
- The audit department that reviews the claim report to determine its accuracy (audit department—auditor)
- The accounting department that pays the claim (accounting department—accountant)
- The postal department that mails the check to the customer (mail department—postal worker)

Job design activities are used to make job-related employment decisions such as establishing interviewing criteria and selection requirements used when hiring new employees. Job analysis is also used to clarify job requirements and the relationships among jobs, forecast human resource needs, and identify training, transfer, and promotion requirements. Additionally, it is used to evaluate employee performance, conduct compensation reviews, enhance career planning, and develop job classifications. Moreover, job design uncovers opportunities for performance improvement and employee growth and development. It is used to improve career counseling activities, resolve grievances and jurisdictional disputes, improve working methods, and identify job classifications useful in developing selection, training, and compensation systems (Cascio, 1995).

## Performance Coaching

As organizations contemplate their future, they often overlook one of the most common problems preventing them from achieving their desired business results—*managerial malpractice*. Simply stated, managerial malpractice is maintaining and using managers who are unqualified, poorly trained, misguided, or inadequately prepared (Gilley and Boughton, 1996, 4). These managers do not have the interpersonal skills required to enhance employee commitment and improve organizational performance. This problem has plagued organizations for years and has become the Achilles' heel of thousands of firms.

Managerial malpractice is a simple problem that is seldom addressed by organizations—and if left unchecked will prevent firms from achieving the effectiveness and efficiency they desire. In fact, organizations would never allow their strategic planning activities, financial management, product quality, service reliability, organizational structure and cultures, and policies and procedures to be such a low priority.

Since managers are at the heart of every organization regardless of its size, complexity, or purpose, they are assigned the task of securing results through people. They serve as guides, directors, decision makers, and energizers for their employees. Managers further function as trainers, performance improvement consultants, career counselors, and mentors in an effort to maximize results needed by the organization. They are the conduits of organizational change and development, without which organizations struggle in mediocrity.

Unfortunately, many organizations typically pluck managers from the ranks of day-to-day operations because they possess advanced technical knowledge. Little or no attention is paid to the interpersonal and leadership skills necessary to secure results through people. Promoting individuals in this manner discounts the importance of the interactive people skills necessary to achieve desired business results. As a result, employees are subjected to inexperienced, ineffective, or incompetent managers. Because organizations fail to focus on the necessary interpersonal skills needed to enhance manager-employee relationships, they miss opportunities to develop effective performance management practices.

As a result of managerial malpractice employee morale and productivity remain low, which leads to poor-quality products and services and higher costs. The daunting question looms—"What should an organization do to overcome managerial malpractice?" The answer rests in the successful transformation from managing to performance coaching.

The purpose of performance coaching is to help improve employee performance, solve problems, and secure desired organizational results. At its heart, performance coaching is a person-centered management technique that requires face-to-face communications, personal involvement with employees, and establishment of rapport. This is an active process requiring constant shifts from one role to another. It transforms managers from passive observers to active participants with employees. Performance coaching is based on good questioning, listening, feedback, and facilitation skills as opposed to autocratic, controlling techniques.

Peterson and Hicks (1996, 14) believe that coaching is a continuous process, not an occasional conversation, that equips people with the tools, knowledge, and opportunities they need to develop themselves and to be more effective employees. Further, they maintain that the performance coaching process allows managers to embark upon three uniquely separate frontiers. These include working one-on-one with employees, guiding employees to learn for themselves, and orchestrating resources and learning opportunities by which employees maximize their growth and development potential.

Performance coaching occurs whenever and wherever a need arises—bolstering the relationship between managers and employees. Thus, the key to effective performance coaching is to handle problem situations without causing resentment on the part of employees. An overzealous manager wishing to demonstrate superior knowledge and power easily creates resentment. Consequently, performance coaching is a minute-by-minute, day-by-day activity that replaces the traditional directing, organizing, coordinating, and controlling activities so common to synergistic partnerships.

To be an effective performance coach, managers must be able to create an environment that brings out the best in employees. To accomplish this, Gilley and Boughton (1996, 43–45) believe that managers need to establish clear performance goals, provide accurate feedback, and be patient with employees who are experiencing difficulty on the job. They also need to create fear-free environments, expect success of employees, and encourage excellence. To achieve this end, managers need to ask more questions, allow employees to make mistakes, and govern their own performance.

Peterson and Hicks (1996) believe that managers need to possess several personal qualities to be effective at performance coaching. Managers need to be enthusiastic, self-controlled, impartial, honest, self-confident, genuine, friendly, optimistic, visionary, open-minded, flexible, and resourceful. In addition, effective managers must be willing to accept criticism, maintain a sense of humor, be willing to allow others to offer suggestions and recommendations, and be willing to accept employees' successes and failures.

## Conducting Developmental Evaluations

Most organizations require regularly scheduled employee performance appraisals whereby change agents judge employee performance and grant compensation increases accordingly. As we discussed in Chapter 5, one reason for the disparity between performance appraisal theory and practice is in the execution of the performance appraisal process. Although performance appraisals are used to improve performance and facilitate change, this is seldom the result. Most organizations rely on performance appraisal forms that allow managers to painlessly evaluate their employees by assigning numbers to predetermined performance categories. Unfortunately, by making the process as simple as possible, it prevents you and your employees from thinking developmentally. In fact, these forms are more damaging than beneficial because they prevent you from working collaboratively with your employees in their development. Overcoming this barrier requires you to be given degrees of freedom to work with your employees to identify performance problems, solutions, and developmental opportunities. By eliminating useless, wasteful performance appraisal and review forms, you can substitute them with a one-on-one interaction known as a developmental evaluation (Gilley, Boughton, and Maycunich, 1999).

Developmental evaluations are an excellent tool for analyzing employee performance and making recommendations for improvement. They help you to isolate barriers that prevent exemplary performance and to identify strategies to overcome them. Consequently, development evaluations provide formal, summative evaluations of an employee's current performance, skills, and aptitudes and are designed to help employees adopt corrective actions or identify activities that will enhance their future potential.

## Creating Employee Growth and Development Plans

Growth and development plans are the cornerstones of performance management systems because they help shift the emphasis from short-term performance results to long-term development strategies. They are based on a process between you and your employees designed to help employees acquire new knowledge and skills and apply them to their jobs.

Development plans should identify career interests (both short-term and longer range), technical, managerial, and interpersonal qualifications, future development requirements, and employees' perceptions of development activities (Simonsen, 1997). Additionally, you are responsible for providing a brief review of the employee's accomplishments, an assessment of his or her qualifications in terms of strengths and areas needing improvement, development opportunities, career recommendations, potential next assignments, and an assessment of the individual's stated career route and goals.

There are several benefits to growth and development plans (Simonsen, 1997). First, organizations have a record of employees' interests, mobility, and goals. Second, information can be available in a database for promotional consideration and human resource planning. Third, development plans serve as a need assessment that can be used in designing and developing learning interventions. Fourth, they reveal employee involvement in career management. Fifth, development plans can help identify employee readiness to upgrade skills and keep them current. Finally, an annual development plan is a means of accountability.

## Linking Compensation and Rewards to Growth and Development

The practice of adhering to an entitlement philosophy of performance evaluation is a thing of the past. Gone are the days when employees were appraised as *effective* and given lock-step raises and promotions as a result. No longer are employees rewarded for simply putting in another year of service. Even in many unionized work environments, seniority is much less important than it used to be.

Typically, compensation and reward programs have been based on performance, with little consideration given to rewarding employees for enhancing their skills or competencies. However, performance improvement without increased knowledge and skills (growth and development) prevents an organization from maintaining the growth phase of the organizational life cycle. Failure to perpetuate the growth phase leads to organizational stagnation and eventual decline. Consequently, compensation and reward programs need to be focused on rewarding employee growth and development to ensure that employee skills and competencies continue to evolve in the context of organizational performance (see Chapter 12).

Once employee compensation and rewards are linked to employee growth and development, performance increases dramatically (Gilley and Maycunich, 2000a). Thus, compensation and rewards become a vehicle for increasing employee development as opposed to mere performance achievement. However, the shift from rewarding performance to growth and development involves a remarkable transformation. You must develop a compensation and reward philosophy, align compensation and rewards with guiding principles, and select appropriate compensation and reward strategies (see Chapter 6). Additionally, you identify long-term performance growth and development goals and offer rewards that enhance employee growth and development. Finally, you link compensation and rewards to performance growth and development outcomes.

## Change Facilitation

The change agent's final area of expertise is to become proficient in change facilitation. A facilitator is an individual who guides a group toward a destination (Hunter et al., 1994). The destination for a change agent is to bring about a change (types identified in Chapter 1) within an organization. To achieve this objective, change agents need to develop the change facilitation area of expertise.

Change facilitation is a process rather than a technique or outcome. Therefore, you direct your energies toward helping employees understand the purpose of change and their roles and responsibilities in implementing it. During change facilitation you gather employees' opinions, suggestions, and recommendations regarding the best way of generating the desired change in the workplace. In short, you use your relationship and communications skills to encourage participation in the change process. This is done for the purpose of developing support for proposed change and making employees feel more comfortable with the disruption brought about by change.

Facilitating change effectively is an art; it offers you a unique opportunity to work alongside and for people in such a way that allows them to enhance and fulfil their responsibility. It also allows you to be a *peaceful warrior*, responsible for bring about needed change through forthright engagement (Hunter et al., 1994). Change facilitation requires you to eliminate unproductive or sabotaging behavioral patterns that will interfere with implementing change. It requires you to be vigilant and ready for action. Finally, it requires you to protect individual employees from becoming casualties of change by engaging in a constant awareness of their concerns, expectations, and actions during the change process.

Change facilitation means guiding employees through processes to achieve the desired outcomes. For example, you guide learning, performance improvement, employee development, conflict resolution, creative problem solving and decisionmaking, strategic planning, and performance and change management processes.

During change facilitation, you do not advise or make decisions for your employees but seek agreement between them. This is accomplished by encouraging employees to develop an appreciation for each other's differences and the complexity of change. Additionally, you improve participation by enhancing your employees' tolerance for ambiguity. Finally, you enhance optimism, hope, and opportunity by encouraging employees to discover their own solutions to problems brought about by change.

During change facilitation, you maximize learning opportunities. Your primary purpose is to assist employees through the change curve by helping them understand their concerns, expectations, thoughts, and fears (see Chapter 3). In this area of expertise, you act as a catalyst for employees by introducing them to the fundamentals of change, which in turn helps them appreciate its importance. Consequently, you become a mentor to employees by allowing them to explore and uncover their own knowledge. This is achieved by encouraging employees to question, confront, and challenge their own assumptions about change, thus enabling them to be willing to embrace and accept alternatives and differences. In other words, providing employees with perspectives regarding the learning that has occurred will greatly influence their ultimate success when implementing change.

In this area of expertise, you focus primarily on processes, ensuring that all employees are permitted adequate time to voice their experiences, opinions, concerns, and reflections regarding change (Sofo, 2000). During change facilitation, you encourage problem solving through personal reflection and application of learning on the job. In group situations, you help employees examine their behavior, which includes their ability to listen, provide feedback, generate solutions, plan intervention, and challenge one another.

There are several key practices that you can use to get extraordinary things done in organizations. You can achieve these feats through sharing control and enabling others to act. The act of engaging others is the chief distinguishing feature of facilitating; that is, you make things easier for your employees by sharing responsibility and enhancing their ability to act as contributing members of the organization.

During change facilitation, you must relinquish some of your control. When you fail to do this, you reduce your effectiveness. Therefore, you relinquish your traditional area of expertise of issuing detailed instructions, controlling work flow, and observing employees to ensure that they produce adequate outcomes. Your new area of expertise places more emphasis on facilitating and coaching within a team environment, which enhances employee development over the long term. During change facilitation, you engage in several activities:

- Helping employees learn from their work through action research methods
- Developing your employees skills
- Employing coaching and mentoring as part of your daily work routine
- Encouraging responsibility for self-motivation and achieving organizational goals
- Using participative and facilitative methods to resolve conflict
- Inspiring a shared vision
- Challenging processes by confronting, experimenting, and searching for opportunities (Sofo, 2000)

As a change agent, your facilitation expertise benefits employees as well as the organization in a variety of ways. First, you create a work environment based on understanding, acceptance, and involvement, which enhance rapport, trust and honesty, and self-esteeming behaviors (see Chapter 6). Second, you enhance openness by encouraging cooperation and collaboration. Third, you foster inclusiveness and engagement by developing a solution-oriented culture. Fourth, you cultivate communities of inquirers by allowing employees the opportunity to participate openly in the change process. Fifth, you enhance creativity by encouraging innovative problem solving. Sixth, you enhance communications and synergy by improving employee relationships, which results in a more collegial work environment.

## How Facilitation Accelerates the Change Process

During change facilitation, you help employees discover how to learn on their own and how to create new meaning. This can be accomplished by asking questions, breaking complex ideas and tasks into smaller parts, determining the extent that learning occurs, and focusing learning on a specific goal or action (Heiman and Slomianko, 1990).

It should be stressed that you are instrumental in helping employees reflect on their learning. Reflection is an intentional and complex activity during which they review and replay experiences, address feelings associated with experiences, and reevaluate experiences in light of their description and feelings.

During change facilitation, you are particularly effective if you are able to help employees focus on learning, question their current assumptions, or overcome negative past experiences (Kouzes and Posner, 1996). This occurs by providing unbiased advice and direction regarding employees' patterns of thinking. Effective change agents allow and encourage employees to assume responsibility for learning. In fact, many employees may not need to rely on you once they understand these principles.

### Questions for Improving Change Facilitation

Certainly, change facilitation is a challenging endeavor. Change agents are better prepared for this area of expertise by addressing the following questions:

1. What is the need for the learning intervention?
2. Who is the change sponsor?
3. What are the expectations and commitment of the client or sponsor?
4. What other key decision makers in the organization have an interest in this intervention?
5. What are the expectations of change sponsors, technical advisers, appliers, coaches, change agents, and employees?
6. What is the scope of the learning intervention?
7. What is the time frame of the learning intervention?
8. What other individuals or groups may be affected by the change initiative (i.e., departments, units, divisions)?
9. What related learning interventions have been implemented in the organization?
10. What were the results?
11. What sources of support exist for the learning intervention?
12. What are the possible constraints to the intervention?
13. What other economic, political, or cultural factors may affect the success of the intervention? (Spitzer, 1992)

## Conclusion

To become a change agent, you need to develop several areas of expertise useful when implementing and managing change. Each of these areas of expertise positively improves organizational effectiveness, but partnership building, learning enhancement, performance management, and change facilitation have the greatest impact (Figure 7.1). Acquiring this expertise is a time-consuming and complex process. However, once obtained it will enhance your credibility within the organization.

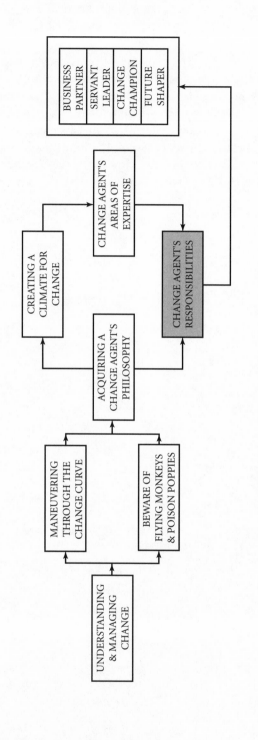

THE MANAGER AS CHANGE AGENT BLUEPRINT

CHANGE AGENT'S RESPONSIBILITIES

BUSINESS PARTNER

SERVANT LEADER

CHANGE CHAMPION

FUTURE SHAPER

CHANGE AGENT'S AREAS OF EXPERTISE

CREATING A CLIMATE FOR CHANGE

ACQUIRING A CHANGE AGENT'S PHILOSOPHY

MANEUVERING THROUGH THE CHANGE CURVE

BEWARE OF FLYING MONKEYS & POISON POPPIES

UNDERSTANDING & MANAGING CHANGE

# The Change Agent's Responsibilities

As a change agent, you need to accept a variety of new and exciting responsibilities. Each is designed to maximize the effectiveness of change initiatives and achieve change goals (such as improve communications, enhance employee relationships, improve organizational performance capacity, enhance the organization's culture, improve employee resiliency, and improve work environments). The ultimate outcome achieved by way of these responsibilities is improving organizational effectiveness. The responsibilities include:

- Demonstrating organizational knowledge
- Improving organizational communication
- Solving problems
- Building consensus and commitment for change
- Facilitating learning
- Conducting analysis
- Implementing and managing change
- Enhancing resilience (Figure 8.1)

These responsibilities can be arranged by their impact on organizational effectiveness. The responsibilities at the bottom of the pyramid occupy the majority of a change agent's time but have the least *direct impact* in improving organizational effectiveness. Although important, these lower-level responsibilities can neither bring about long-term systemic change nor can they independently enhance these outcomes. However, they do serve as the

FIGURE 8.1    Change Agent's Responsibilities

foundation of a change agent's efforts. If these responsibilities are neglected, a change agent will not have the credibility required to engage in higher-level responsibilities. Finally, there is a direct correlation between these seven responsibilities and the areas of expertise of a change agent discussed in Chapter 7 (Figure 8.2).

## Demonstrating Organizational Knowledge

You must demonstrate your understanding of your organization as a way of illustrating your capacity to initiate change initiatives. This includes your understanding of how your organization operates, how decisions are made, and how business gets done, which enhances your credibility within the organization. Failure to actively demonstrate your organizational knowledge and thus your lack of credibility may prevent you from implementing change. Finally, this responsibility includes being able to communicate effectively and efficiently with executives and stakeholders.

Organizations are complex, hierarchical structures comprised of impersonal relationships organized to produce products and services. However, we often forget that organizations are made up of people. People constitute all aspects of organizational life. They do not haphazardly reside within organizations; each has his or her selected purpose for existence and responsibilities

| Areas of Expertise | Responsibilities |
|---|---|
| Organizational Knowledge | Demonstrating Organizational Knowledge |
| Employee Relations | Improving Organizational Communication |
| Partnership Building | Solving Problems |
| | Building Consensus and Commitment for Change |
| Learning Enhancement | Facilitating Learning |
| Performance Management | Conducting Analysis |
| Change Facilitation | Implementing and Managing Change |
| | Enhancing Resilience |

FIGURE 8.2    Relationship Between Change Agent's Areas of Expertise and Responsibilities

for tasks and activities that produce outputs necessary for the survival of the firm.

As a change agent, it is occasionally useful to think of organizations as icebergs where you only see the part above the surface. This represents the formal components of an organization's perceived image, business logo, or what executives want you to think the firm represents. Beneath the water's surface lies the real organization, the hierarchical layers, departments, units, functions, policies, procedures, practices, managerial relationships, and so forth.

Another way of thinking about an organization's system is by examining the dynamic interdependence of its essential elements. Figure 8.3 provides an overview. The arrows in both directions convey an open system principle— what changes in one factor will eventually affect the whole. If an organization is healthy and produces positive results, these seven interdependent elements are working in harmony. When an organization fails to achieve desired results, you can look to the relationships among these elements to reveal potential breakdowns, areas of weakness, or both. Once a breakdown has been discovered, it is useful to examine these elements in greater detail. Although it is essential to examine each one carefully, it proves more important to assess their interdependence and relationship to discover the potential for embracing change. Consequently, change initiatives can be targeted to improve various elements of organizational system. Thus, you will have a systematic

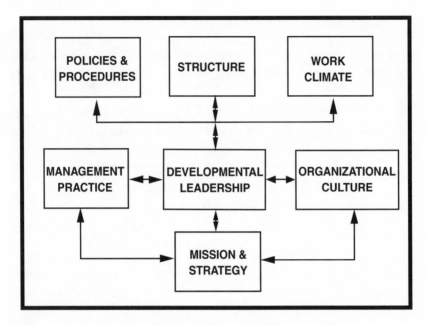

FIGURE 8.3    Organizational System (Gilley and Maycunich, 1998)

approach to examine weaknesses as well as looking for opportunities for improvement between and among these seven elements.

The center of an organizational system is leadership. We believe that leaders are at the heart of every organization. Their skills and abilities impact and
influence the organization's direction and energize, excite, and influence its
workforce. Moreover, leadership directly impacts the four most important
functions within the firm—structure, culture, managerial practice, and mission and strategy.

Indirectly, leadership influences policies, procedures, and work climate,
which are greatly impacted by such things as organizational structure, culture, and managerial practices. The distance between various functions is also
significant. For example, changes in organizational structure may not directly
affect its culture unless leadership and work climate change simultaneously.
Moreover, structural changes may or may not have an impact on the organization's mission and strategy unless leadership deems it necessary. Similarly,
improvements in managerial practices may not significantly affect an organization's work climate unless the structure, leadership, and culture are altered
to reflect these improvements. Changes in policies and procedures may not
impact work climate or culture unless structural considerations and leadership are fully supportive of these changes. Although leadership blesses policy

or procedural changes, in reality many changes occurring inside individual departments are rarely, if ever, fully disclosed to senior management. Consequently, departments may vary drastically in their interpretations of organizational rules and regulations that, over time, may foster a somewhat schizophrenic work climate and culture. Improving the interaction between these elements will affect your ability to bring about change within the organization.

## Improving Organizational Communications

As a change agent, you are responsible for interpreting and sharing information to motivate employees to adopt change. Communications is essential in this process.

### Sharing Information

One of the questions in the Stakeholder Analysis (Chapter 2) asks, "What is important to this stakeholder?" That answer holds the key to much of your success in transforming a potential problem into a supporting partner. Ultimately, your goal is to build strong relationships, starting early in the change initiative and maintaining those relationships in ways that are meaningful and useful to each stakeholder. In many cases, as emphasized throughout this book, the answer to this question is as simple as providing information. When individuals have access to accurate and timely information, they feel they are part of the organization and of the change initiative; they are equipped with a basic tool that makes them feel comfortable and included.

Inclusion can be realized by simply providing courtesy copies of updates and reports to your various stakeholders. The content will vary, naturally, by the needs of each group and by the sensitivity of the information. But as we pointed out earlier in the discussion of formal and informal power, those with informal power can many times be your most threatening barriers. Basic and ongoing information may be the only thing they really want in the first place.

Your dilemma may be that those with more formal power are wary of sharing much information too soon or at all. Unfortunately, we still have leaders today who see that information is power. By giving up information to the "public," they perceive themselves as losing that power of knowledge and information that only a select few were privy to before.

Discuss with these leaders the value of open, honest, and ongoing communications in moving change initiatives forward. Share with them, or even involve them in, the development of your stakeholder analyses. In doing so, they will clearly see that one of the most frequently recurring needs of others is nothing more complex than information and updates.

When you share information, you are fulfilling the traditional role of a change agent. As such, your primary responsibility is to provide information needed by others to define problems and make decisions. As such, you are responsible for supplying information, helping employees cope with change, and handling defensive reactions.

## Creating and Communicating a Change Vision

Change agents should create a change vision to help them develop strategies for achieving that vision. *Vision* means a picture of the future with some implicit or explicit commentary on why people should strive to create that future.

An effective vision serves three important purposes. First, it clarifies the general direction for an organization. Second, vision motivates people to take action in the right direction and helps overcome employees' natural reluctance to change. Effective vision acknowledges that sacrifices will be necessary but makes clear that these sacrifices will yield particular benefits and personal satisfactions that are far superior to those available today—or tomorrow—without attempting to change. Third, an effective vision coordinates the actions of different employees by aligning them in a remarkably efficient way. Without a shared sense of direction, interdependent employees may constantly conflict, whereas a shared vision clarifies the direction of change and helps employees agree on the importance and value of change (see Chapter 12).

*Building a Communications Plan.* Too many organizations view communications as a onetime, splashy announcement that publicizes the initiation of a change effort, after which there is dead silence for the duration of the effort. Some authors warns against this one-event communication (Katzenbach, 1995). Both formal and informal communication should be used to provide the lubrication needed to mobilize employees into action. Thus, it is essential that your communication efforts be viewed as two-way, interactive approaches, which are always more powerful than one-way communication. Otherwise, you can neither be assured of staying in touch with your employees nor can you be assured that communications are being received as sent. Therefore, there is a continuous need to ask, "What's going on? Why? How does this fit together?"

Change agents need to use every vehicle possible to communicate their vision. To achieve this goal, they should create a communications plan. An effective communications plan should be stated in a simple jargon- and technical-free document. It should paint a verbal picture incorporating all possible media forums (such as memos, e-mail, newsletters, and formal and informal interactions). Such plans utilize repetition, which allows ideas to sink into employees' subconscious. Finally, an effective plan relies on leadership by example; the behavior of change agents must be consistent with the message being communicated.

No change initiative should be considered complete without time built in for creating and implementing a communications strategy. A thorough and complete communications strategy can be as lengthy, complex, and detailed as an actual change initiative. Ulrich, Zenger, and Smallwood (1999, 25) contend that it is important to have "an extraordinary concern for communicating with all stakeholders. . . . Constant and extensive two-way communication using all media and sharing all types of vital information is the rule."

It is not the intent of this book to teach you how to build a detailed communications strategy. A number of outstanding resources are available on this subject; we strongly advise you to read as much as you can on the subject. For now, realize that you need to address, at minimum, the following issues as part of an overall communications strategy and plan:

• Audiences: What are the major categories of employees with whom you will need to communicate and what are their information needs?
• Messages: How will you articulate your messages to identify with the particular frames of reference related to the audiences you just identified?
• Media: For each audience, what is its preferred means of receiving information (for example, e-mail, paper memos, informal meetings with the boss, presentations)?
• Frequency: Depending upon each audience group and the impact they will feel (both perceived and real), what is an appropriate time line for each audience that will provide them with a rate and flow of information that keeps them moving smoothly through the change curve?

*Build an Internal Communications Network.* The corporate grapevine, where the spin of gossip and rumor can rival a Kansas tornado, is oftentimes viewed as an unavoidable threat to projects, one of the "givens" that simply requires reactive responses after the damage has been done.

Rather than reacting negatively to the grapevine, consider doing what one Midwest organization did when they rolled out a global enterprise resource planning (ERP) system: Use this grapevine to help further your cause. In this case, the project team identified key people in the organization who, for whatever reason, always seemed to get the attention of their coworkers whenever it came to knowing the corporate gossip. Employees looked to these informal resources as their first source of information and oftentimes as their "reliable" source of information.

The organization invited these key people to become part of an official information network. The project team agreed to provide these individuals with the "bleeding edge" information related to the project, and in turn asked them to deliver the messages and information to their respective circles of coworkers and associates. They could deliver these messages in the format and style appropriate to their peer groups (for example, e-mail, verbal, informal meetings, bulletin boards, and so on). The project team then publicized these grapevine names to all employees, encouraging employees to go to them with questions and concerns.

In support of a true, two-way communication network, the project team also asked these grapevine individuals to keep the project team apprised of the state of emotions and thoughts that existed within each respective employee group. As soon as an employee brought a question or rumor to the grapevine source, the source contacted the project team for information and clarification, which he or she could then promptly relay back to the individual and the group. These clarifications and answers also served as the basis for a frequently-asked questions (FAQ) list that was provided on the project web site that was accessible to all employees.

These networked resources acted as a two-way conduit for information flow between the project team and the employees. They could help identify in advance any potential bad news or monkeys that might be waiting to attack. Frequently, they would help identify ways to counteract the flying monkeys (see Chapter 4).

This type of network has great potential for a win-win, proactive communication solution. Partner with individuals who have the potential to be the primary barrier, those who can inflict considerable damage to your change initiative. By providing them with official information in advance of anyone else, you help them achieve more "formal" credibility among their peers. They, in turn, can serve as your closest and most immediate sensors for what the moods and emotions are among the rest of the employees at any given stage of the change cycle. Instead of being part of the problem, they are now part of the solution.

## Solving Problems

Unfortunately, many organizations cannot correctly identify or solve their own problems. Consequently, they rely on your skills and abilities as a partnership builder. The type and complexity of problems vary from organization to organization and within an organization. As problem solvers, your primary responsibility is to make certain that the perceived problem is indeed the one that needs solving. To be effective, you should spend the majority of the time determining the accuracy of the problem rather than providing solutions to problems that do not exist. A useful approach involves working with the problem as "defined" by employees in such a way that more useful definitions emerge.

Surfacing and dealing with problems can actually help you reap benefits. You may gain more and better ideas, simply from listening to others and reflecting on their perspective of a situation as a way of gathering new insight. A problem can prompt you to search for alternative approaches, which many times may help you reap better results than what your original plan envisioned. It is possible that you may be the first person within a group to address the issues of change and encourage individuals to verbalize their resistance. As a result, you may discover that other, older issues and problems might surface and can be resolved in the process.

Encouraging others to become involved in the change process frequently results in improved creativity and innovation within an organization. Once they've been encouraged to come forth and participate in the change process, employees who were previously silent can frequently achieve surprising results. Certainly you will see a greater involvement in problem solving, ownership, and commitment to solutions once you've successfully involved others.

Every time you address a problem, you have an opportunity to clarify personal interests, values, and expectations. You may find yourself continually refining the vision statement to the point where everyone has a better understanding of the value and impact of the change.

The entire problem-solving process can enhance your personal development and growth in areas like problem resolution, communication, interpersonal relationships, and change leadership. Certainly, that can only lead to increased respect from your colleagues and superiors, but even more important, increased self-respect.

## Build a Solution Partnership

You may be tempted to think that you know the answers from the very beginning of a change initiative. It's simply a matter of the stakeholder stepping aside and letting you do your job. You impart your knowledge and skills, and you're on your way. You can be assured that at least one employee is waiting on the sidelines who will resent your stepping forward with every answer. That individual will accuse you of being insensitive to the unique needs of your employees and claim that you are doing nothing more than bringing a boilerplate solution that you've used and repackaged multiple times.

To circumvent this potential problem, present alternative solutions instead of a single solution. Offer analysis of the pros and cons for each alternative. By discussing these alternatives, you engage clients in a greater degree of "ownership" of the final solution or approach. They will inherently assume a shared responsibility for the ultimate success or failure of the solution.

## Advocating Solutions

Advocating solutions requires change agents to influence the organization to choose particular actions or solutions that improve performance, efficiency, and quality. Meeting this responsibility requires change agents to be very directive, proactive, and persuasive in performance-related issues. It could be said that change agents are "selling" organizational leaders during this activity.

As a change agent, you establish a vision of your organization's future. Consequently, it is important that change agents function as futurists, providing multiple options, ideas, and possibilities. The value of this activity is in the several alternatives generated for the organization.

## Present the Tough Answers

The hardest part of being a change agent is presenting your stakeholders with bad news. You have just been encouraged to use your mind in presenting good, positive news whenever possible, but the reality is that there will be times that you need to present the other side of the picture. It is critical that you take a "no surprises" stance in the relationships you build to reduce the chance of reflexive retaliation. Let your stakeholders know at the very beginning that you value and require honesty in both directions.

Prepare your stakeholders for the outcome, whether it is the one they will like or want. Sooner or later the "truth" will surface—don't think you can avoid the inevitable. The Wizard of Oz is a classic example of someone who continually came up with ways to mask and hide the truth. Only when Toto tore back the curtain and exposed the Wizard as a mere mortal hiding behind smoke and mirrors, bells and whistles, was the group able to work together, constructively, for a satisfactory resolution. Indeed, the solution was not necessarily what was originally anticipated or promised. But the story still had a happy ending.

### Providing Objective Observations

When solving problems, you ask reflective questions and help employees clarify or alter a given situation. Thus, you serve as philosophers and verifiers by asking reflective questions that improve the quality of change initiatives. Furthermore, you observe the effects that performance standards have on quality and performance, the effectiveness of performance appraisals and reviews, the impacts of job design and redesign activities, and the impact and results of other organizational change interventions. Objective observation is a nondirective activity that enables you to witness the affect that change has on your employees and helps you guide them in their effort to overcome their resistance to change.

### Asking Tough Questions

Courage is your willingness to ask questions that enable you to check and validate assumptions during your analysis. Challenge your own assumptions at several times during the change initiative. Likewise, challenge the assumptions you hear from others.

One of the most difficult things you may need to do is to ask others for honest, direct feedback about your own performance. But don't wait until the end of the initiative as part of the evaluation phase. You should seek input and feedback from your stakeholders on an ongoing basis, always looking for ways to fine-tune your performance and behavior so that your clients will perceive you as someone who is willing to listen and adjust. Your behavior, in fact, can serve as a model for others.

As a change agent, you take an active role in the problem-solving process. Your objectivity helps you evaluate existing problems and explain possible solutions. In addition, you use a synergistic approach, collaborating with employees in the perceptual, cognitive, and action-taking processes involved in solving organizational problems.

Feeling needed is a basic human principle. Recall the discussion of client relationship skills in Chapter 3. For some stakeholders, all they want is a chance to be heard, to be included, to share their ideas and thoughts. In some cases, involving others is as simple as listening rather than talking, especially in the early stages of a change initiative. The more you listen and observe, the easier it will be for you to identify where individuals are on the change curve, which in turn enables you to plan communication and change strategies that meet their needs. As you listen to employees' concerns and needs, ask for their ideas and suggestions when appropriate. Identify people who will be flattered that you ask for their support and assistance and seek their input and help, which in turn will enable them to move to exploration and commitment and overcome the potential for resentment and subversion.

## Building a Consensus and Commitment for Change

Any change useful to an organization will rely on employees working together. As a change agent, you build consensus and commitment among organizational decision makers and in bringing about lasting and needed change. Each employee is encouraged to consider the overall good of the organization before considering personal objectives or goals. Therefore, you provide sound and convincing recommendations and present them persuasively.

Building consensus and commitment requires you to use a collaborative, participatory approach with employees during problem identification and resolution. This requires you to establish a collaborative working relationship with each employee. From the beginning, an effective relationship becomes a collaborative search for acceptable answers to employees' real needs and concerns. Ideally, this will be a mutually beneficial relationship, where trust and a readiness for change are developed quickly during the change process.

Employees are encouraged to define existing problems and test alternatives for an effective resolution. To execute this responsibility correctly, you can use a partnership approach where you focus your attention on identifying problems and selecting, evaluating, and implementing alternatives. This responsibility requires you to identify your employees' readiness and commitment to change. The following questions can be used to achieve this end:

- How willing is the organization to implement change?
- Are senior managers willing to learn and use new management methods and practices?

- What types of information does the organization readily accept or resist?
- What are employees' attitudes toward change?
- What are senior managers' attitudes toward change?
- To what extent will employees regard their contribution to overall organizational effectiveness as a legitimate and desirable objective? (Gilley and Maycunich, 2000)

Another way of gauging readiness for change is to examine the level of enthusiasm for a particular recommendation. By identifying the level of enthusiasm, you instantaneously measure resistance or support for a given solution. Once identified, you are able to withdraw or encourage recommendations prior to implementation.

## Establishing a Sense of Urgency

Another way to build consensus and commitment is to establish a sense of urgency for change (see Chapter 2). This is important to gain needed cooperation. When complacency is high among employees, they are not willing to embrace change. Consequently, change usually goes nowhere. Without a sense of urgency, it is nearly impossible to energize employees to address problems within the organization. Thus, the momentum for change never materializes.

Employees find a thousand ingenious ways to withhold support from change when they sincerely think it is unnecessary. Some organizations promote a kill-the-messenger culture, which adds to complacency, others maintain a heightened capacity for denial, and others have overconfident executives and senior managers who resist change. Any of these excuses can lead to apathy and indifference.

There are five positive ways to raise the urgency level within employees (Conner, 1992). First, you can make available more data about employee satisfaction and performance, which demonstrates the competitive weaknesses vis-à-vis the competition. Second, you can insist that employees interact regularly with dissatisfied employees, unhappy suppliers, and disgruntled stakeholders. Third, you can provide more relevant data and honest discussion during performance reviews and employee meetings. Fourth, you can promote honest discussions of problems and insist that senior managers stop providing "happy talk" about real, serious problems. Fifth, you can provide employees with information on future promotional opportunities or increased financial incentives for capitalizing change opportunities.

## Facilitating Learning

A fundamental element of change is learning. It could be said that change couldn't take place unless learning occurs. As a result, one of your most important responsibilities includes providing employees with learning opportunities, making certain they have access to references and tools needed during learning and providing coaching and feedback when needed. Further, you are held accountable for conducting developmental evaluations, which enables employees to develop growth and development plans (see Chapter 7). Finally, you are responsible for linking compensation and rewards to learning (that is, growth and development).

During the learning process, you are responsible for helping employees acquire new skills, knowledge, insights, awareness, and attitudes needed to implement change. For example, employees will need skills or knowledge in problem solving, performance feedback, performance measurement, self-directed learning, interpersonal communication, causal analysis, listening, goal setting, conflicts resolution, and group diagnosis to be able to become independent employees. By developing such skills or knowledge employees will rely less on you as they apply what they have learned.

On occasion, you facilitate learning activities to improve performance and create organizational change. In some situations, you are simply asked to recommend which learning processes are best. At other times, you may be asked to provide professional development activities to help your employees obtain needed knowledge and skills. Change agents rely on their understanding of the teaching and learning process, appropriate use of instructional methods, application of experiential-learning activities, and presentation, listening, and facilitating skills (Gilley and Eggland, 1989). Finally, you must have the ability to *teach* or create learning opportunities. This ability should not be reserved for formal classroom activities, but should be utilized on the job, during meetings, and within the mainstream of the overall change effort.

As a change agent, you have a special responsibility in assisting employees to use interactive, self-directed strategies to enhance their own capability. In this case, the facilitator's role consists of helping employees shape their curiosities, challenging and developing their ideas for exploring and investigating, directing participants to useful resources, and linking people and ideas to forge collaborative efforts.

Facilitating learning involves a transactional process, a relationship with a person (the change agent) that promotes initiative, autonomy, freedom, and growth. There are six important principles of effective practice in facilitating learning (Brookfield, 1987, 9–19). First, facilitation relies on voluntary participation, which means employees are highly self-motivated to learn and want to participate. Second, facilitation requires mutual respect among employees for each other's self-worth and uniqueness. Third, facilitation involves a collaborative spirit, a cooperative enterprise. Fourth, facilitation is a cyclical process. That is, employees reflect on a learning activity, engage in collaboratively analyzing the activity, participate in a new activity, further reflect and collaborate on an analysis of the activity, and so on. Fifth, facilitation fosters critical reflection, an attitude of healthy skepticism and development of critical thinking skills that seeks to appreciate diversity and alternative points of view. Sixth, facilitation nurtures self-direction, encouraging employees to become autonomous, proactive, initiating, and creative learners.

## Conducting Analysis

When change agents rely on their performance management expertise, they are responsible for conducting analysis activities used in identifying organizational and employee needs. There are four common needs: business, performance, learning, and work environment (Robinson and Robinson, 1996). An understanding of each is essential for change agents to develop an appropriate response.

*Business needs* are expressed in operational terms such as goals for a unit, department, or organization, and represent the quantifiable data measures used to monitor the organization's health. There are two types of business needs: problems and opportunities. *Business problems* define a gap between what is occurring at the present and what should occur operationally. The gap exists when two conditions are present. First, there is a deviation between what should occur operationally and what is occurring. Second, someone in on the senior management team feels "pain" about the deviation and is therefore motivated to address the problem.

*Business opportunities* focus on a future possibility that needs to be optimized. In this situation no current problem needs to be fixed. Business opportunities exist when some senior managers desire to maximize gain from an opportunity. In other words, business problems require pain while business opportunities leverage perceived gain.

*Performance needs* describe employee requirements if business needs are to be addressed. In short, they are the on-the-job behavioral requirements of employees who perform a specific job. These serve as targets for employees when achieving productivity requirements and serve as a yardstick for you to gauge the adequacy of performance.

*Learning needs* identify what people must learn if they are to perform successfully. They represent areas where performers lack the skill or knowledge to perform satisfactorily. These needs are the foundations for training programs and knowledge acquisition plans.

*Work environment needs* identify the systems and processes within the employee's work environment that must be modified if performance and business needs are to be achieved (Robinson and Robinson, 1996). Once identified, you can modify the existing organizational system to ensure that the needed performance is adequately supported. They also help determine actions that need to be taken to achieve performance needs.

Although these needs vary in importance, they should be examined together. For example, business needs are the most important because they are the very reason organizations exist. Further, learning and work environment needs are linked to business needs through performance needs because positive learning and environmental change brings about improved performance, which results in the accomplishment of business needs.

## Conducting Performance Analysis

Performance analysis is a major and vital phase of a change initiative. As a change agent, you use this process to identify the critical performance roles and factors that must be improved to implement and sustain change. Thus, performance analysis is used to "assess individual and organizational performance" (Hale, 1998, 46). Additionally, performance analysis is critical to make certain that improvement factors are not overlooked.

Performance analysis presents a clear picture of existing and desired conditions surrounding performance. As a result, analysis answers four key questions:

1. What results (performance outcomes) are being achieved?
2. What results are desired?
3. How large is the performance gap?
4. What is the impact of the performance gap? (Hale, 1998)

Performance analysis typically identifies the level of performance improvement needs. They are:

- Primary needs—specific improvements in performer behavior or results needed to positively achieve desired business objectives.

- Secondary needs—performance analysis reveals that employees cannot increase performance on their own, but that they need some sort of performance support tool to aid their development.
- Tertiary needs—performance analysis also reveals additional needs in the work environment, such as for a new organizational structure to facilitate or support a performance initiative (Robinson and Robinson, 1996).

To identify and describe past, present, and future human performance gaps, you assess desired versus actual performance. For example, a sales department has failed to meet its sales quota for three consecutive months. As a change agent, you are responsible for determining "why" this problem exists. The following questions can help you conduct a performance analysis useful in determining the answer to this question:

- What is the performance gap or difference?
- Who is affected by the performance gap? Is it one person, a group, an organization, or a work process?
- When and where did the performance gap first occur—or when and where is it expected to begin?
- When and where were its effects, side effects (symptoms), and aftereffects (consequences) first noticed?
- Have they been noticed consistently or inconsistently?
- How has the gap been affecting the organization?
- Have the effects been widespread or limited?
- Is the performance gap traceable to individuals, work groups, locations, departments, divisions, suppliers, distributors, customers, or others?
- What are the immediate and direct results of the gap?
- How much has the gap cost the organization?
- How can the tangible economic impact of the gap best be calculated?
- How can the intangible impact of the gap be calculated in lost customer goodwill or worker morale? (Rothwell, 1996b, 13)

Once these questions have been addressed, you will have a better understanding of the situation, how it affects the organization, its costs, and effects on members of the department. However, you will not know the real reason(s) for the performance gap until you conduct a second investigation known as cause analysis.

Conducting Cause Analysis.    Cause analysis reveals the real reason(s) problems or gaps exist. It is also used to identify factors that impede and contribute to performance. Determining the causes of performance gaps requires you to consider the following:

- Do employees have the knowledge, ability, skills, time, and other resources necessary to perform?
- What are employees' expectations of performance?
- Are employees motivated to perform adequately?
- Do performers possess the ability to perform their jobs correctly?
- What is the adequacy of environmental support and feedback?
- Are employees providing sufficient data and information regarding their performance?
- What are the rewards and incentives for performing correctly, and are they adequate to motivate acceptable performance?
- What are the results and consequences for performing inadequately?
- Are performers penalized or otherwise given disincentives for achieving desired work results?
- How well are people given the data, information, or feedback they need to perform at the time they need it? Are performers given important information they need to perform on a timely basis?
- How well are performers supported in what they do by appropriate environmental support, resources, equipment, or tools?
- Do performers have the necessary job aids and working conditions to perform satisfactorily?
- How well are individuals or groups able to perform?
- Do performers want to achieve desired results? What payoffs do they expect? How realistic are their expectations? (Rothwell, 1996b)

Once a cause analysis has been completed, you will be able to determine the real cause(s) of the performance gap. Once identified, you can develop a change intervention that will address the root cause of the problem, thus closing the gap between the actual and desired state.

## Implementing and Managing Change

Change agents are responsible for implementing and managing change. This stems from a need to make certain that change is supported at the operational level of the organization. In other words, employees must support change or it does not become a permanent part of the organizational culture.

According to Ulrich (1997), change agents must turn knowledge about change into know-how for accomplishing change and success factors for change into action plans for accomplishing change. The first step is to have a clearly defined change model. A model identifies key factors for a successful change and the essential questions that must be answered to put the model into action. Specific questions determine the extent to which key success factors exist within an organization. The seven key success factors are:

- Leading change: Having a sponsor of change who owns and leads the change initiative.
- Creating a shared need: Ensuring that individuals know why they should change and that the need for change is greater than the resistance to change.
- Shaping a vision: Articulating the desired outcome from the change.
- Mobilizing commitment: Identifying, involving, and pledging the key stakeholders who must be involved to accomplish the change.
- Changing systems and structures: Using management tools (staffing, development, appraisal, rewards, organization design, communication, systems, and so on) to ensure that the change is built into the organization's infrastructure.
- Monitoring progress: Defining benchmarks, milestones, and experiments with which to measure and demonstrate progress.
- Making change last: Ensuring that change happens through implementation plans, follow-through, and ongoing commitment (Ulrich, 1997).

Resolving the paradox of change means transforming the seven key success factors from a theoretical exercise into a managerial process. Using the following questions, the seven factors' capacity for change in a given organization can be profiled. Ulrich (1997, 73) believes that change agents assigned to integrate change should answer these questions to ensure that the resources needed for implementing and managing change are available.

- To what extent does the change have a champion, sponsor, or other leader who will support the change (leading change)?
- To what extent do the people essential to the success of the change feel a need for change that exceeds the resistance to the change (creating a need)?
- To what extent do we know the desired outcomes for change (shaping a vision)?

- To what extent are key stakeholders committed to the change outcomes (mobilizing commitment)?
- To what extent have we institutionalized the change through systems and structures (changing systems and structures)?
- To what extent are indicators in place to track our progress on the change effort (monitoring progress)?
- To what extent do we have an action plan for getting change to happen (making change last)?

Change agents do not implement change, employees do. However, they must be able to *get the change done*. By identifying and profiling key factors for change, they lead employees through the steps necessary for increasing change capacity. The probabilities of implementing and managing any change initiative improve dramatically when these seven success factors and their corresponding questions are assessed and discussed (Ulrich, 1997). Human resource development professionals leading the change should ask questions that reveal underlying assumptions.

## Enhancing Resilience

Although organizational effectiveness implies continuous change and development, employees, senior managers, and executives differ in their ability to adapt to or recover from change. The capacity of these members to absorb change without draining the firm or individual energies is referred to as resilience. Change agents are challenged to strengthen their employees' adaptability to change, both personally and professionally. There are two approaches to breaking the downward spiral and thus becoming more resilient. First, employees can increase their energy by developing adaptive skills. Second, they decrease their energy expenditures by accepting the inevitability of change and adjusting accordingly.

As a change agent, you are responsible for discovering ways to help employees strengthen the skills needed to adapt to change and thus remain resilient during change. Moreover, you must create an environment that provides support for change and resiliency. Consequently, your primary responsibility is to help the organization and its employees increase resilience by increasing your employees' capacity and ability to adapt to change.

Resilient employees realize when change is inevitable, necessary, or advantageous and use resources to creatively reframe a changing situation, improvise new approaches, or maneuver to gain an advantage. They take risks despite potentially negative consequences and draw important lessons from change-related experiences that are then applied to similar situations. They respond to disruption by investing energy in problem solving and teamwork and influence others to resolve conflicts.

Resilient employees are "positive, focused, flexible, organized, and proactive" (Conner, 1992, 238). They display a sense of security and self-assurance based on their view of life as complex but filled with opportunity (positive). They view disruptions as the natural result of a changing world, and see major change as uncomfortable but offer opportunities for growth and development.

Resilient employees believe there are important lessons to be learned from challenge and see life as generally rewarding. They are employees who clearly focus on what they want to achieve by maintaining a strong vision that serves both as a source of purpose and as a guidance system to reestablish perspectives following significant disruption. Resilient employees feel empowered during change, recognize their own strengths and weaknesses, and know when to accept internal or external limits. They challenge change and, when necessary, modify their assumptions or frames of reference. Finally, they rely on nurturing relationships for support and display patience, understanding, and humor when dealing with change.

As a way of managing ambiguity, resilient employees develop structured approaches that help them identify the underlying themes embedded in confusing situations. They identify priorities that they are willing to renegotiate during change. If necessary, resilient employees have the ability to manage several simultaneous tasks. They compartmentalize stress so that it does not carry over to other projects or parts of their lives. They know when to ask others for help and engage in major action only after careful planning. Finally, resilient employees engage in change (proactive) rather than defend against it.

## Improving Organizational Effectiveness: The Outcome of Change

When each of the eight responsibilities have been executed, the ultimate outcome is improved organizational effectiveness. As we discussed in Chapter 2, organizational effectiveness can be measured in a variety of ways. Regardless of the method you use, meeting your responsibilities should result in improved:

- Motivational systems
- Compensations and reward programs
- Work environment culture transformation

- Organizational communications
- Employee development
- Job design
- Performance management systems
- Performance and causal analysis
- Problem solving
- Strategic and change partnerships
- Organizational analysis
- Change alignment
- Performance coaching
- Conflict resolution
- Vision setting

Additionally, you are able to help your organization improve its ability to adapt strategies and behaviors to future environmental change by maximizing the organization's employees' contribution. Thus, improving organizational effectiveness implies that you are dedicated to developing and maintaining the most important systems and linkages to improve performance and enhance organizational readiness and competitiveness through change initiatives.

## Conclusion

The change agent's responsibilities are designed to maximize the effectiveness of change initiatives and achieve change goals. The ultimate outcome achieved by way of these responsibilities is improving organizational effectiveness.

# Part C

# Integrating Resources, Roles, and Competencies

## Holistic Model for Change Agent Excellence

*Introduction to the Competencies of a Change Agent*

The Scarecrow, the Tin Man, the Lion, and Dorothy were each on a quest. The Scarecrow longed for a brain with which to understand and intellectually influence the world around him; the Tin Man for the heart to meaningfully connect with it; the Lion for the courage to confront his challenges and proactively change it; and Dorothy for the vision to understand her place in the world and to define what it should look like in the future. What these characters sought—a brain, heart, courage, and vision—are personal resources that, when *combined* in real-world organizations, can enable you to achieve excellence as a change agent. Achieving that goal depends on your ability to develop these personal resources and then draw on them as you operate within four *core roles* as a change agent:

1. Business partner—Master your organization as well as the tools of your profession.

2. Servant leader—Meet your employees' needs, both personally and professionally.
3. Change champion—Exhort your employees to strive for excellence throughout the change process.
4. Future shaper—Assist your employees in defining the long-term future of the organization

Each core role is independent of the others, yet *interdependent* at the same time. That is, each provides you as change agent with a *decidedly different* platform from which to drive change, and yet intentionally progressing through each of the core roles results in your operating in an increasingly broad sphere of influence.

## The Core Roles as Spheres of Influence

### The Business Partner Sphere of Influence

The brain must serve as your initial source of credibility as you strive to build internal and external networks. Without first establishing this "brain-powered" credibility, your efforts as a change agent are doomed to failure. Without it, change agents are regarded as "empty suits" with "soft" hearts, unnecessary change missions, and misguided visions of the future.

### The Servant Leader Sphere of Influence

Once a credible business partnership is established, the heart becomes the source of selflessness necessary for you to gain the full commitment and trust of your employee groups. Your main goal as servant leader is to demonstrate wholeness in your approach to organizational life and work, a wholeness that will compel your employees to fully engage (hands, mind, heart, and spirit) in the effort at hand and to trust that you are committed, first and foremost, to their success.

### The Change Champion Sphere of Influence

Garnering the commitment and trust of your employee group through selflessness will earn you the right to employ courage and champion change throughout your organization. Based on credible business and organizational analysis conducted primarily within the business partner and servant leader spheres, you can proactively address organizational dysfunction and manage change efforts to improve organizational performance.

## The Future Shaper Sphere of Influence

This final and broadest sphere of influence allows you to leverage vision and become a major driver of long-term strategic direction for your organization. To operate effectively in this sphere of influence, you need to demonstrate a proven track record of results over a significant period of time within your organization.

It is important to note that although you must initially progress through each of the four core roles to achieve increased breadth of influence, operating in one sphere does not mutually exclude the others. For example, once you have operated effectively in the business partner sphere you will continually "regress" as needed to operate within that sphere; at times, you will concurrently operate in any combination of the four spheres. This dynamic is clearly demonstrated in Figure C.1, which portrays the core roles as increasingly broad, but not mutually exclusive, spheres of influence.

FIGURE C.1   Core Roles as Spheres of Influence

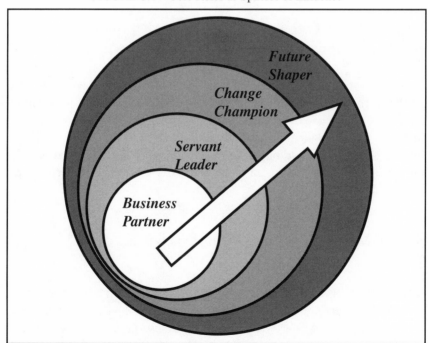

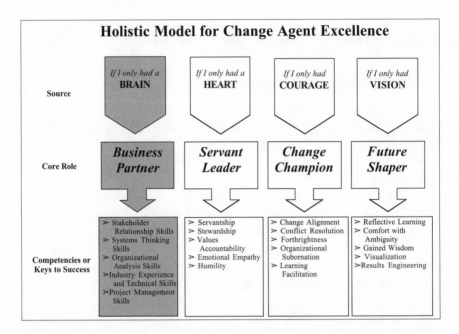

FIGURE C.2  Holistic Model for Change Agent Excellence

# Performing the Core Roles: Required Personal Competencies

Associated with each of the core roles are five personal competencies or keys to success that you must master in your quest for excellence. Each competency is a sine qua non of personal success as a change agent. *None* can be excluded from your tool kit if your goal is holistic employee engagement. These "building blocks" are laid out in the following unified model (Figure C.2) and discussed in detail in the following four chapters. This is your blueprint for excellence; study it closely.

# Holistic Model for Change Agent Excellence

## *Self-Assessment*

Following is a series of questions designed to allow you to assess where you currently stand in your quest to remain or become a holistic change agent. For each statement answer "yes" or "no." Be honest. Each "yes" is worth five points. Then add up your score and check your current standing using the scale at the bottom of the page.

TABLE C.1   Holistic Model for Change Agent Excellence Self-Assessment

**Operating in the Core Role of Business Partner**

| Statement | Points (0 or 5) |
|---|---|
| I can list at least 3 different project opportunities that I am currently developing. | |
| I can describe the value chain for my organization in detail. | |
| I can recreate the top level organizational chart for my organization from memory, including titles and names. | |
| I am considered an expert in at least two competencies or work-skills critical to the success of my organization. | |
| I maintain a detailed plan for all projects that I'm currently managing, including resource allocation and utilization rates, task/event dependencies, milestones, and progress to date. | |

**Operating in the Core Role of Servant**

| Statement | Points (0 or 5) |
|---|---|
| My colleagues would refer to me as selfless. | |
| I have received a poor performance evaluation as a result of a employee of mine receiving a poor performance evaluation. | |
| I am motivated on a daily basis by my work being connected to a higher purpose. | |
| I have shared my feelings with a colleague. | |
| At least 3 of my colleagues can point to specific things that I have learned from them. | |

**Operating in the Core Role of Change Champion**

| Statement | Points (0 or 5) |
|---|---|
| I have developed a personal toolkit of strategies for effectively managing organizational change. | |
| I have proactively defused at least 5 personal or organizational conflicts in the last quarter. | |
| I can accurately articulate the difference between performance evaluation and performance management. | |
| I have voluntarily removed myself from a role or organization in recognition of my inadequacy or the greater organizational good. | |
| At least 10 separate colleagues/employees can point to specific things that they have learned from me. | |

**Operating in the Core Role of Future Shaper**

| Statement | Points (0 or 5) |
|---|---|
| I keep a personal journal or log chronicling significant personal and professional events in my life. | |
| I have given budgetary approval for a least one new project, product, or service in the last year based on "gut feeling." | |
| I am intimately involved in the strategic planning process for my organization. | |
| I can draw or describe a conceptual model or picture of a product or service that my organization will be offering 20 years from now. | |
| I have specific and challenging personal and professional goals articulated for both myself and my team members for the next 6 months, the next year, and the next 5 years. | |

**Scoring Scale**

**Your Total Score** _____

**75 to 100  Holistic Change Agent** – An effective and influential change agent

**50 to 75  Fragmented Change Agent** –
A person making the transition from a manager to a change agent

**25 to 50  Change Follower** – A person that follows other during change initiatives

**0 to 25  Change Resistor** – A person that resist or is a barrier to change

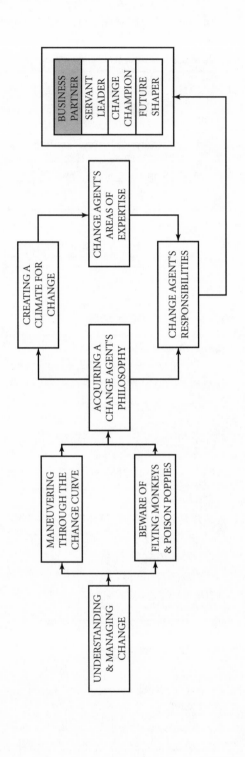

THE MANAGER AS CHANGE AGENT BLUEPRINT

# Business Partner

*Without first establishing a Business Partnership, Change Agents are regarded as "empty suits" with "soft" hearts, unnecessary change missions, and misguided visions of the future.*

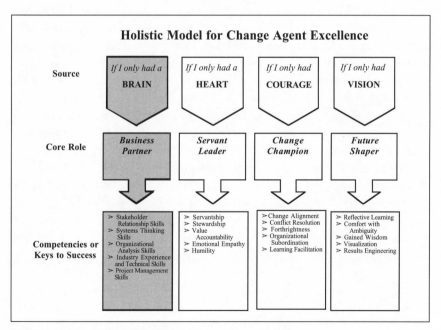

FIGURE 9.01    Holistic Model for Change Agent Excellence

## Operating in the First Core Role: Business Partner

To become an effective change agent, you need to assemble a tool kit of experience, theoretical understanding, interpersonal skills, organizational skills, and task-specific competencies. Such a list will not guarantee you a position as a change agent; rather, it is the ticket to the show, the entry card to become a solid force for organizational renewal.

Many change agents have the desire to make their organization a better place, but lack the frontline skills to gain credibility. Thus, they lack competency to establish a true *business partnership.*

Plumbers need wrenches and pipes, carpenters need hammers, saws, and wood, and change agents need their "tools of the trade." To gain credibility as a change agent in any organization requires the ability to reach into your business tool kit for the knowledge, skills, and abilities the organization will take seriously.

Increasingly, organizations are becoming more project-oriented and this is especially true during periods of change. Consequently, organizations need internal operators to manage projects. Herein lies an enormous credibility problem for those of you who want to become change agents. "How do I get them to know how great I am?" Human resource departments too have fought a similar internal battle for years, wondering, "Why don't we get invited to the strategic planning meetings?" In both cases, the problem is a perceived lack of credibility, a barrier that can be surmounted only if you acquire the skills the organization needs. Organizations will be willing to build such partnerships with you, to invest in you, only if you have something they cannot do without. Once they are convinced you have what they need, the partnership process can begin.

Such a tool kit is, then, an absolute prerequisite for change agents who want to work with their stakeholders as business partners to solve problems, create opportunities, capitalize on strategic windows, and leverage organizational strengths. Becoming a business partner is something to be earned, valued, and nurtured, but preparation is the key. Without something to offer the partnership, you'll never get to first base, never be considered a player, and you'll stay on the bench while the real work of the organization happens around you. What specific skills are essential for you to become a positive force for change within organizations?

## Stakeholder Relationship Skills

Participating in change initiatives requires the ability to work with people and to be recognized as someone who will add value to the organization. A plethora of self-help books, seminars, and programs have been developed to train business professionals on the finer points of becoming a sought-after resource inside the company.

Although it would be wonderful for stakeholders to view the relationship between themselves and change agents as a partnership, it seldom happens (Robinson and Robinson, 1996). Consequently, change agents face difficult challenges in managing stakeholder relationships. As a way of addressing this issue, you should define the change process for your employees. Next, you should explain your role, responsibilities, and activities during the change process and provide concrete examples. You should also clarify employees' responsibilities during solution selection, design and development, and implementation.

### Keep Your Eyes Open, Listen, and Empathize

Listening, observing, and empathizing are skills that are extremely important for change agents. Too often change agents seek to be the one listened to, instead of the one doing the listening. Do you really hear what others are saying? Can you pick up on what is "between the lines" of a message? The first rule in relationship building with a stakeholder must be listening, truly hearing what your stakeholder is saying, both verbally and nonverbally.

Too often change agents want to be the one being watched instead of the one watching. Do you have an accurate idea of the situation confronting you? Do you know where the leverage points are in the organization? What are the norms of behavior? How does the organization get things done? Why are things the way they are? Only by keeping your eyes and focusing your attention on others and their interactions will you be able to move to the most important aspect of stakeholder relationship building, understanding, acceptance, and involvement (see Chapter 3).

People in organizations want to be understood. Although this process begins when you pay attention to others so they feel as if they are being "heard," it is most powerfully unleashed when you make an effort to walk in someone else's shoes. Employees want you to make a connection to their reality in a very real and tangible way. The real question that must be answered is "Do your employees truly believe you can relate to them and help them with their problem?" Developing the reflective skills of watching and listening are key to developing empathy, which translates into greater participation and greater influence in most organizations.

## Plan Early Victories and Broadcast Them!

Once you have established credibility with your employees and other organizational leaders, make sure your change initiative achieves some early deliverables that are *visible, measurable,* and *promotable.* These early (planned) victories encourage support for you as a change agent. Once a change initiative has begun, you should manage the process carefully so that the needs of various stakeholders are satisfied. Next, make certain that you positively promote the outcomes of change and their impact on organizational performance, thus creating a positive image of the change effort. For example, you should notify your primary stakeholders of early success as a way of reassuring them that their decision to support a change initiative was prudent and wise.

Self-promotion is something many people shy away from. However, the ability to promote yourself and your contribution in moderation can be essential. If you don't promote yourself, who will? Promotion, however, can be a dangerous thing if you fail to deliver the outcomes suggested, which can damage relationships with the organization. Underpromising and overdelivering are wise words to live by. Once you deliver, though, be sure to get credit for the delivery and be certain everyone "reads the credits" once the show is over.

## Send Notes

Although George Bush succeeded the "Great Communicator," President Ronald Reagen, he had his own style of communication. He was a prolific note writer. Bush made it a point to send several handwritten notes every day to contacts, subordinates, other heads of state, and contributors. It's a small thing, but everyday communication has power beyond what most people realize. In today's world, e-mail is a tremendously powerful communication tool. Although it is efficient, it is a very impersonal medium because it lacks the human touch. But a simple, well-crafted, handwritten note of thanks or information can provide encouragement and reinforcement as well as establish a connection with an individual. This technique holds particular power during the change process because it keeps employees motivated and informs stakeholders of project progress. This can expand your network and enhance your reputation as a solid change agent.

## System Thinking Skills

Change agents must have the ability to determine the importance of gaps between what is and what should be in the organization's interactions with the external environment (as discussed in Chapter 8). This means using strategic thinking skills and having the ability to compare an idealized vision of the future with organizational reality (Nilson, 1999). Two essential questions that will help change agents in this effort are:

- How will the most important *present* challenges facing the organization eventually play out in its dealings with customers, stockholders, suppliers, distributors, and other important external groups?
- How will the most important *future* challenges facing the organization eventually unfold in its dealings with customers, stockholders, suppliers, distributors, and other important external groups? (Rothwell, 1996a, 149)

Strategic thinking is the ability to anticipate business trends and processes and break them down into manageable units for others to understand and implement. Once accomplished, change agents generate a variety of solutions that narrow the gap between what is needed and what is delivered. They also make the necessary adjustments to ensure organizational success. Strategic thinking is a conceptual-level activity that requires you to establish business priorities. Quite simply, strategic thinking is the ability to look to the future and navigate uncharted waters.

Katz and Kahn (1978) believe that strategic thinking requires the ability to assess which elements of a system are related and determine which inputs, processes, and outputs from one element of a system interact with other elements of that system (Katz and Kahn, 1978). Moreover, strategic thinking requires you to predict which parts of a system are likely to change when another part of the system changes.

Change agents need to develop an understanding of the characteristics of open systems. These characteristics form a framework for appraising an organization's internal environment, isolating performance problems, and identifying relationships critical to organizational effectiveness.

*Importation of energy* is referred to as *production inputs,* which consist of materials, resources, and energies that are directly related to producing products or delivering services. Typically these are generated by an organization's external environment. Internal inputs, such as organizational policies and procedures, guide employees as they carry out their activities as members of the system.

There are several questions that can be used to examine your organization's importation of energy:

- What are the production and maintenance inputs of the organization as a whole? Of each part of the organization?
- How are those inputs changing to respond to external environmental change?
- How *should* those inputs change in the future to respond to external environmental change?
- How do present and future changes in inputs affect program planning efforts?
- How *should* present and future changes in inputs affect program planning efforts? (Rothwell and Cookson, 1997, 105)

*Throughput* is the process of transforming raw materials (inputs) into products and services (Katz and Kahn, 1978). This is sometimes referred to as performance activity, which describes the steps employees go through to create products and deliver services (Rummler and Brache, 1995).

Again, there are several critical questions that help you when appraising an organization's throughputs:

- What are the throughputs (transformation processes) of the organization? Of each part of the organization?
- How are throughputs changing to respond to external environmental change?
- How *should* throughputs change in the future to respond to external environmental change?
- How do changes in throughputs currently affect program planning efforts?
- How *should* changes in throughputs affect future program planning efforts? (Rothwell and Cookson, 1997, 106)

At the completion of the throughput process organizations have created *outputs,* which are products and services critical to their survival. The quality and quantity of the outputs consumed by the stakeholder determines the organization's profitability. As a change agent, you use the following questions to appraise an organization's outputs:

- What are the outputs of the organization?
- How are outputs changing in response to external environmental change?
- How *should* outputs change in the future in response to external environmental change?

- How do changes in outputs currently affect program planning efforts?
- How *should* changes in outputs affect future program planning efforts? (Rothwell and Cookson, 1997, 106)

The input-throughput-output cycle flows smoothly as long as the organization maintains its current processes and procedures. However, change can cause breakdowns or impose barriers that must be addressed. Additionally, you may simply wish to improve the efficiency of processes. Therefore, you need to examine the relationship among inputs, throughputs, and outputs to detect existing or desirable changes and their impact on present and future programs.

Of critical importance is how an organization obtains information from its internal and external stakeholders regarding their needs and expectations. Information such as this permits you to predict and manage change. Mismatches in this area can lead to the loss of external customers, turnover among employees, and poor partnerships (as discussed in Chapter 7). Such losses result when organizational products and services fail to match customers' needs and expectations. Therefore, as you evaluate your organization's *informational input* you may wish to ask the following questions:

- How is the organization obtaining information about stakeholders', employees', and partners' needs?
- How are decision makers and prospective change participants using that information?
- How should they be using that information to make adaptive or even proactive change to meet or exceed customer, employee, and partner requirements?
- How is or should performance improvement intervention that supports efforts to obtain and use information to meet or exceed customer, employee, or partner requirements? (Rothwell and Cookson, 1997, 107)

During change, it is critical to determine how the organization maintains stability amid turmoil. Consequently, change agents need to identify which activities help to preserve order and how these activities react in response to external environmental pressure. You also need to determine how existing policies and procedures help to preserve order. Additionally, you need to identify which programmatic changes are necessary to adapt to or anticipate changing external environmental conditions.

As organizational differentiation and specialization increases, change agents will need to establish ways to control such complex entities. This requires change agents to set priorities, establish organizationwide rules and regulations, increase organizational communications, establish performance standards, identify operating procedures, coordinate production scheduling, and establish quality improvement standards.

## Organizational Analysis Skills

Change agents should think of organizational analysis as a process, not an event. It involves all key decision makers, stakeholders, and employees and should be influenced by a clear understanding of the organization's performance and business needs, as well as its strategic goals and objectives. As a process, organizational analysis is used to examine every aspect of organizational life. Further, organizational analysis is used to determine the effectiveness of organizational communications and the operational efficiency of the organization. It is also used to identify the effectiveness of critical interventions such as strategic planning and change interventions and their impact on the organization as well as the benefits derived.

Organizational analysis should be perceived as a daily philosophy and practice. As such, organizational analysis is an everyday process for change agents. As a result, everything—*everything*—is analyzed. As an operational approach, analyze, analyze, analyze. When uncertain of usefulness, effectiveness, or credibility—analyze. Then and only then will you be able to determine the viability and utility of your activities, initiatives, interventions, and processes. Organizational analysis is seen as a feedback and improvement process designed to enhance service and quality.

Conducting organizational analysis requires interacting with your employees to determine their needs, performance problems, performance and change barriers, learning and developmental expectations, and expected performance outcomes. This activity requires you to communicate with employees in a straightforward and understandable manner.

### Organizational Analysis Process

Regardless of the type of organizational analysis conducted, the process consists of eight simple steps, each of which is essential and based on previous steps. In simplest terms, the organizational analysis process compares results against objectives. The eight steps include:

1. Identifying the problem
2. Collecting data
3. Analyzing data
4. Interpreting and drawing conclusions from the data
5. Identifying the root cause
6. Comparing conclusions to stated objectives
7. Documenting results
8. Communicating results to key decision makers, stakeholders, and influencers

During the organizational analysis process, a variety of data collection techniques are available for use. The most common are questionnaires, interviews, focus groups, organizational reports and records, pretests and posttests, and management's perception of change. Each of these techniques can be used to collect the data necessary to draw conclusions and make recommendations to internal stakeholders.

### Analyzing Organizational Systems

When analyzing the organizational system, you must review the seven elements we discussed in Chapter 8 (see Figure 8.3). These elements tend not to be effected by minor events or activities within the organization. Therefore, you can use previous organizational analysis as a baseline to determine if the organizational system has changed dramatically since the previous analysis. For example, you can use a previous analysis to determine the affects of a change such as the reporting relationship in a department. Any changes that may have occurred in the leadership, structure, work climate, organizational culture, mission and strategy, change agent practice, or policies and procedures should be documented and examined carefully. Any strategic planning activities or change initiatives that were designed to alter any of these components within the organizational system should be examined as well.

Since the organizational system tends not to change dramatically from one point in time to another, it is important for you to capture any gradual, evolutionary changes that might occur over time. Therefore, it may be appropriate to go back several years to examine previous organizational analysis activities and compare them to current realities. Only then will the gradual shifts that may be occurring within the organizational system be evident so that they can be documented and accounted for, and adjustments made in customer service activities, practices, procedures, or interventions.

## Analyzing Performance Management Systems

Perhaps one of the most important organizational analysis actions is the examination of the performance management system. This involves a comprehensive and continuous review of the impact and effectiveness of the performance management system. One of the best ways to analyze such a system is to assess overall performance improvement activities that have occurred from one specific point in time to another. By looking at the aggregate of such activities, you determine which interventions have been successful and which have not. You can also determine whether or not a breakdown has occurred between any of the functions within the performance management system (that is, performance appraisal, learning acquisition and transfer, compensations and reward program, selection and recruiting process, performance coaching, and job design), then identify changes to improve the overall performance management system.

Organizational analysis should be viewed as a type of circuit analysis designed to make certain that the performance management system is working to its designed specifications. This is not unlike your home electrical system requiring periodic checks to make certain there are no shorts or breakdowns that could shut down the system, or, in a worst-case scenario, start a fire that could destroy the home. Organizational analysis helps guarantee that the performance management system is viable, functional, operational, and working in harmony to produce the desired results.

## Analyzing Human and Material Resources

Change agents must continually examine the adequacy of human and material resources within the organization. Since these are inputs used to produce desired results, they must exist in the right quantity and quality to achieve organizational effectiveness. Analyzing the effectiveness of human and material resources requires consideration of their placement, accessibility, and interchangeability. Each of these criteria will help determine whether these resources are being used efficiently.

## Analyzing Learning Systems

When analyzing the learning system, you examine the program design and development process, the delivery system, and the learning acquisition and transfer process. Each of these critical areas offer tremendous information regarding the effectiveness and quality of learning interventions. In Chapter 8, we discussed a change agent's activities before, during, and after a learning activity. Each element should also be analyzed to determine their application and effectiveness.

### Analyzing Job Design

Analysis of job design focuses attention on four components: competency maps, performance activities, performance standards, and performance outcomes. These four components can be used in the construction of a job design audit for any position within the organization. The components are circular in nature, beginning with competency maps and ending with performance outputs. That is, the outputs of one action are the inputs of another. For example, competency map outputs are the inputs of performance activities, and so forth. As a result, analysis may commence "at the end" (performance outputs) to determine whether or not each previous step has been successfully completed (see Chapter 11).

### Analyzing the Selection and Recruiting Process

When analyzing the selection and recruiting process, you examine the interviewing techniques used to ascertain whether they are successful in identifying the most qualified candidates. You also examine the skills and abilities of the individuals conducting employment interviews to determine their competency level. Moreover, the selection and recruiting process is investigated to determine whether it uses the most effective method possible. You determine whether the organization's recruiting and selection philosophy is consistent with its guiding principles and mission. Finally, you determine whether there is a direct connection between selection and recruiting processes and the adequacy of human and material resources.

### Analyzing the Performance Appraisal Process

When analyzing the performance appraisal process, your focus is on outcomes. For example, what is the quality of your performance improvement strategies? Do employee improvement plans include a learning transfer strategy? Is the compensation and reward program based on employee performance, growth and development, or other criteria? You examine the congruence between your performance appraisal philosophy and its actual execution. Finally, you determine whether performance appraisal activities such as data gathering, feedback discussions, conflict resolution, and reaching agreement on next steps are conducted in an effective manner.

## Analyzing Compensation and Reward Systems

Compensation and reward programs provide the primary motivating force for most employees. Therefore, you must be concerned with the effectiveness and impact of such programs on long-term performance improvement, as well as achieving organizational goals and objectives (see Chapter 7). In other words, you need to determine whether the compensation and reward program's intent and philosophy is being maintained. Further, you need to determine the types of outcomes that such programs reward, such as entrepreneurial activities, long-term results, teamwork, and performance behaviors that realize needed business results. By examining these issues, you make certain that the compensation and reward program indeed helps the organization achieve its strategic business goals and objectives.

## Analyzing Career Planning Activities

When analyzing career planning, you conduct four types of examinations. First, you determine how work design and the learning system influence the career planning process. Second, you examine the human allocation process to ascertain whether employees are being matched properly with job assignments. This includes comparing employees' knowledge and skills with job descriptions and task analyses to gauge the match, and determining whether the correct number of employees are assigned to each job classification within the organization. Third, you analyze the developmental planning process. This examination focuses on a realistic review of future career options and opportunities and the creation of activities thar will prepare employees for future job and career decisions. From this analysis, you can determine whether employees are being given opportunities to obtain the type of experience necessary for future job assignments and career advancement. Analyzing the developmental planning process may require studying performance improvement plans created by employees (during the performance appraisal process), which reveal the nature of development plans, their rigor, and their quality. Fourth, you examine the performance planning process, which centers around the identification of specific job demands, goals, priorities, and reward expectations associated with current job assignments. Specific learning acquisition and transfer plans, performance activities, performance priorities, and financial compensation are linked to successful completion of stated goals and objectives. Ultimately, you are responsible for determining the organizational impact of performance planning activities.

## Analyzing Organizational Communications

During this type of analysis, you determine the organization's appetite for and ability to produce effective organizational communications. You also determine how well organizations communicate interpersonally and intrapersonally (groups) within the firm. Finally, you ascertain the impact of technology and organizational structure on organizational communications and which strategies are most appropriate for overcoming areas of deficiency.

## Analyzing Strategic Planning Activities

Change agents can greatly improve the strategic planning process by carefully examining each of its five components. First, you determine the scope of the strategic plan by ascertaining whether it is designed for the entire organization or an independent department or unit. Second, you analyze the strategies used to conduct an internal and external analysis employed to determine the internal strengths and weaknesses of the organization as well as external opportunities and threats that confront the organization. This is sometimes referred to as a SWOT analysis. Next, you determine the accuracy of the organization's vision and the process that was used in its creation. Finally, you examine the planning and implementation strategies employed to determine their effectiveness and whether or not they meet the standards and expectations derived at the outset of the strategic planning activity.

## Industry Experience and Technical Skills

Effective change agents, *with brains,* ensure that they have significant industry-specific or technical training in their tool kit. Positions and projects abound for those who have prepared themselves for the task. In organizations, specialized change agents are needed in a variety of roles and functional areas, including compensation and benefits, performance management, leadership development, quantitative methods, and more. However, you cannot expect to be taken seriously in any of these fields without first having cut your teeth in a related field of experience with significant responsibility.

If you lack credible experience, organizations may pay lip service to you as a change agent, but will secretly harbor doubts about the effectiveness of the solutions you offer and may soon come to believe that the emperor has no clothes. For example, if you were a stakeholder needing assistance with a process flow problem, you would certainly look for an expert with tools and techniques appropriate to systems design, process flow analysis, and the like. If you needed an actuarial analysis, you might look for individuals that have advanced statistical modeling techniques and an understanding of life-expectancy theory. The bottom line is this: The industry experience and technical expertise that you develop in the process of becoming a change agent must include experiences appropriate to the task and the problem your organization wishes to resolve. A carpenter shouldn't use a saw for a hammer any more than a financial expert should attempt to assess corporate culture using only quantitative methodology.

Effective change agents think like their stakeholders, which requires an understanding of how things are accomplished inside the organization and how decisions are made. Although some managers can point to their long tenure with an organization, it does not mean that they have an understanding of the organization's structure, leadership, or practices, knowledge of its processes and procedures, advanced capabilities, or appropriate industrial expertise. Industry experience and technical skills involve awareness of how organizations operate and why they exist, including knowledge of business fundamentals, systems theory, organizational culture, politics and procedures, and specialized knowledge that add value to an organization. Industry experience and technical skills help you to be perceived as a member of the organizational family, which enables you to generate solutions to business problems.

Successful change agents avoid using jargon when explaining performance problems, instead relying on straightforward language to describe processes and approaches to solving them. Moreover, you describe solutions in business terms rather than in technical terms, which helps establish clear communications and permission to proceed. Change agents understand the financial and marketing language that other executives and senior managers utilize every day. "Talking their language" allows you to establish joint partnerships.

By reading the organization's annual report and demonstrating an *understanding* of it, you are able to establish an in-depth knowledge of the business (Robinson and Robinson, 1996). Additionally, you can demonstrate your knowledge by conversing with senior managers and executives regarding the critical ratios used to measure the firm's operational health in order to compare current performance with goals. From such conversations you are able to determine return on equity, whether operating revenue is on target and if not why, what business actions must be taken to close any gap, and the external forces that challenge the organization's ability to meet its business goals.

Moreover, you are able to discuss competitors' strategies and actions and their implications for the organization. Finally, you are able to skillfully use the business terminology unique to the organization and the industry.

Because business challenges and goals change, effective change agents take the initiative to remain current. This includes reading trade journals relevant to the organization and reviewing organizational documents that provide information about the firm's vision, mission, strategic goals, and performance. This includes volunteering to serve on task forces or committees formed to address particular business issues and volunteering to work on special assignments in areas such as manufacturing, customer service, or maintenance. Finally, identifying critical performers in a business unit or division and asking permission to "shadow" them for a few days is another way to develop additional insight and knowledge.

## Project Management Skills

One of a change agent's basic roles is that of project manager; however, we continually discover that many managers have very little idea of what a project is and how to manage a project to its successful completion. If you are going to be a change agent, a seasoned set of project management skills is essential. The best project managers use a practical approach to deliver the project on time, deliver the project on budget, and deliver a strategic solution that addresses the agreed-upon problem for the stakeholder.

Every performance improvement intervention, change initiative, and special assignment is a project. Consequently, you need project management skills to lead such projects from beginning to end. Project management skills overlap with the skills required to be a change agent in that you will need to define the relationship with the project sponsor and define the change initiative clearly (Fuller and Farrington, 1999, 165–166). Additionally, you need to analyze risks to project completion, engage in contingency planning to help minimize risks, write requests for proposals, and select and manage employees. You need to make certain that the project's requirements are being fulfilled, that people working on the project are aware of their roles and responsibilities, that timing and scheduling of the project are going according to plan, and that the budget is within limits. This also includes managing communications between you and your employees, senior managers, and among employees.

### What Is a Project?

Projects vary in size and scope from a simple, one-day training seminar to a comprehensive organizational redesign. A project is really nothing more than an organized effort with planned activities and schedules. Change initiatives and performance improvement interventions are projects, thus they are one-time efforts and have specific time-bound results. Although the concept appears to be simple from this perspective, projects do have multiple, interrelated tasks and usually involve many people across several functional areas in the organization. As such, project management is a skill that must be understood completely and practiced regularly, if you are to count it as a feature of your change agent brainpower.

## What Is Project Management?

Above all else, project management is a way of thinking; a process of keeping desired results in focus. As project manager, you act to achieve specific objectives within a given budget and schedule. Project management, just as all the proficiencies demanded of a business partner, requires the use of proven tools and techniques.

Project management involves planning and identifying objectives and activities that produce a desired result. It also includes organizing people to get the job done and directing them by keeping them focused on achieving the results. Project management requires you to measure your project team's progress and give them feedback to keep the project moving ahead.

Project management begins with determining your stakeholders' expectations, including specific and measurable goals and results. Once determined, these expectations become your benchmark to measure the project's progress systematically. During the project management process, you are responsible for constantly monitoring progress toward and deviation from the project's goals. This monitoring activity allows you to make decisions that redirect the project and provide corrective action to narrow the discrepancy between stakeholders' expectations and your performance.

Project management is a complex skill that should not be underestimated. A project's many facets include creating a work breakdown structure and a schedule estimation, determining the interdependencies in the schedule, optimizing the schedule, and researching the project (Fuller, 1997).

## Project Constraints

The reality of project management is that every project is bound by three constraints: schedule, cost, and quality. As illustrated in Figure 9.2, they form an equilateral triangle that must remain equilateral. That is, if changed on any side, the overall size of the triangle may increase or decrease, but the form must remain the same. The size of each side of your project triangle must be agreed upon in advance by you and your stakeholders. In addition, you should attempt to agree on the fact that if time shortens, for instance, either the quality of the deliverable will decrease or extra resources, either human or financial, must be attained to retain the shape of the original agreement.

## The Phases of Project Management

As a process, project management progresses through at least five phases, all of which are critical to carrying out the project on time, within budget, and up to the desired level of quality.

*Project Definition.*    The first step in project management is to define the size and scope of the project. Once defined, it will be your job to break the macroproject into microtasks and a series of miniprojects. This defines the project as a set of interrelated work packages. A work package is a group of tasks or activities that an individual can complete.

*Project Scheduling.*    A primary purpose of a project schedule is to name the task interdependencies of a project. Another equally important purpose of project scheduling is to identify when resources are most likely to be available. Then you will be able to schedule tasks in the proper sequence and allocate resources for maximum efficiency.

One common scheduling tool in project management is a bar or Gantt chart (Figure 9.1). It is simple to draw, yet it captures a great deal of information about the project plan. Assigning different colors to different project stages or team members makes a Gantt chart a particularly powerful tool.

Managing a project is very rarely an endeavor with a level schedule. Because of time and resource constraints, your project may be front loaded, with substantial work at the beginning of the project, or rear loaded, with a last-minute rush to completion. Your task is to smooth out the schedule wherever possible and monitor the progress toward completion at all times.

*Project Budgeting.*    Once the project is defined, broken down into its component parts, and scheduled, you can then develop a budget appropriate to the size and scope of the project. To maximize control, you should begin building the budget at the microcomponent level of the project, so each budget item is linked to a part and subpart of the project. Then, as the project progresses you will be able to examine budget items and carefully link them to your plan.

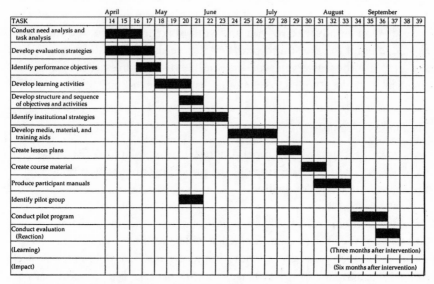

FIGURE 9.1   Gantt Chart for an Employee Growth and Development Plan

Clearly identifying with your stakeholder all costs—fixed, variable, direct, indirect, and allocated—early on in the project will decrease the opportunity for disagreement later on. If you name each of these types of cost for every part and subpart of the project, your budget will be more accurate, and if your stakeholder wants to change the triangle of the project later, you can clearly show which aspects of the project budget will be affected.

*Project Controls.*   Project controls help you successfully complete a project by comparing your actual progress against your plan. Controls also enable you to compare your performance against your stakeholders' expectations. Then you can make adjustments to reduce discrepancies between performance and expectations. Project controls focus on one or more of the three major components of a project: time, costs, or quality standards. Monitoring and controlling the project accomplishes three things: tracking progress toward completion, detecting deviations from your plan, and taking corrective action.

Three basic types of controls you may use on a project include:

1. Steering Control—Initiated at critical checkpoints along the way, steering controls give you the power to carry out corrective action if activities and tasks don't meet your expectations.
2. Go-No-Go Control—Although it is similar to steering control, go-no-go control gives you the freedom to shut the project down if

quality, time, or costs are beyond your threshold limits at any critical checkpoint of the project.

3. Postaction Control—Postaction controls allow you, your project team members, and your stakeholder to evaluate the project after completion. This feedback mechanism can be a very powerful learning tool for all involved.

## Project Leadership and Communication

Drawing on the relationship and communication skills mentioned Chapter 3, you develop and rely on excellent communications and leadership skills for project management to be successful. You clearly and specifically define each project team member's role and responsibility, define standards of performance, and communicate those performance standards so project team members can evaluate their own performance and take their own corrective action, if needed.

## Project Management Pitfalls

No matter how experienced or efficient you are at project management, it is impossible to run any project without occasional changes that must be incorporated into the plan, managing information flow, and managing the size of human involvement.

*Changes in the Scope of Your Project.* Changes in scope of the project occur for several reasons including:

Icebergs—as the project proceeds, you discover new information requiring shifts or expansions in the plan.

Technology changes—state-of-the-art changes develop as a result of innovations in the market or can be created by the project itself. A vendor or project team may need to design new technology specifically for your project.

Project member changes—team members may resign, be transferred, promoted, or terminated, which changes the rhythm of the work plan.

External forces—changes in the marketplace, state or federal regulations, or even "acts of God" can change the scope of a project.

Although many of these changes are difficult to predict, they can be anticipated and accounted for in the plan. For example, you should have a contingency plan that accounts for each of these factors. This means that you account for changes in requirements by having alternative ways to achieve the project objectives. Additionally, you identify alternative technologies and human resources prior to the beginning of a project in case your current resources are needed on another project. Finally, assess the conditions of external forces so that immediate corrections can be made to ensure that project quality, cost, and timeliness is achieved.

Other changes in project scope occur when the stakeholder or project team has a better idea. Being flexible and amenable to improvement demonstrates concern for the stakeholders' needs. Inadequate communications and poor project management planning contribute to the project's disaster, referred to as *scope creep*. This is an unfortunate event that can surface unexpectedly and create a great deal of damage to the project and your credibility. Scope creep refers to an ever-evolving change in focus by stakeholders. For example, the stakeholder may change the focus of the project each time you meet, thus applying continuous pressure to change direction. This makes it difficult, if not impossible, to set a concrete project goal and control costs, and can be the primary reason that the project is not completed on schedule or within budget.

The solution: Project scope boundaries and content must be unambiguously documented at the beginning of the project. Initial reports must provide the most clear and complete scope definitions. All stakeholders must publicly agree on the scope of the project. Any changes in scope must be documented in detail and communicated to everyone who is affected by them. Further, stakeholders must understand that as the project progresses, additional costs will result if the scope is modified.

*Excess or Lack of Detail.* Too much detail in the management system can choke the project. For example, scheduling on a day-by-day or hour-by-hour basis may be far too extreme. As a result, you may become buried in detail. At the other extreme is too little detail. Scheduling quarterly or annually may lack the proper management needed to move the project along successfully.

The solution: Consider carefully the time unit to be used for scheduling. The more frequent the time checks or intermediate deadlines, the more supervision is being supplied to the project. How much guidance does the project staff need? A team that is experienced, has a good understanding of the project, or is accustomed to working together may not need short inter-

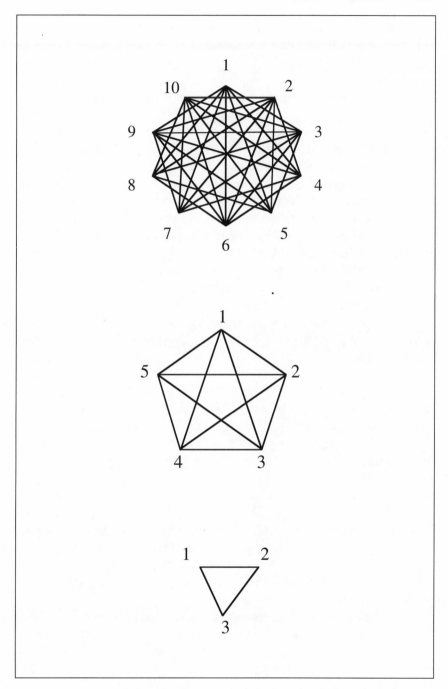

FIGURE 9.2   Interpersonal Relationships

vals between deadlines. For most projects, a time unit of days or weeks works best. The complexity of a project will help determine the amount of supervision and structure needed.

*Too Many People on the Project Team.*   Any experienced change agent can provide examples of projects that have failed because too many people were involved. Rarely do projects fail solely because there were not enough people involved. Each time a staff member is added to the project, the number of interpersonal relationships affecting the project is increased. Three members require three relationships, five members require ten relationships, and ten members require forty=five relationships (Figure 9.2). Each time a member is added to the project, relationships increase geometrically. If the project becomes overstaffed, progress slows and decisions are subject to frequent changes. Recall how much trouble Dorothy had getting her three friends to the Emerald City. Now imagine how complicated the journey would have been trying to get forty-five individuals there.

The solution involves only the people who are vital to project success on the team. Avoid including people for political or business etiquette reasons. Others can be brought in briefly for their specific expertise without becoming permanent project members.

*Lack of Communication.*   If project members do not know or understand the project goals, it is doomed from the outset. A lack of communication leads to a lack of commitment. Members who perceive no sense of importance for the project or do not see the overall scope of its purpose will not be highly motivated to contribute to it. Do you think Dorothy could have convinced the Scarecrow, Tin Man, or the Lion to face the dangers along the road without their desire to find the brain, heart, and courage they so wanted?

Always conduct a project kick-off meeting to review the project, all its parts and subparts, the schedule, a communication plan, and the relevant budgetary items. Make it clear that you expect to be notified of problems early and that you don't shoot messengers. Attempt to develop an atmosphere of "no surprises," which will assist you in delivering a quality project on time and on budget to your stakeholder.

The solution: Communicate goals at the beginning of the project and update progress regularly. Make schedules and their revisions available to everyone. Announce project results at the conclusion of the project. If there is any doubt as to whether something needs to be communicated to the project team or to the stakeholders, always decide to communicate.

# Conclusion

We hope we have identified the knowledge, skills, and abilities necessary to use your intellect to influence the world around you. Although it may a bit overwhelming, don't be discouraged. In Chapters 10, 11, and 12 you will learn how to use your heart, courage, and vision to sustain you throughout the process. If you persevere, collect these tools, and continue to hone your ability to use them, you will become an effective agent for change. And re-member—if you succeed, you're in elite company. Today's organizations need good people who can produce solid *business* results.

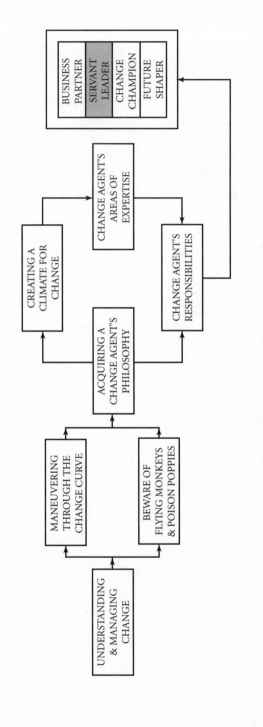

THE MANAGER AS CHANGE AGENT BLUEPRINT

# Servant Leader

*Do nothing out of selfish ambition or vain conceit,*
*but in humility consider others better than yourselves.*
*Each of you should look not only to your own interests,*
*but also to the interests of others.*

The Apostle Paul

**Holistic Model for Change Agent Excellence**

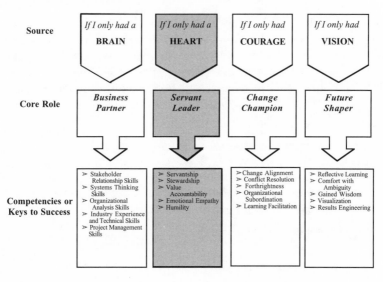

FIGURE 10.01   Holistic Model for Change Agent Excellence

## Operating in the Second Core Role: Servant Leader

The Tin Man desperately wanted a heart, because without it he was "empty and frustrated." Conversations with employees who have unsuccessfully engaged ineffective managers revealed that they often feel the same way—frustrated and incomplete. Many cited incompetent, abusive, critical, or unfocused managers as the cause. Quite simply, dissatisfied employees' needs have not been met.

As a change agent, you put your employees' needs first, devoting your time and energy to providing superior service that meets and exceeds their expectations. Thus, employee needs are at the heart of any change engagement.

Satisfying employees requires thorough understanding of their mission, vision, goals, values, objectives, culture, strengths, weaknesses, resources, management practices, and so forth. Developing such knowledge challenges a change agent to immerse himself in the employee system and take ownership of the opportunity. Doing so fosters a partnership dedicated to meeting the employee's specific need(s), which may bring lasting and improved performance.

Accessing the hearts of others requires being humble, as the chapter-opening quote elucidates. A change agent must become a servant leader, focused first and foremost on the success of employees, recognizing that their success is, ultimately, his success. It is not an overstatement to say that as a change agent, your success absolutely depends on the success of those around you. Make no mistake about it, this is imperative to truly gain the trust and commitment of the employee base. Without trust and commitment on the part of employees, a change agent's efforts are doomed to failure.

Operating in the core role of servant leader requires internalizing and modeling the following five personal competencies: servantship, stewardship, values accountability, emotional empathy, and humility.

## Servantship

> *The Servant-Leader is servant first . . . it begins with the*
> *natural feeling that one wants to serve, to serve first.*
> *Then conscious choice brings one to aspire to lead.*
> Robert Greenleaf (1996),
> *On Becoming a Servant Leader*

A servantship approach does not imply weakness or an inability to make difficult decisions. It simply implies a personal philosophy of humility and a willingness to work for the betterment of employees. Moreover, servant leaders help their organization by advocating, assisting, growing, and developing its most important asset: its people. Simply stated, servantship means being a caretaker without regard for one's own personal needs or the rewards that are typically afforded to managers responsible for the professional lives of others, a tremendous responsibility that should not be taken lightly.

In his seminal work on leadership and power, Greenleaf introduced the American corporate world to the notion of leadership as a servant to their followers. To be sure, Greenleaf's message initially fell mostly on deaf ears. However, in recent years, Peter Senge, Max DePree, Peter Block, David Ulrich, Ed Lawler, and other pioneers of modern managerial and organizational thought have lent significant focus and legitimacy to the idea. Although it is still relatively new to dialogue in the corporate world, this leadership paradigm has been eloquently modeled through the lives of service and enduring accomplishments of some of history's most influential change agents. Most can be viewed as change agents who brought about transformational change through radical selflessness and radical expressions of love.

## Radical Selflessness

Does radical selflessness mean that success as a change agent depends on the willingness to submit to execution on behalf of employees? Yes and no. Servantship in the business world may not entail physical death, but it often entails putting your professional neck on the line for employees—taking unpopular stands, occasionally in direct opposition to the powers that be. More directly, success depends on the ability to demonstrate a servant heart toward others, intentionally serving the needs and goals of employees first, making them the overriding focus, the purpose for being a change agent in the first place. This is how real trust and commitment are born. Equally important, this is the way one's track record of servantship eventually becomes a source of leverage that can be used to operate in the core roles of change champion and future shaper, as we will discuss in Chapters 11 and 12.

## Radical Expressions of Love

Radical expressions of love does not mean that success as a change agent depends on the willingness to literally wash the feet of employees. Rather, the message is how important it is to communicate appreciation for employees in meaningful ways and to walk on common ground with them; to roll up your sleeves and help others, even though they don't expect it. For example, stay late to help the administrative staff prepare a report needed for an important early morning meeting so that they don't have to spend additional time away from their families; send an employee an encouraging e-mail, just because; demonstrate in concrete ways that you are all in this together, in good times or bad; publicly praise employees for their work, especially for a job well done. The following contemporary examples demonstrate servantship in action through coming alongside your employees and sharing the glory with them.

## Come Alongside Employees

A major consulting firm based in Fairfax, Virginia (one of the top fifteen in terms of worldwide revenues), was retained to reengineer the business processes and develop a new information systems infrastructure for a state taxation agency. Halfway through the project life cycle significant technical problems with the new computer systems emerged. The problems necessitated major work-arounds and manual data entry of tax returns as the April 15 income tax deadline approached. Many of the state employees and consultants assigned to the joint project team were required to work data-entry shifts from 6:00 P.M. to 12:00 midnight twice a week in addition to their normal workloads. Understandably, motivation levels among the 125-member project team began to dip considerably. However, just one week into the "crisis mode" schedule the project team members received a pleasant surprise. When they looked at the data entry station next to them, these employees and consultants saw the secretary of revenue and the consulting firm's senior partner (essentially the CEOs of both organizations) doing the same data entry right alongside them—three or four nights a week instead of the required two. The result? Motivation on the project team rose to an all-time high, and the state taxation agency set operational performance records for that tax season despite the system problems and manual work-arounds.

## Share the Glory

Maytag Corporation is a mature company competing in a mature industry characterized by pricing pressures and slow growth. The once "sleepy" *Fortune* 500 appliance manufacturer headquartered in rural Iowa has set company records for sales and earnings over each of the last three years. Much of the credit for Maytag's renewed growth is focused on Lloyd Ward, the charismatic and servantship-oriented chairman and CEO who joined the company as heir apparent in 1995. A senior vice president for Best Buy Co. (a major customer of Maytag) comments that since that time, "Ward has been able to almost reinvent Maytag." A major piece of this reinvention puzzle has been the success story of the Neptune, a front-loading, water-saving, $1,000 washing machine driven to market by Ward. Recently Ward sought out a longtime salesman at a Sears store in Des Moines, Iowa, who had persuaded a woman to buy a Neptune over the phone, sight unseen. Ward greeted him heartily with a warm grin: "I'm Lloyd Ward with Maytag." Taken aback somewhat, the salesman commented, "I know who you are, I read about you in the newspaper." Ward's response, typically self-effacing and sincere, was quick: "You're the one whose picture should be in the paper if you sold a Neptune over the phone!" Ward had done what he came to do—to deflect the praise to one of his employees in a radical way. To share the glory. The result? Sales of the revolutionary Neptune have exploded, allowing Maytag to increase their market share of major appliances from 15 to 19 percent since 1996. With a slate of more than twenty new products introduced in 2000 alone, along with a major organizational restructuring initiative announced last quarter, it doesn't appear as though Maytag will be a very "sleepy" company again for quite some time.

The message for change agents is clear. Radical selflessness and radical expressions of love can create radical commitment to change among employees.

## Stewardship

> *Stewardship depends on a willingness to be held accountable for results without control or caretaking as the means to reach them . . . stated simply, it is accountability without control or compliance.*
>
> Peter Block (1992), *Stewardship*

Although servantship entails intentionally putting the needs and the success of employees above those of a change agent, stewardship takes it a step further and requires being held accountable for meeting those needs and ensuring those successes. A change agent must do so without employing a traditional command-and-control style, lest he slip back from being employees' steward to being their patriarch. As mentioned earlier, more than seventy-five years of management studies and theory have clearly indicated that patriarchy leads, at best, to minimize employee dissatisfaction but not to true employee motivation. It's one thing to operate as a brilliant yet humble change agent, consistently sharing the glory and giving employees credit for *your* successes. It's another thing altogether to ensure that they have actually achieved the success on their own, and thus have truly earned the praise. Add to that the competitive realities of today's global marketplace and the stakes become clear. Unless a change agent can do more with constrained resources (both human and capital) and meet increasingly sophisticated customer demands, both while concurrently creating trust, commitment, and most important, self-sufficiency among your employees, success as a change agent is tenuous. The challenge must be approached as a steward that equips and engages employees.

## Equip the Employees

Stewardship requires equipping employees with the knowledge, work skills, and resources necessary for success. Make significant up-front and ongoing investments in their competencies and development. Spend a good portion of every day imparting personal wisdom, expertise, skills, and experience with at least one key employee, always remembering that the goal in doing so is not to impress, but to equip. Do these things and two significant outcomes will be realized: Employees will become more self-sufficient and they will feel more valued—a double win.

## Engage Employees

Being a steward means that, once employees have been equipped for a battle, you let them fight it. Give them the authority and autonomy to allocate resources, redesign work processes, and create new ways to meet customer needs. This does not mean sending them out to the wolves without any protection. Legitimize their involvement, formally articulating to the organization the extent and reason for their autonomy and confidence in their abilities. Blaze a trail for them. If a change agent cannot or is unwilling to do this, then he's not ready to empower them. Remember, their failure is the change agent's failure.

Ultimately, stewardship is about equipping and engaging employees in such a way that, as Peter Senge comments, they wholeheartedly endorse the following ancient wisdom about change agency and leadership:

*The wicked leader is he who the people despise.*
*The good leader is he who the people revere.*
*The great leader is he who the people say, "We did it ourselves."*

## Connect with Employees

It takes more than industry knowledge and the courage to express convictions to ensure success in reaching the destination; One also needs compassion and empathy. They must establish a healthy, honest employee–change agent relationship. Further, numerous resources on the subject of building employee relationships yield common threads. Truth and the ability to create trust are vital components for a successful relationship. This stands to reason, considering that "truth" emerges as a basic fundamental in all relationships, both personal and professional.

Working as a change agent for a mid-size Ohio firm, Sally was given a special, one-of-a-kind assignment. The organization had recently purchased a small company with approximately 100 employees in Columbus. Sally's assignment was to temporarily relocate to Columbus, stay one to two years, and educate the new group on the established culture, office procedures, and work ethic of the main firm. Eventually the Columbus operation was to resemble the main location as much as possible. The goal was to make Columbus employees "like" working for their new parent firm and want to remain.

During her first week in Columbus, the parent firm's president addressed all the employees and assured everyone that their jobs were secure. There were no plans to downsize their operation. He encouraged everyone to stay and give the new relationship a chance. After the meeting, the president spoke privately with Sally, reassured her that there were no plans to change anything, and asked her to bring the new employees into the flock and help build a new, much needed addition to the operation. One month later, over 25 percent of the Columbus employees were let go. Sally was notified five minutes before employees were informed.

It seemed impossible, and somewhat naïve, but Sally and the remaining employees were convinced that another look at the operation had made this change in position necessary and that the worst was over. Everyone, once again, was assured that their jobs were secure. Sally dedicated herself to regaining the trust that had been obliterated by the downsizing. After six months of building relationships, regaining trust, and restoring morale, the second shoe dropped. Another downsizing was announced. Although only five people were involved, the damage was irreparable. Empty assurances and bad-faith promises destroyed any hope of a healthy management-employee relationship and eventually destroyed the employee–change agent relationship as well. Sally was later reassigned to the home office but was never able to overcome the lack of trust she now felt. Shortly thereafter she resigned from the company. Eventually, all the work performed by the branch office was transferred to the home office and the Columbus operation was closed. Everyone was let go. No one was surprised this time.

"Only truth leads to the right decisionmaking, and success. An immense amount of organizational energy can be spent avoiding and suppressing the truth. This is surely the essence of folly" (Lucas, 1997, 42).

So what does it take to create a successful employee–change agent relationship? We are back to "truth." Employees' trust depends on two things. The first, according to Bob Graham, a noted project management consultant, is "WIIFM," What's in It for Me? (Pinto, 1998). Employees must perceive substantial benefit to the relationship before committing time and resources. They are not likely to support or offer help on a project unless it is in their best interest.

The second question that must be answered to gain employee trust is "How are you going to make me look good?" There are five steps to gaining employee trust.

1. Establishing commonality and empathy with the employee.
2. Maintaining credibility in everything.
3. Defining intentions or reasons for actions and how those actions can help the employee.
4. Being responsive to employees' needs, goals, and objectives.
5. Being accountable for actions and project results.

Ultimately, a personal connection with employees is necessary to change success. Change agents must add value to the organization, be seen as totally credible, and above all, understand their employees' problems and opportunities.

A certain set of skills is necessary to develop a successful employee–change agent relationship. Not coincidentally, these are some of the same skills needed to be a successful leader, such as listening, negotiation, and problem-solving skills. Throughout the relationship change agents will serve as diplomats, the bearers of difficult news, and marketers of change successes. They will make professional and succinct presentations, conduct focused, stakeholder interviews, and provide both positive and negative feedback using effective communication skills. The more of these skills a change agent masters, the more successful his relationships.

In order to build a successful, long-lasting relationship, both employee and change agent must be willing to relinquish some control and promote mutual trust. Be willing to share information relating to the change initiative, including progress on important goals, financial information, and any contemplated organizational changes. Be willing to share information gathered without sifting it through personal perceptions or assumptions. The result is a connection with the employee that improves project results and leads to future opportunities.

## Demonstrate Passion

Change agents should be concerned about and aware of the passions of employees or stakeholders. A mistaken focus on planning at the exclusion of passion can lead to micromanagement of a change initiative which, in turn, can result in a loss of any sense of purpose or spirit. "People need an incredibly high level of freedom and trust in our response before they'll release the passion that can lead to exceptional achievement" (Lucas, 1997, 12).

Operating in the core role of servant leader requires embracing the spiritual dimension of work and organizational life and willingly accepting accountability for the "spiritual well-being" of employees. When employees can put their spiritual values to work, their quality of work life increases; when the quality of work life increases, individual motivation and performance levels increase; when individual motivation and performance levels increase, the aggregate organizational motivation and performance level increases. So once again, a win for employees is a win for the change agent and the organization. Tapping into the spirit of employees is what enables a change agent to change holistically—hands, mind, heart, and spirit.

There are many myths about passion. Here are a few:

- Passion is always a good thing.
- Actions intended to improve things will evoke positive passions.
- Negative passions won't last in a professional organization.
- We can trust our instincts on what people will get passionate about. (Lucas, 1997)

Remember, people's passions cannot be managed or controlled. There will be opportunities to create situations that will excite passions or manage situations to control them. None of us, however, have the ability to control the passions themselves. Taking time to develop a relationship of mutual passions for common project goals ensures the success of the change initiative and relationship.

## Value Accountability

*How we put our spiritual values to work can make a huge difference to our own quality of life, and that also is the foundation for each organization in our society to become prosperous, successful, and healthy.*
William C. Miller

There is nothing more central to an individual than their core value system. Values are defined as broad-based qualities of the individual self that are important and affect behavior. Values are the standards that guide our lives. People use these guideposts to make life choices in all areas of their lives. Values are the abstract qualities that we care about. We cannot commit to values without caring. In short, we can say that the area of personal values serves as the principle governing body of the personal system.

Values tend to be picked out in a haphazard, piecemeal fashion from friends, parents, the media, teachers, popular heroes, and clergy, in that order. Value systems and beliefs are important to know where you stand, but they must be one's own values, not someone else's. If knowing yourself and being yourself were as easy to do as to talk about, there wouldn't be nearly so many people walking around in borrowed postures, spouting secondhand ideas, trying desperately to fit in rather than to stand out. As Emerson says, "What you are speaks so loudly I cannot hear what you say."

Eliminate the false dichotomy between the "secular" and the "sacred" to be value accountable. For too long now the corporate world has viewed the topic of spirituality as taboo—a subject for the sacred world of churches, charities, and the Boy Scouts, and certainly not applicable to the secular world of big business. Thus, employees are often expected to leave their terminal values at the door and keep them out of the organizational dialogue. This expectation is narrow-minded, and as spiritual beings, it is a difficult and unnatural thing for employees to do. Clearly articulate to employees that you recognize the value of and the place for spirituality in *all* of life. This includes business organizations and the work conducted within them. There is a higher purpose for working together than simply earning a paycheck or even becoming a more efficient and profitable organization, for that matter.

Although attitudes and opinions change quickly, values are enduring and often last a lifetime. They represent the guiding principles in our lives—concepts such as achievement, humanism, and individualism. Because they represent such fundamental beliefs, our values systems strongly influence our views of how we ought to live and what decisions we ought to make. They affect the jobs we do, the people with whom we spend our time, and the brands we buy. It's been said that we are the sum of the choices we make. Our values say who we are because they determine what we choose.

Values exist at a deeper level than attitudes and are more general and basic in nature. We use them to evaluate our own behavior and that of others. As such, they vary widely among individuals. Values are enduring beliefs that a specific mode of conduct or end state of existence is personally or socially preferable (Rokeach, 1973).

| INSTRUMENTAL VALUES | | |
|---|---|---|
| Honesty | Ambition | Responsibility |
| Forgiving nature | Open-mindedness | Courage |
| Helpfulness | Cleanliness | Competence |
| Self-control | Affection / Love | Cheerfulness |
| Independence | Politeness | Intelligence |
| Obedience | Rationality | Imagination |
| TERMINAL VALUES | | |
| World peace | Family security | Freedom |
| Happiness | Self-respect | Wisdom |
| Equality | Salvation | Prosperity |
| Achievement | Friendship | National security |
| Inner peace | Mature love | Social respect |
| Beauty in art/nature | Pleasure | Exciting, active life |

FIGURE 10.1   Instrumental and Terminal Values

When examining values, we can separate them into two categories. First, value can be classified as those that represent a means for achieving goals such as being honest or dishonest, responsible, independent, and so forth (instrumental). Second, they can be classified as outcomes or ends such as wisdom, freedom, world peace, and so forth (terminal). In Figure 10.1, we list examples of both of these types of values. Terminal values are deeper rooted and do not change dramatically over time since they represent an end state, whereas instrumental values can change in accordance with current efforts in achieving a goal. Another way of differentiating between these types of values is by thinking of them as either an expression of behavior (instrumental) or desire states (terminal). By separating values into these classifications, it is possible to better understand your daily behavior as well as your long-term mission in life. Most important, make certain that daily behavior helps achieve your life mission. Being incongruent in this area will lead to frustration and anxiety and missed opportunities.

Values tend to form the foundation of a person's character. Although some of one's values may change over the course of a lifetime, they tend to remain fairly deeply entrenched in one's personality. A person develops a sense of right or wrong, good or bad, beginning quite early in life. Many of one's ideas change through the teenage years, but as mature adults one tends to hold onto and defend some basic core within that tells one what is really important in life and basic to one as an individual. Examples of values would be such ideas as:

- Always being honest with others.
- Always standing on your own two feet and not burdening others with your problems.
- Always facing up to life's difficulties and not running away.
- Never deliberately hurting another's feelings.
- Never letting anyone feel you have not lived up to your responsibilities.
- Always doing your best at any activity you try.
- Never going "overboard" about interests.

These are the kinds of values that a person normally refuses to violate; they determine people's integrity as individuals. Following one's values enhances the basic sense of personal worth; failing to follow them causes guilt, shame, and self-doubt. Values that are most severely challenged with little or no change are the strongest. An untested value may really be little more than an attitude or belief.

Values also tend to exist in a hierarchy. Some are likely to be somewhat more critical than others. Decisions are based on values. When people experience value conflicts this hierarchical arrangement often helps them to make a decision.

## Values and the Organization

Organizations are everyday arenas for considerable conflict, primarily because of our differences in values. Businesses have shown increasing interest in values over recent years. Often value conflicts are very hard to resolve. For example, imagine yourself in a position where you must dismiss an employee for being absent too much owing to alcoholism. One of your values is to always be honest and another is to always be kind. How would you balance these values with one another? Can you find a way to honor them both? For some people being honest with an employee might be an unkind act or even a dishonest act. Think of examples in your own life where you found a value conflict. For example, this occurs when personal values conflict with those of the organization. The organization takes action based on its core values and the law of the land. An organization whose values include protecting employees' welfare is morally obligated to "walk the talk" and establish activities in support of this. Your values are more personal and affect decisions and actions, which might be inconsistent with those of the organization.

It is not unusual to be in circumstances where values conflict with needs or goals. Suppose, for example, in order to be successful, advance, and be recognized by superiors in an organization you had to engage in behavior that you considered unacceptable (for example, political backbiting, concealing information about a defective product, using the rumor mill to make a rival look bad, and so on). Your goal of advancement—perhaps even the need to survive in an uncertain job market—could push you to behave in ways that conflict with your values. What you end up doing might then reflect your adopted values. Think of current or recent situations that illustrate this.

Values focus on why people behave as they do. Since organizational values can powerfully influence what people actually do, we think that values ought to be a matter of great concern to change agents. In fact, shaping and enhancing values can become the most important job a change agent can do. Research has found that successful companies place a great deal of emphasis on values (Deal and Kennedy, 2000). In general, these companies shared three characteristics:

- They stand for something—that is, they have a clear and explicit philosophy about how they aim to conduct their business.
- Management pays a great deal of attention to shaping and fine-tuning these values to conform to the economic and business environment of the company and to communicating them to the organization.
- These values are known and shared by all the people who work for the company—from the lowest production worker right through to the ranks of senior management.

## Organizational Culture and Values

Organizational culture is derived from beliefs that are set forth by guiding principles, which may be external to the organization (for example, the Ten Commandments), and are demonstrated daily by every action. Actions set corporate culture in motion, not memoranda. Corporate culture cannot be changed by sayings. Management must sincerely believe in the corporate culture and demonstrate values on a daily basis for it to pervade the company. Corporate culture must be continually reevaluated to account for rapidly changing perceptions about job expectations and increasing workforce diversity.

Culture is composed of the beliefs, values, and behaviors a group shares in an environment and is demonstrated in actions. Values left undemonstrated are not values.

Values are fundamental notions of ideal behavior, usually unattainable but worth striving for. Values are seldom explicit but very much shape how employees interpret events and form expectations about behavior. For example, in some groups members believe that it is "right" that individuals should always put group needs ahead of personal interests. Individuals are expected to subordinate their desires for the betterment of the total group. Various members of a group or even one member may hold conflicting values, and this can cause serious tension at crucial times.

Recent attempts to help organizations manage external relationships suggest the need for new interventions and competence among managers. A change agent must have not only social skills but also political skills. He must understand the distribution of power, conflicts of interest, and value dilemmas inherent in managing external relationships and be able to manage his own role and values in respect to those dynamics. Interventions promoting collaboration and systems maintenance may be ineffective in this larger arena, especially when there are power and dominance relationships between organizations and competition for scarce resources. Under these conditions, more power-oriented interventions may be needed, such as bargaining, coalition forming, and pressure tactics.

Mission, vision, and values become objective standards for directing the activities of employees. You must write the mission, vision, and values statements in simple and meaningful language so people can use them to make decisions. These are valuable documents to avoid and resolve conflict, but to be truly useful they must be more than just documents. The company must painstakingly act consistently with its mission, vision, and values. Disparities between action and mission, visions, and values become sources of conflict.

The workplace of the future is upon us. With it brings a shift in focus from quality to value creation as the primary objective of an organization.

### The Role of Change Agents in Defining Value

The genius of leadership lies in the manner in which leaders see and act on their own and their followers' values and motivations. "The leaders' fundamental act is to induce people to be aware or conscious of what they feel—to feel their true needs so strongly, to define their values so meaningfully, that they can move to purposeful action" (MacGregor, 1978, 78). Shared values are the bedrock on which change agents build the edifice of group achievement. No examination of leadership would be complete without attention to the decay and possible regeneration of the value framework (Wren, 1995).

For credibility to be attained, a credit agent must do what he says he will do, maintain a level of integrity beyond reproach, and keep confidences. Additionally, be willing to challenge the way things are done, push for continuous improvement, and demonstrate a willingness to take risks. The mark of a great change agent is the ability to bring out the best in others to meet goals. A change agent needs to be able to solidify those goals and align them to the organization's success, at the same time developing the talents of those around them. It takes courage to stand up for your values, but more important, it takes a lot of understanding and listening to what's going on in the organization. The presence of a "conscience" (change agent) at the side of the CEO means that deviations from right behavior (and the temptations can be many) are nipped in the bud and almost always are avoided entirely.

### Steps in Demonstrating Values Accountability

Make an overt commitment to access the terminal values of employees, to make your values known to them, and to allow those values to be a constant source of personal and corporate meaning and motivation. The following list provides several steps necessary to take as a change agent to demonstrate and embody values accountability:

1. *Be transparent and uncompromising about your terminal values.* For employees to feel comfortable with the idea of bringing their whole selves into the workplace, including their terminal values, they will have to see the change agent model the principle first. This doesn't mean "proselytizing" or attempting to convert employees to *your* terminal values. It simply means openly sharing with them what you are passionate about when it comes to your work and your life. Quite simply, what do you view as the ultimate purpose for your life? Once you have answered this question, conduct your work and life activities as much as possible in harmony with the terminal values that you have espoused. Nothing damages the potential influence of terminal values quicker than hypocrisy and compromising behavior on the part of a change agent. You *are* under a microscope, with employees looking through the lens.

2. *Make a concerted effort to know and understand employees' terminal values.* Once employees feel comfortable that they really know the change agent, both professionally and personally, it's his job to then draw them out if necessary. In most cases, employees will naturally and willingly share their terminal values. However, sometimes change agents need to make a more concerted effort to know employees holistically. Be creative, persistent, and patient—look for opportunities to connect with them around values. Ask questions like, "Why is that important to you?" "What have you been doing outside of work lately?" Responses to such questions can give you immediate insight into employees' terminal values.

3. *Make concrete connections between your terminal values, your employees' terminal values, and your work together as often as possible.* This is really the lynchpin to realizing the direct work-related benefits of being a spiritually sensitive change agent. Making these connections is what enables one to intentionally leverage understanding of employees as a source of motivation and effort. Not surprisingly, it is the inability and unwillingness of most organizations to do this that results in many of their vision and mission statements being "soul-less" and "empty," as opposed to deeply meaningful, shared, and *purposeable* statements of terminal values.

Jack Welch, perhaps the most influential change agent of the past quarter century, commented that he views his main job as "unleashing the spirit" of the employees at General Electric, resulting in an employee base that feels rewarded and fulfilled "in both the pocketbook and the soul." Given his track record of success as a change agent and General Electric's corporate success under his watch as chairman and CEO, it is clear that being a spiritually sensitive change agent not only makes good "heart sense," it makes good "business sense" as well: yet another win-win for you and your employees.

Like Welch, you must be willing to accept values accountability for your employees, at least as it relates to your work together. If employees are unable to holistically engage in the task at hand, *you* are at fault, and your efforts as a change agent will suffer.

## Emotional Empathy

> *Accepting strong emotions and acknowledging the importance of patience in dealing with change are vital.*
> Todd Jick (1993), *Managing Change*

As a change agent, you will find that organizational life is all about change both for you as the initiator and for employees as the recipients and participants in change. You view change as a personal mandate, a challenge, a calling to proactively guide the organization in the right direction. However, change is messy, and at times decidedly emotional, especially for employees, who usually don't have the same adaptability to change as you do.

Thus, the turmoil of organizational change will often result in a great deal of emotional, personal, and professional conflict between the change agent and employees. This conflict needs to be handled with great care and sensitivity—or put simply, with emotional empathy. The following steps are necessary for you to follow as you employ emotional empathy in working with your employees.

1. Clearly articulate to employees that it is normal and even healthy for them to feel what they are feeling.
2. Openly share your own feelings and emotions surrounding the change with employees on a regular basis.
3. Provide individual or group forums and outlets for employees to express their emotions and feelings about the change.
4. When employees share their feelings and emotions listen to them in an open and nonjudgmental yet discerning manner.
5. Based on what you learn, design and implement additional individual or group interventions as necessary.

As we have said, being a servant leader involves being transparent about your personal feelings and emotions surrounding the change effort at hand; more important, it requires being empathetically attuned to the emotions and feelings of employees. Remember, these emotions are not only normal and inevitable, and therefore cannot be ignored, but practicing emotional empathy also allows for the change agent to more holistically understand and engage employees, thereby gaining more change leverage.

## Humility

> We must become willing to reveal our uncertainties, to be
> ignorant, to show incompetence—knowing that these are
> essential preconditions to learning because they set free
> our innate capacity for curiosity and experimentalism.
> Peter Senge (1990), *The Fifth Discipline*

According to history, the British ambassador came to the United States in 1863 to visit President Abraham Lincoln at the White House. When he arrived he was escorted to the president's private office where he found President Lincoln shining his shoes. It has been reported that the British ambassador was shocked by what he witnessed. He abruptly stated, "Mr. President, you can't shine your own shoes." President Lincoln paused, slowly looked up, and calmly replied, "Then whose shoes should I be shining?" Such an account clearly demonstrates the humility needed to be a servant leader. As an Appalachian saying goes, "be careful not to grow too much above your raisin." This simple and honest expression reveals the importance of remembering one's humble beginnings and not letting success vault you too high above those who raised you. Humility can become a guiding principle that shapes behavior and personal philosophy. If you remain grounded you can focus better on the needs and expectations of others.

By remaining humble, a change agent actually becomes more influential and powerful because employees perceive him as approachable, open, and friendly. This enables employees to remain at ease during interactions, which improves communications. It allows employees to feel closer and more willing to support thoughts, ideas, and suggestions. Consequently, the mental wrestling match so common in leader/employee relationships simply disappears.

When you ask employees to change their behavior, apply new skills, or implement change that will increase business results and outcomes, a servantship approach is critical. This approach requires the demonstration of several characteristics (Boyett and Boyett, 1995). First, to be a servant, driven by the need to learn and serve. Next, lead by listening to followers. Help people articulate their own goals and those of the group by reaching a consensus that inspires trust. Further, take people and their work seriously, exhibiting commitment to employee growth, development, and independance.

Recognizing that power and control rests with the employees, exercise servantship to help them become all that they can be. Well-served employees realize that they have the power to grow and develop, become masters of their careers, and achieve professional success.

True humility is demonstrated by being willing to put the needs, expectations, interests, and success of employees above oneself. As a servant leader, advocate, support, and promote employees and accept your career development responsibilities by working continuously to help employees grow and develop. Assist workers as they struggle to become the best they can be, share organizational success, and make certain that other decision makers in the organization are aware of employee contributions to achieving desired business results. As a humble leader, a change agent operates without regard for his own well-being or career advancement because he believes employees are the organization's most important asset. Most important, be a humble leader because it is the right thing to do. Finally, accept responsibility for employees' failures and celebrate their successes.

Humility is also demonstrated through the *law of legacy* whereby a leader's lasting value is measured by succession (Maxwell, 1998). This law maintains that leaders are willing to let their employees grow and develop above and beyond themselves. Thus, the change agent creates a legacy only when he puts the organization in position to do great things on its own. As a result, the change agent delegates tasks and responsibilities to others because he realizes that employees need these opportunities for growth and development. Understand that you will receive credit for a job well done since part of the job was being delegated.

The willingness to engage employees by becoming personally involved in their careers and professional lives is another characteristic of servant leaders. This encourages employees to discuss important issues openly and honestly, without fear of negative repercussions or reprisals. Thus, the change agent becomes a real person who is willing to demonstrate personal vulnerability rather than hide behind a guarded and controlled personality. When this type of behavior is exhibited, honesty and openness will be reciprocated by employees (see Chapter 3).

If you believe that being a successful change agent means always having the right answers, then you are dead wrong. History has shown us that many of the greatest leaders in the business world recognized the need to surround themselves with people smarter than they were and to learn from them. Henry Ford's epitaph conveys this nicely: "Here lies a man that enjoyed success because he was wise enough to surround himself with people smarter than himself." Remember, Ford is the same man that essentially sparked the American Industrial Revolution with his invention of the modern-day assembly line.

Senge (1990) has written extensively about this idea in connection with his groundbreaking work on organizational learning. In the context of this work, Senge emphasizes the need for change agents to foster *dialogos* with their employees—that is, the free-flowing and nonjudgmental exchange of ideas, knowledge, and wisdom. Unfortunately, the traditional model of change agency all too often results in only one-way *dialogos* taking place, where the teaching is done by the change agent and the learning is done by the employee, which in reality isn't *dialogos* at all, but rather is classic command-and-control communication. The leader has all the knowledge and good ideas and the followers simply soak up what the leader espouses and spit it back as "good" employees are supposed to do. Under such a model the risk of the organization making poor decisions is greatly increased because the livelihood of the group is dependent on the ideas, knowledge, and wisdom of just one person as opposed to many. The consequences often include severely handicapped organizational performance at a minimum, and outright disaster at a maximum. Your poor decisions may never result in consequences as grave as these, but the applicability to success as a change agent is clear.

An important connection to make here is that having humility as a change agent not only enables you to personally practice continuous learning, but more important, almost always results in employees following suit. This in turn leads to greater levels of organizational learning. Others have exhorted us to keep in mind that over the last twenty years it is precisely an organization's ability to learn that dictates its long-term economic success. In a groundbreaking study that involved over 175 *Fortune* 500 firms and extended over ten years, operational and financial data was used to determine the relationship, if any, that corporate culture has on long-term organizational performance (Deal and Kennedy, 2000). Their conclusion? That corporate culture is indeed one of the *most valid* predictors of long-term organizational performance and more specifically, that firms that fostered continuous learning and flexibility throughout their ranks consistently performed at higher levels than their inflexible, "nonlearning" peers. And what do you think was one of the most important patterns among these higher performing, learning organizations? They were led and staffed by executives that demonstrated *humility*.

Walter Wriston, former chairman and CEO of Citibank, once commented that "the person who figures out how to harness the collective genius of the people in his or her organization is going to blow the competition away." Be a teachable change agent and do exactly that—tap into the ideas and expertise, the "genius" of your employees, learn from them, and achieve greater success.

## Conclusion

The heart is the source of all that truly motivates and engages us as human beings. The multitude of management theories and studies developed over the years, including seminal works like Maslow's Needs Hierarchy (1970) and

Herzberg's Two Factors Theory (1971), attests to that. Accessing the hearts of others is what enables you as a change agent to bring about true individual and organizational transformation—aggregate self-actualization and motivation, if you will.

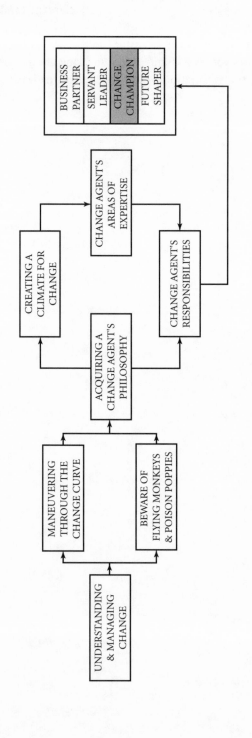

THE MANAGER AS CHANGE AGENT BLUEPRINT

**Flowchart contents:**

- UNDERSTANDING & MANAGING CHANGE
- MANEUVERING THROUGH THE CHANGE CURVE
- BEWARE OF FLYING MONKEYS & POISON POPPIES
- ACQUIRING A CHANGE AGENT'S PHILOSOPHY
- CREATING A CLIMATE FOR CHANGE
- CHANGE AGENT'S AREAS OF EXPERTISE
- CHANGE AGENT'S RESPONSIBILITIES
- BUSINESS PARTNER
- SERVANT LEADER
- CHANGE CHAMPION
- FUTURE SHAPER

# Change Champion

A good rule of thumb in a major change effort is: Never
underestimate the magnitude of the forces that reinforce
complacency and that help maintain the status quo.
                                                    John Kotter (1996)

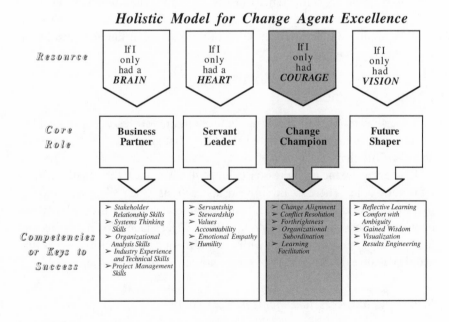

FIGURE 11.01   Holistic Model for ChangeAgent Excellence

## Operating in the Third Core Role: Change Champion

Change facilitation is not for the weak. It requires one to possess certain expertise, sales aptitude, problem-solving skills, and the ability to tolerate rejection, even failure. Many change agents are still considered "outsiders" even though they are members of the organization. They must overcome organizational apathy, politics, and inertia. Further, they are often thrust into the latest organizational "political hot topic," for which they may be conveniently blamed, at some future date, for its failure or less than satisfactory impact on the firm.

The Lion in *The Wizard of Oz* longed for the courage to face his fears and defeat his foes. He desperately wanted the courage to better his own position in life and proactively change his environment, singing boldly of his personal stature and plans: "If I were king of the forest . . . ," he cried. Courage is the personal resource that empowers a change agent to lead others through the change process, ensures accountability to individual and organizational performance goals, and facilitates continuous learning. As Kotter's quote clearly suggests, a healthy dose of courage will be necessary to confront the inevitable organizational complacency and inertia. The world of change agency is not one for cowards. However, buck up your courage by mastering the following five personal competencies or keys to change champion success.

To demonstrate courage, change agents must develop change alignment, conflict resolution, forthrightness, organizational subordination, and learning facilitation competencies.

## Change Alignment

A change champion has a thorough understanding of the organizational behavior (OB) dynamics associated with the change process. Far too many change efforts have attempted to design a fail-safe, lock-step change process without adequate focus on the overarching OB elements of the equation. These efforts are futile. "There are no sure-fire instructions which, when scrupulously followed, make change succeed, much less eliminate or solve the problems accompanying any change process" (Jick, 1993, 27). Detailed, foolhardy "recipes for success" should be replaced with a broader set of change imperatives that greatly enhance the probability of success for any change initiative.

### Seven Keys to Successful Organizational Change

To be a change champion with the courage to see the process through to the end, you must be equipped with and willing to hold yourself and the orga-

Seven Keys to Successful Organizational Change

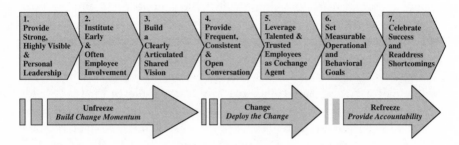

FIGURE 11.1    Seven Keys to Successful Organizational Change

nization accountable for seven keys to successful organizational change (Figure 11.1).

Conceptually it may help to connect the seven keys to Lewin's classic change model—the first three with "unfreezing," the next two with "changing," and the last two with "refreezing"—as illustrated in Figure 11.1. Your overarching strategy for effective change management is clear. Employ the seven keys to successful organizational change to build momentum for the change effort, deploy the change plan, and provide performance accountability for your employees and the organization. Failure to do so will result in being derided as a change agent who lacks common sense or courage.

The seven keys to success may appear to be "commonsensical," but it is amazing how few organizations take the time to develop such an overarching list, let alone commit to one. *The Wizard of Oz* describes *lions, tigers, and bears* as fears of the unknown. Such fears are perceptual and lack concrete evidence of threat but prevent one from achieving objectives. However, *flying monkeys* are genuine threats to your plans that make commitment difficult in the change process. The Cowardly Lion's first impulse was to run from danger. But the change agent's goal must be to have the courage to clearly articulate these seven principles as nonnegotiable elements of his change initiative strategy and then remain unswerving as he employs the list and insists on employees' ongoing commitment. Relying on practical strategies as the seven keys are implemented is an essential part of keeping the courage needed to sustain the process.

*Provide Strong, Highly Visible, and Personal Leadership.*    Display an unswerving commitment to the goals of the change initiative at hand. Further, claim a personal stake in the success of the change initiative and demonstrate willingness to be held accountable for achieving that success through teamwork rather than through individual effort alone. Additionally, ensure that a clearly dedicated and visibly executive sponsor is 100 percent behind the change initiative and is driving it at all levels of the organization.

Hold personal discussions with employees to discuss commitment to the change effort and what is in it for you, for the work unit, and for the organization. Further, make sure you discuss with each employee what is in it for them. Next, provide "highly visible" leadership, which means taking the time to get to know employees on both a professional and a personal level. Take the time to walk through your area and hold "pulse check" conversations with your employees. Try to do this for each employee at least once a week.

Try to ensure that all of your actions support the change initiative vision. Moreover, be sure to express to employees that you have as much to gain or to lose as they do in the change effort, that you are all in it together and your success depends on their success. Hold personal conferences with each person you directly supervise to discuss their work skills and competencies and map out a plan to capitalize on their strengths, address their weaknesses, or both. Finally, ask employees for feedback on your performance as their team leader and as one of the leaders of the change effort. Try to do this informally at least once a month.

*Institute Employee Involvement Early and Often, at All Levels.* Ensure that as many employees as possible, as early as possible, are actively involved in planning and conducting the change effort. To accomplish this, make certain that at least one employee from each of the areas of the organization that will feel the impact of the change effort is assigned to the change initiative team full-time. Encourage employees to share their ideas and concerns via colleagues assigned to the change initiative or other formally designed feedback mechanisms, such as a change initiative hot line or a change initiative suggestion box. Establish a biweekly change initiative brown-bag lunch series and encourage all the employees to attend. Make it clear that meaningful employee involvement in the change effort is valued by working with the organization to free up time for key employees to be involved.

*Build a Clearly Articulated, Shared Vision.* Take the time to develop a shared and formally articulated vision for the change effort at hand, personally endorse it, and build support for it throughout the organization. This can be accomplished by working with employees to draft a vision statement for the change effort. The vision statement must capture what the team is striving to achieve and must be fairly short and memorable. Display the final product prominently in the change initiative work area.

Work with your employees to draft mission statements and team charters for each subteam within the larger change initiative team. Mission statements must articulate each subteam's purpose, and the team charters must describe each subteam's values and how the team will work together. Be sure that all the employees have a personal copy of these documents for their respective subteams.

Ask each employee to draft a personal vision statement that captures what is important to them both personally and professionally and connects the goals for change and the organization's desired future state. Encourage employees to sign their statements and display them in their work areas.

Work with employees to design and develop a banner or other promotional material that captures the change initiative vision statement. Display the banner or promotional material prominently in the change initiative work area and encourage each employee to sign it as a public statement of their personal commitment to the successful transformation of the organization.

Work with employees to plan and hold a half-day or full-day retreat on a quarterly or semiannual basis. Hold the retreat off site, away from the constant distractions at the organization. Dedicate a significant portion of the time at such retreats to readdress the change initiative vision statement and the subteam mission statements and charters as necessary.

Whenever a new person joins the change initiative team, hold a special meeting to welcome that person to the team. Select a facilitator and ask the employees with whom the new person is going to work to write down and openly discuss their answers to the following questions at the welcome meeting:

- What do you want to know about the new team member?
- What do you want the new team member to know about you?
- What are some pitfalls for the new team member to avoid?
- What must the new team member focus on first?
- What is your best advice to the new team member as a friend?

Finally, circulate articles, case studies, or quotes that clarify and support the change initiative vision.

*Provide Frequent, Consistent, and Open Communication.* Ensure that as much information as possible is passed along to all the members of the organization at the appropriate times and in the appropriate manner. It's better to err on the side of providing too much rather than too little information, even if the details are still being developed.

Work with the leadership from the areas affected by the change effort to establish stakeholder groups that meet weekly or biweekly throughout the life cycle of the change initiative. Use these groups to exchange change initiative–related information, set goals for the change effort, monitor progress, and ensure the involvement of associates from all affected areas.

On the heels of the stakeholder group meetings, hold regular meetings with leadership teams from the organization to debrief and ensure that everyone is up to date and on the same page. Next, ensure that minutes are kept for the stakeholder group and leadership group meetings and disseminate minutes to all the employees in the work areas involved. Moreover, encourage employees to openly communicate concerns or ideas that they may have. Emphasize the open door policy. When an important message needs to be disseminated to employees, use several media (for example, paper memos, electronic memos, verbal announcements) to ensure that information filters do not cause misinterpretation.

Additionally, have separate work areas that are affected by the change effort hold regular plenary meetings on the heels of their respective leadership team meetings. Ensure that these meetings are open forums for questions and change initiative–related discussion, ensuring that the information that is being provided to the individual work area teams is consistent with the information discussed in the leadership team meeting. Encourage leaders of the separate work area teams to answer all questions as candidly and honestly as possible, even if the details surrounding the question or concern at hand are still being determined. This will help to relieve fear of the unknown.

Communicate as much as possible as early and often as possible, including using e-mail or an intranet site to develop and disseminate a weekly change initiative update to all employees.

*Leverage Talented and Trusted Employees as Cochange Agents.* Identify employees who are most enthusiastic about the transition effort and have the highest level of credibility among their peers; give them opportunities to lead the charge by exhibiting modeling behavior.

Encourage several key employees from the relevant work units to volunteer to attend the change initiative brown-bag lunch meetings and to provide written and/or verbal overviews to their colleagues. Hold personal discussions with several key employees to emphasize to them the importance of their role as change agents. Encourage them to be as involved with and supportive of the change effort as possible. Stress the benefits of their actions not only for the organization but also for themselves (that is, what's in it for them).

Next, encourage several key employees to "lead the charge" in all activities. Make it clear that their involvement is a priority and publicly display that commitment to the rest of the employees. As enthusiasm for the change effort spreads to the rest of the team, do whatever possible to involve those employees as well. The goal is for the change agents to model behavior that will catch on in the rest of the team, and eventually with the organization at large.

Moreover, assign all employees who are working on the change initiative full-time to take regularly scheduled updates back to their respective work areas. These updates should be done both formally (meetings and/or presentations) and informally (personal and/or small group discussions). Finally, establish a change initiative *contact/liaison program* to involve influential employees (those not already assigned to the change effort full-time) in making connections and providing change initiative–related information to all employees in their respective work areas.

*Set Measurable Operational and Behavioral Goals.* Work with your employees to develop meaningful goals for the change initiative. Be sure to establish milestone dates against which the progress of the change effort can be measured. Use your stakeholders (as outlined above) as sources of accountability and progress tracking for these goals.

When appropriate, work with employees to set daily/weekly/monthly operational goals and prominently display them in your work area and/or publish and circulate them in your business plan and other relevant documents. Also work with organizational leaders to set behavioral goals in line with the change initiative vision and the overall goals of the change effort. It is critical to ensure that these behavioral goals are given equal weight as the operational goals, as discussed further in the section on performance management.

*Celebrate Successes and Readdress Shortcomings.* Hold yourself and the organization accountable for individual and organizational goals set through teamwork. Take every opportunity to publicly and positively reinforce successes, and readdress shortcomings in the spirit of development and opportunity. To accomplish this, regularly compare progress against the daily/weekly/monthly operational goals. Celebrate any successes associated with meeting the goals, as Dorothy and her friends did when they were finally admitted to the Emerald City. The celebration does not have to be elaborate, and can be as simple as just getting the change initiative team together to make an announcement and congratulate one another.

Prominently display the change initiative team's daily/weekly/monthly operational results. Regularly revisit the change initiative team's daily/weekly/monthly operational goals and adjust as necessary. This is especially important if the team always meets or exceeds the goal (thus the target needs to be pushed out to provide a new challenge) or always falls short of the goal (the target needs to be pulled back so as not to become demoralizing).

Take the time to personally congratulate employees on an informal basis for their hard work and day-to-day accomplishments. Work with employees to regularly review their career development plans and ways the change initiative experience they are gaining fits into the larger picture. Take the time to personally coach employees when a shortcoming occurs. Be sure to approach each employee in the spirit of development, highlighting the occurrence as an opportunity rather than a reprimand. When the Fearful Lion jumped out snarling at Dorothy and the others, Dorothy had the courage to point out the truth: "Why, you're just a great big coward!" But she also inspired him to admit the truth and come along on the journey to see the Wizard and find out if it was possible to change.

*Build a Personalized Change Management Tool Kit.* Clearly, the list of strategies for employing the seven keys to success is neither an exhaustive nor mandatory list in the sense that every change agent must apply every idea. Of course, as alluded to earlier, the list does not represent a sure-fire recipe for a problem-free journey. Thus, we strongly encourage using this list as a starting point to build your personalized tool kit of "best practices." However, the overarching imperatives reflected in the seven keys to successful organizational change must continue to guide the change agent's efforts, and he must continually ask, "In what ways am I enacting the seven keys to success in support of the overall change effort?"

## Conflict Resolution

> *Skill at negotiation obviously matters for excellence in professions like law and diplomacy. But to some extent everyone who works in an organization needs these abilities; those who can head off trouble are the kind of peacemakers vital to any organization.*
>
> Daniel Goleman (1998)

Conflict is a common by-product of organizational life. Therefore, the ability to confront difficult issues is essential for change agents because much of their work consists of exposing issues that organization members are reluctant to face. A change champion must have the courage to work proactively to both prevent unnecessary conflict and aggressively resolve the inevitable conflicts that do arise. Doing so elevates one to the vital role of peacemaker (Goleman, 1998). Moreover, and perhaps more important to you as a change champion, it is also true that healthy conflict and appropriately aggressive conflict resolution can be leveraged to catalyze organizational change. This is precisely the conclusion arrived at following ten years of research and consulting work with over 140 *Fortune* 500 firms (Pascale, 1990).

Since conflicting goals, ideas, policies, and practices make it almost impossible to implement meaningful change, change agents must develop conflict resolution skills, which allow them to guide executives, managers, and employees through the change process in a way that minimizes resistance. These skills enable one to develop an understanding of why resistance occurs and how to respond accordingly, maintain an objective viewpoint, and demonstrate fairness. Such insight is advantageous in overcoming resistance to change.

## Leveraging Conflict

The phrase *vectors of contention* captures the essence of how successful companies use constructive conflict to adapt to changing marketplace dynamics (Pascale, 1990). Leveraging conflict has also been referred to as *creative tension* (Senge, 1990, 142). In either case, the message for you as a change champion is the same—have the courage to embrace conflict as a natural and often beneficial outcome of the change process, and work with employees to bring those conflicts to a healthy resolution. Leveraging conflict in this way depends on the ability to do the following:

1. Proactively monitor employees and the organization for sources of conflict. Always keep *conflict radar* in full deployment, recognizing that the sources of conflict may be both human (personality clashes, team dysfunction) and inhuman (business process inefficiency, information system crashes).
2. Once conflict is detected, work aggressively to constructively resolve it. If the conflict is allowed to fester, it will simply become a cancer to the organization and to change efforts. As the old saying goes, *deal with the elephant in the room.*
3. *Bring the parties involved in the conflict together to work through the issue. Attempting to resolve the conflict without directly involving all the parties concerned at the same time may make it possible to avoid some heated*

*discussions, but the end result is simply a prolonged conflict life cycle and a greater potential for lingering resentment and misunderstanding. Jack Welch has championed a conflict resolution and organizational improvement process at GE called* Workout *that, simply put, involves sitting the people involved in a conflict in a room together until the conflict is brought to a constructive resolution. In other words, you need to develop the courage to bring people together to* slay the elephant.

4. Ensure that the proposed resolution is implemented immediately. Nothing will damage a change agent's reputation for leveraging conflict more quickly than lack of follow-through on the resolution. Have the courage to decisively implement the solution, even when it will cause individual and organizational pain.

Addressing and resolving conflict will undoubtedly be messy, and even personally and professionally painful at times. However, remain steadfast in your commitment to proactively and aggressively search out conflict, embrace it as a change catalyst, and constructively resolve it. If you don't, the elephant will eventually sit right on top of you, effectively crushing your efforts as a change agent.

## Forthrightness

During the change process, it is sometimes necessary to examine employees' behavior or performance. How can this be done and still maintain a positive working relationship? It certainly cannot be accomplished through aggressive, rude, abusive, or sarcastic tactics typically used by managers to force changes in behavior. These methods only create resentment and seldom help resolve the problem. Moreover, avoiding problems and pretending they do not exist will not help resolve them either, because it causes resentment that leads to anger and mistrust. Unfortunately, most problems are not addressed until behavior or performance has deteriorated to such a point that drastic action must be taken. Often such action makes the situation even worse.

To become a competent change agent you must balance the need to get the work done with the need to have a positive working relationship with employees. The only way this is achieved is through forthrightness. It involves nonjudgmental descriptions of the behaviors requiring change. Forthrightness allows one to disclose feelings about an employee's behavior without affixing blame. It clarifies the effects of employee behavior, the change opportunity, and the organization. Change agents have more fulfilling relationships with employees and enhance change opportunities by communicating needs, expectations, and concerns in a way that demonstrates respect for employees.

True forthrightness is a way of behaving that confirms a change agent's individual worth and dignity, simultaneously confirming and maintaining the worth and dignity of employees. Forthrightness is demonstrated when methods of communication are used that maintain self-respect, personal happiness, and satisfaction. This type of communication allows you to stand up for your rights and express personal needs, values, concerns, and ideas in direct and appropriate ways. Simultaneously, don't violate the needs of employees, but help them retain a positive self-concept.

Forthrightness requires you to convey specific feelings, experiences, and behaviors when interacting with employees. An assertive message contains three parts:

1. A nonjudgmental description of the behaviors to be changed.
2. Disclosure of feelings.
3. Clarification of the effects of the employee's behavior on the change agent. (Bolton, 1986, 140)

## Nonjudgmental Description of Behavior

The description should be specific so that employees know precisely what you mean. Otherwise, they may not clearly understand which behavior may prevent employees from incorporating change. Avoid drawing inferences about employees' motives or attitudes but focus on "what they did" that concerns you. The behavioral description should be as brief as possible to avoid confusion. Try to make the description an objective statement rather than a judgment. In other words, don't imply that, because their behavior is inadequate in one area, the employees are lazy, stupid, or bad.

The following are some examples of nonjudgmental behavioral descriptions:

- When you are frequently late for work . . .
- When you overspend your budget . . .
- When you don't take accurate phone messages . . .
- When you don't turn in your report on time . . . (Gilley and Boughton, 1996, 150)

We will use these examples later to illustrate the other two parts of an assertive message.

*Disclosure of Feelings*

The second part of a forthright message allows the change agent to communicate how he feels about the employee's behavior. It is a genuine disclosure of the emotions experienced as a result of the employee's behavior. When an employee's performance is unacceptable, the easiest way to express how you feel is to use "I" messages. In other words, "I feel . . ." describes what is going on inside. The feelings can be identified immediately after an inadequate or poor performance.

*Clarification of the Effects of the Behavior*

What we mean by *effects* are the things that directly affect you as a result of employees' behavior. For example, money, time, extra work, quality, and teamwork are all things affected by employees' behavior.

Let's look again at the four previous examples of nonjudgmental behavior descriptions, and add a disclosure of feelings and clarification of effects for each:

- When you are frequently late for work . . . I feel angry . . . because it costs us money to delay the production line.
- When you overspend your budget . . . I feel annoyed . . . because it means I must make cuts that will affect the quality of the project.
- When you don't take accurate telephone messages . . . I feel upset . . . because I lack information and can't return calls that may be important.
- When you don't turn in your report on time . . . I feel frustrated . . . because I can't get an accurate picture of our current financial position. (Gilley and Boughton, 1996, 151)

The use of forthright messages can greatly enhance employees' understanding of the change agent's concerns and feelings and the effects of their behavior. These messages should help you and your employees to remain rational in difficult times.

## Organizational Subordination

> *Put a good employee against a bad system and the system wins every time.*
> Gary Rummler

When managers allow their organizations to get in the way of employees' positive contributions, ideas, and efforts, employees' importance and value diminishes. By doing so, they are communicating that the organization is more important and valuable than their employees. This sets up confrontation that results in increased employee turnover, disloyalty, mistrust, poor performance and productivity, low morale, and ultimately, organizational sabotage on the part of some employees. These undesirable outcomes are inconsistent with a change agent's philosophy and practice.

Organization subordination is a process by which change agents place the contributions, involvement, and loyalty of employees above those of the organization. They strive to guarantee organizational subservience to employees' efforts to improve productivity, efficiency, and approaches essential to competitive readiness and organizational renewal. Furthermore, they *get out of the way* and allow employees to work effectively and efficiently, enabling workers to demonstrate creative, insightful, and innovative approaches to business problems and performance difficulties (Ulrich, Zenger, and Smallwood, 1999).

The *organization-first* approach must be reversed if you wish to achieve the benefits of evolving to change agent status. A change agent can demonstrate organizational subordination by eliminating policies and procedures that interfere with, prevent, or discourage employee growth and development as well as eliminating organizational structures that inhibit two-way communication and discourage or prevent employee growth and development (Gilley, 2001). Making certain that the formal structure does not interfere with employees' efforts to achieve their performance objectives in an efficient manner can do this. Next, demonstrate this activity by eliminating negative and personally destructive work climates and creating organizational cultures where employee growth and development are encouraged and sponsored. Further, perform this activity by creating performance management systems that foster employee growth and development, creating work environments where continuous learning and change are the norm, and transforming performance appraisals into developmental evaluations designed to foster employee growth and development (see Chapter 7). Such an activity is demonstrated by creating compensation and reward systems that recognize and reward results (see Chapter 12). Additionally, organizational subordination is demonstrated when selecting managers and supervisors for their employee development and interpersonal skills rather than their personal performance records. Further, organizational subordination is demonstrated by eliminating political favoritism in favor of a performance-oriented promotion system based on continuous employee growth and development. Finally, organizational subordination is demonstrated by encouraging employee career development and linking it with long-term human resource planning initiatives, selecting employees based on their readiness to learn, change, grow, and develop, and linking employee growth and development to the organization's goals and objectives.

## Learning Facilitation

> *Leaders in learning organizations are responsible for building organizations where people are continually expanding their capabilities to shape their future—that is, leaders are responsible for learning.*
> Peter Senge (1990), *The Fifth Discipline*

Since the publication of his seminal work on organizationl learning Senge has called leaders and change agents to the critical task of learning facilitation. Taking on such a responsibility requires courage to master *the art of balancing advocacy, teaching employees,* and inquiry, *engaging your employees in the learning process.*

### Teach Employees

Learning facilitation requires the courage to teach others throughout the organization (see Chapter 7). To that end, a change agent must have the courage to employ the following list:

1. *Clearly articulate knowledge transfer as a top priority.* Far too often, training practitioners dispense their wisdom and expertise and leave employee confusion and dependency in their wake. Unequivocally commit to knowledge transfer from yourself to your employees and build into the change initiative plan infrastructures and design interventions that will enable this to happen. This also includes accepting the lion's share of employee development responsibility.
2. *Take advantage of "teachable moments."* In the regular course of organizational life, let alone in the middle of a tumultuous change effort, numerous situations arise in which ideal opportunities to teach arise. Have the courage to seize these moments as opportunties to reinforce knowledge transfer, whether the moments are positive or negative.

3. *Hold employees accountable for learning.* Integrate learning expectations and measurements for employees and the organization into your performance management process (see earlier section on performance management [developmental evaluations]).

### Engage your Employees in the Learning Process

To be an effective facilitator of learning for employees, draw them out and engage them in critical dialogue (see Chapter 10, "Humility"). To do so requires the courage to employ the following strategies:

1. Ask questions. It is as simple as that. Continually ask questions, never falling into the cowardly routine of pretending to know something or understand a situation simply because you don't want to appear ignorant. Equally important, if you sense the same dynamic in an employee, ask the question for them, and then use the opportunity (in private) as an ideal teachable moment for the individual and as an ideal opportunity (in public) to reinforce your commitment to knowledge transfer.
2. Make connections. Draw out the ideas, knowledge, and expertise of your employees, and take every opportunity to make connections among that collective body of critical information.
3. Forgive failure. Some of the greatest learning that you and employees will experience will happen as a direct result of individual or organizational failure. "It is necessary to fail" to truly learn (Gilley, 1998). For too long now, the organizational paradigm has been unforgiving of mistakes and failure. Such an absolute leads to fear of experimentation and can sound the death knell for your efforts as a facilitator of learning.

## Conclusion

Remember, at the end of *The Wizard of Oz,* it was the Cowardly Lion who led the way as Dorothy's friends tried to save her, so it is the Cowardly Lion of whom the Scarecrow and Tin Man say, "You put up a great fight, Lion. I don't know what we would have done without you." Operating effectively in the third core role, as a change champion with courage, the same will be said about you and every member of the change initiative team.

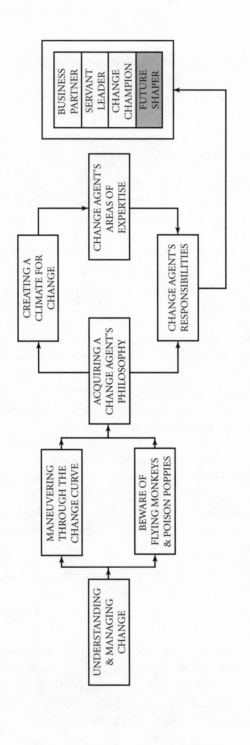

THE MANAGER AS CHANGE AGENT BLUEPRINT

# Future Shaper

The essence of management lies in the exercise of two
major talents. One of these is operating talent: the ability
to carry the enterprise towards its objectives in the situation, from day to day. . . . The other is conceptual talent:
the ability to see the whole in the perspective of history–past and future–to state and adjust goals, to evaluate, to analyze, and to foresee contingencies a long the
way ahead. Leadership, in the sense of going out ahead
to show the way, is more conceptual than operational.

Robert Greenleaf,
*On Becoming a Servant Leader* (1996)

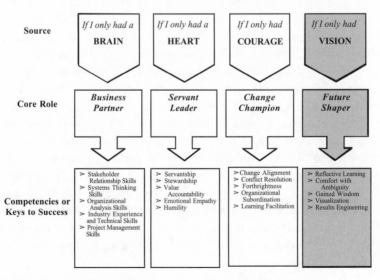

FIGURE 12.01    Holistic Model for Change Agent Excellence

## Operating in the Fourth Core Role: Future Shaper

The final piece of the puzzle in the process of becoming a change agent is the development of this conceptual talent that Greenleaf (1996) writes about above. Effective change agents have clear visions for their organizations in both human and financial terms. Such a vision helps focus disconnected employees toward achieving a common set of outcomes. It gives daily activities serious meaning and determines an organization's success or failure. Furthermore, change agents clearly know what they want to achieve and how employees can better serve their stakeholders (internal and external customers). Effective change agents are successful in communicating this purpose and developing a vision that ensures employee support and involvement. Quite simply, visionary thinking identifies the purpose of one's organization.

"Anyone can steer the ship, but it takes a leader to chart the course" (Maxwell, 1998, 33). As a future shaper, you are responsible for identifying the path ahead and make midcourse corrections to avoid dangerous water. To do so, rely on past experiences as a source of information and wisdom. Moreover, solicit the wisdom of employees and other leaders and examine conditions before making commitments. Accordingly, demonstrate faith in others and dynamically balance optimism and realism, intuition and planning.

Developing a strategic vision requires directing attention to the department and the organization's future. As a change agent, it is necessary to have the ability to anticipate business trends and processes and break them down into manageable units for employees to implement and manage. Dismantling business trends and processes into manageable components generates a variety of solutions that narrow the gap between what is needed and what is delivered, making the necessary adjustments to ensure organizational success. For example, a strategic vision should include a description of the idealized organization (department, division, work team, and so on). Moreover, identify the type, quantity, and quality of resources required to realize the idealized organization. Describe the type of work climate you envision and the type of communications that exists. Describe the type of result that will be achieved by the idealized organization and contrast them with current results. Finally, describe the type of initiatives that will be required to achieve idealized status. Although this activity may appear to be an exercise in futility, it provides "targets" to strive for in the effort to transform the organization.

When designing and developing a vision for employees, use an inclusive approach that encourages employee participation in the creation of this vision. This allows them to share opinions and ideas and accept responsibility for activities that help the organization realize its dreams. Thus, the change agent's support and involvement is necessary for the collaborative vision to resonate throughout the firm, thereby creating an environment of employee and organizational success.

By contrast, some employees view vision statements as *just a bunch of words that have no meaning for those of us in the trenches.* This sad commentary stems in part to lack of effective change leadership—poor change agents take more pride in creating well-written vision statements than in building acceptance among employees for its execution. Additionally, some managers who are not yet change agents have difficulty achieving buy-in from employees becaise of failure to adequately communicate their vision of the organization. Ineffective change agents often identify the organization's purpose but are unable to articulate its vision.

Recently, we worked with an organization that allowed its employees to develop and implement a new organizational vision. We established focus groups that helped them:

1. Identify the organization's *big picture*
2. Its purpose
3. Stakeholders served by the organization
4. Processes that need to be changed
5. Strategies to be used in implementing the organizational vision

Thus, employees created a vision that they were willing to embrace, which is an extremely powerful process that dramatically impacts organizational productivity and profitability.

In some rare cases, visionary ability seems to be a birthright, but in most people we've observed such talent comes only over a period of time. Just as fine wine needs to age and single malt whiskey needs to mellow, the true development of a change agent as future shaper is most typically a developmental process. There is very rarely a moment of enlightenment one can point to as "when I finally got it." Instead, change agents who wish to become visionary future shapers will find themselves on a journey that can only be described as a process of becoming.

We have also observed many people in organizations who don't wear well with age. These are the myopic organizational "others" who seem to bide their time and wield very little organizational influence, no matter how long they abide. These folks are the *living dead* and the *paper shufflers* of the world for which change is a frightening experience. They long for stability, for stasis, for regularity in their work. However, in today's knowledge-based work environment of constant change, such people are maladapted to survival and companies with large groups of such people are slated to become the dinosaurs of the organizational landscape.

Dorothy's vision was to return to Kansas, which represented her ultimate goal. Kansas was home, the past she desired to return to represented her future, the desired state—and getting there would require her to summon all of the brains, heart, and courage she had. Change agents, too, possess vision, which guides their actions and interactions with employees, just as Dorothy's vision framed the journey she and her friends took to Oz. Clear vision can be a powerful motivator for both change agents and employees.

Successfully achieving vision involves maximizing one's knowledge, skill, and behavior via brains, heart, and courage. How to develop these resources were explored fully in Chapters 9 through 11. Occasionally, one is challenged to help employees define, refine, or achieve their vision. By helping employees define "What do we aspire to be?" you guide them through in-depth assessment of and action on their long-term goals, opportunities, weaknesses, and strengths. Doing so separates the "smoke and mirrors" manager from the true change agent.

In the quest to be a change agent, how can one be sure to continue to "become?" How can one guard against the atrophy of organizational talent? How can one ensure continued movement through the spheres of influence from business partner to servant leader to change champion to future shaper?

Successfully navigating the Yellow Brick Road requires change agents to check their vision. First, remove those rose-colored glasses. Second, learn to look beyond the obvious, beneath what appears to be reality, and past today. Change agents must possess the vision to see what is really going on during the change process and with the project at hand, but also to see where the process is going. They ask, "What will things look like in a day, a month, or a year after the change initiative is completed?" Will the poppy poison that clouded their judgment wear off and reveal their mistakes or will they see a beautiful Emerald City, just as imagined?

As future shapers, change agents understand that leadership is a 24/7/365 activity. Thus, they inspire employees and encourage their continuous growth and development. Change agents constantly attend to every minute detail and spend time nurturing and developing employees. They establish trust with employees, demonstrate respect by sharing power, and promote mutual success and accomplishment. To achieve this end, there are several competencies that future shapers must develop and demonstrate.

## Reflective Learning

One characteristic we have observed again and again in those who lead organizations well is a voracious appetite for learning. What seems to separate true visionaries from the crowd is their inquisitiveness and impatience with the status quo—both in themselves, in others, and in the organizations they impact. Long-term effectiveness as a change agent appears to be directly correlated with a personal commitment to intentional and reflective lifelong learning (see also Chapter 10 on teachability). This is true for organizations as well, which is the main reason behind the explosion of the term *learning organization.*

If a commitment to individual learning and openness to change is important at the personal level, then organizations themselves need to have the same commitment and openness to survive in a world of increasing globalization and rapid change. The rapid state of change in organizations today— *permanent white water*—suggests not only getting used to this rapid pace of change but also emphasizes that companies accept the extended turbulence and build an organizational culture capable of taking strategic advantage of such turbulence (Vaill, 1998).

In essence, what is required to build visionary ability in organizations is leadership development. McCauley, Moxley, and Van Velsor (1998) contend that organizations like the Center for Creative Leadership offer leadership development process models, which requires assessment (identifying a gap in present and desired states), challenge (experiencing disequilibrium), and support (reflective guidance before, during, and after the experience). Such a process is at its core a learning process. Thus, employees and change agents begin with an honest critical assessment of where they stand today in relationship to their future goals (think Dorothy), they expose themselves to new experiences and experiment with different solutions (following the Yellow Brick Road), and through the process metamorphose into new people (change). The recognition of this process is learning, a skill that must be mastered by agents of positive organizational change.

Learning and development can only happen if all three of the components are present. Assessment itself will not change anything. Experience without assessment and reflection is simply a ride. Reflection lacking prior assessment and experiences on which to reflect is empty.

Again, this process is not strictly personal; it must also be an organizational function. Organizations of all types must have leadership development progams that encourage assessment, risk taking, and reflection.

Building change capability and nurturing change agents should be a primary goal in all organizations (Ulrich, 1997). In a world of constantly shifting competitive pressures, a workforce of change—friendly, adaptable, and flexible employees—is a sustainable strategic competitive advantage for any firm.

## Comfort with Ambiguity

Some believe that the change agent's effectiveness depends on his or her ability to tolerate ambiguity (Burke, 1992, 177–178). Since every organization is different, and what works in one may not work in another, it is important that every change initiative fit the unique circumstances within an organization. Accordingly, to become an effective change agent, develop within yourself a comfort level with ambiguity. Too often we have observed managers struggle with this issue from two different directions. On the one hand, control-oriented managers struggle with *analysis paralysis*, a particularly dangerous form of discomfort that will not allow decisions to be made until all the unknowns become known. Although we understand such a malady, it is simply unacceptable in today's organizational context. The notion that decisions cannot be made until all the facts are in and all the variables are known simply will not work with the rapid pace of change in most industries. A second type of struggle is the *backseat driver* approach to management. Here, the decision maker appears to be comfortable with delegation and decisionmaking. However, he hovers so closely to "inspect" subordinate performance that performance is stifled.

In both of these cases, future shapers and visionary leaders must strive for a certain comfort level with organizational ambiguity if they are to truly move the organization forward. Decisions must be made with wisdom and intuition based on the known available facts at hand. However, they must also be made in "real time" as opportunities and threats face the organization. Moving the organization forward to meet its strategic goals and objectives can only happen if the power of individual performance is unleashed through real delegation in a "freedom to fail" environment.

The parenting analogy is very powerful in understanding the ability to be comfortable in uncertain circumstances and when the outcome of a situation is somewhat unknown. Good parenting does not imply controlling every variable in a child's life from birth through adulthood, nor waiting until the child is nearing adulthood to allow interaction with unknown circumstances and people; rather, varying degrees of freedom are necessary for proper development of a child. Early in the development process, parents certainly have (or should have) a greater degree of control. However, as time progresses the parent must release control and become more of a mentor or guide to allow the necessary degrees of freedom for the child to develop properly and independently. Once the child reaches early adolescence, the degrees of freedom become greater and into adulthood the parent releases even more control so that the child can come into their own. As this freedom and development occurs, good parents realize that strict control will not guide the child in the correct way, but that a certain degree of boundary setting and gentle nudging toward positive choices may produce intended results. The future for every child is certainly not known in advance; however, waiting for certainty or hovering inappropriately will not allow for proper development.

As a change agent, develop good "parenting" skills for projects or organizational responsibilities. The real power of the organization will only manifest itself if you allow for degrees of freedom for people to develop and take change responsibility for themselves and their own situations. To do this effectively, exercise restraint and do not seek to control outcomes that are by their very nature uncertain. You must develop a comfort with ambiguity that can allow the people and processes in your organization to develop.

In reflecting on leadership, some researchers recognized the need for leaders to accept a degree of comfort with ambiguity in their work, stating

> Leader is not always a position. Whatever one's position, the amount of ambiguity is directly proportional to the amount of leadership required. Healthy organizations exhibit a degree of chaos. A leader will make some sense of it. The more comfortable you can make yourself with ambiguity, the better a leader you will be. Organizations always delegate the job of dealing constructively with ambiguity to their leaders. (De Pree, 1992, 57)

Quite simply, if you want to lead, get used to dealing in the gray areas of management and develop skills to deal with uncertainty.

In today's global environment, cultural differences play an important role in understanding the ability for individuals to deal constructively with ambiguity in the organizational context. Some have observed marked differences in people of differing cultural backgrounds relating to their ability to deal with uncertainty and ambiguity at work (Hoppe, 1998). For example, in their landmark study Deal and Kennedy (2000) discovered that more than forty cultures found *uncertainty avoidance* to be one of four major cultural dimensions that define differences in national cultures as they relate to management. A weak uncertainty avoidance society (such as the United States or Sweden) is one that does not feel threatened by the uncertainty of the future, but is generally tolerant and secure. A strong uncertainty avoidance culture (like Germany or Japan), on the other hand, tries to overcome future uncertainties by developing legal, technological, and religious institutions that create security and avoid risk. Change agents working in cross-cultural contexts should be aware that even within seemingly similar cultures, employees' ability to deal with these matters can differ greatly based on cultural norms, values, and traditions.

## Gained Wisdom

> Listen, my sons, to a father's instruction; pay attention
> and gain understanding. . . . Do not forsake wisdom,
> and she will protect you; love her, and she will watch
> over you. Wisdom is supreme; therefore get wisdom.
> Though it cost you all you have, get understanding.
> Proverbs 4:1, 6–7

Written 3,000 years ago by King Solomon, the "wisest man who ever lived," these words have a timeless applicability to a change agent's efforts. As a change agent you will experience many things and work with many different individuals who will enable you to develop wisdom. Embrace those opportunities. Eventually, as you operate in the core role of future shaper, you will have opportunities to draw on that wisdom as you map out the future state of the organization.

An important reality to accept right away is that, as stated above, wisdom is most often gained through experience and instruction from more experienced colleagues. As a hard-charging change agent of the twenty-first century this may be a difficult reality to swallow, but one that is consistent with the makeup of a servant leader (see Chapter 10 on teachability) and a change champion (see Chapter 11 on learning facilitation).

To this end, commit to the following list of absolutes in the quest to develop gained wisdom.

1. *Tap into the wisdom of the "elders" in your organization.* Despite the "generation gap" that exists between you and your older colleagues it is imperative to tap into *their* wisdom and understanding. Often their insights into the culture, history, and people of the organization will prove to be invaluable to your efforts as a change agent, and available from virtually no other source. Listen to their stories. Observe the artifacts in their offices. In short, honor their wisdom and absorb as much of it as possible.

2. *Build a "wisdom war chest."* As your experience base grows so too will your battle scars. Have the hindsight and vision to see those experiences within the broader contexts of both the past as well as the future. Continually ask the following questions: "What can/did I learn from this project/incident/experience?" "How can I apply the lessons from this project/incident/experience in the future?"

3. *Patiently and progressively wield your wisdom-based influence on an organizational level.* Don't be in too much of a rush to display your rich wisdom to the rest of the organization. Remember that wisdom is *gained,* and you must patiently earn the right to influence the direction of the organization when drawing from your wisdom base as the source of that influence. Once you have done so, gradually broaden the scope of your wisdom-based influence.

4. *Share wisdom with others on an individual level.* Once a change agent has become established as a true source of gained wisdom at the organizational level, he must then commit to sharing insights with others throughout the organization. This must be done in an intentional yet casual way, as a mentor of future change agents who will in turn become future sources of wisdom for the organization.

Understanding and employing this list will enable you to differentiate yourself as a wise change agent as opposed to a foolish one. A change agent who has earned the right to influence and shape the future for your organization. A change agent whose source and breadth of influence is much more significant than mere intellectual knowledge, or even seniority, as Figure 12.1 shows.

When you have achieved *gained wisdom status,* you will find it necessary to be supportive and serve as a leader with employees—performing the role of mentor. A mentor renders several activities for employee growth and development. As a result, change agents often serve as confidants in times of personal and professional difficulty, providing feedback, observation of performance, and personal reactions. Mentors provide insight about the mission, goals, and strategic direction of an organization. Moreover, help employees develop political savvy and awareness to enable them to function efficiently and effectively within the organization. Provide employees with insights into organizational philosophy, operations, and the functional system. Help employees with long-term career planning, advocating for growth, encouraging risk taking, and providing advancement opportunities. Enable your employees to participate in visible projects and programs that may further advance their careers. Finally, serve as an honest, open, and direct adviser.

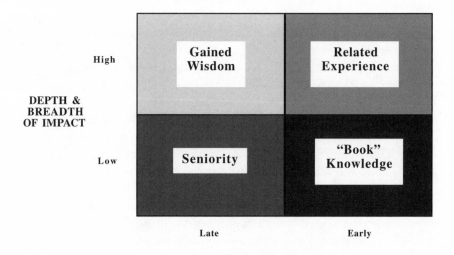

FIGURE 12.1    Sources of Organizational Influence

At the heart of a mentoring relationship is an eagerness to improve employees and help them become the best that they can be. Thus, mentoring encourages a change agent to share experiences with employees, helping them gain additional insight, understanding, and awareness that will be invaluable in the progression of their careers. Mentoring allows employees to benefit from your experience, both the successes and failures—thus alleviating employees' fears, concerns, frustrations, and pains, and promoting celebration of successes, victories, and job accomplishments. Mentoring allows a change agent to demonstrate his supportive, interactive nature and helps him become more caring, sympathetic, and patient. Simultaneously, mentoring helps the change agent grow as well.

Mentoring is a process of ultimate sharing, providing the opportunity to unlock the mysteries of the organization for employees. Mentoring helps employees avoid costly mistakes and pitfalls that can be so damaging to their careers and helps them adjust to the organizations' culture and better assimilate into the work environment.

Mentoring requires a change agent to develop a synergistic, self-esteeming relationship with employees, which demonstrates an attitude that the success of the organization is based on the success of its employees. When this attitude is present, you function effectively as a mentor—and are on the road to overcoming resistance to change. By contrast, traditional managers who maintain an authoritative, noninvolved style based on "my way or the high-way" mentality have difficulty performing as mentors.

Change agents who value relationships with employees and strive to over-come managerial malpractice can make excellent mentors. To be effective, it is important to demonstrate substantial knowledge of the organization, in-cluding thorough understanding of its vision, direction, and long-range goals and objectives, as we have argued throughout this book. Maintain an appro-priate network that will enable employees to make critical contacts through-out the organization. Share technical competence to help employees overcome skill deficiencies. Mentors possess the ability to persuade others, and encourage employees to share their opinions and ideas. Change agents have credibility within the organization and are willing to bear responsibility for employees' growth and development.

Your mandate as a change agent evolving into a future shaper is clear. Be patient, be persistent, and invest your hard-earned wisdom in the organiza-tion's next generation of future shapers.

## Visualization

*The first responsibility of a leader is to define reality.*
Max De Pree (1992), *Leadership Jazz*

De Pree sums up the essence of leadership in one short sentence; however, the ability to carry out his instruction is a much more difficult process. Lead-ers serve a unique role in today's organizations. In a sea of change, choppy water, and uncertainty, leaders are called on to find the horizon for those on board. The definition of what the company is fundamentally about, what it will and will not do, where it will and will not go, and where the boundaries are is the work of leadership.

In concert with gained wisdom, the ability to define reality is generally as-sociated with either sheer brilliance or years of experience. Michael Dell and Bill Gates are two special people who have been able to see a reality in the personal computer industry that others have not been able to focus on. Their type of future shaping has come relatively early in life. In fact, Dell dropped out of college to start his computer business, focusing on a "build to order" paradigm that no high-level strategists at IBM and Compaq had ever even considered. Gates was a self-acknowledged geek in high school who went on to found the most highly capitalized company in the history of the world on the basis of making using a computer as easy as "point and click." Why these two? Simply, they defined reality for themselves and their organizations in ways others had never considered. Commonly known today as "thinking out of the box," this trait is unfortunately anything but common.

Accomplished athletes use the technique of visualization often in preparation for competition. Michael Jordan , Jack Nicklaus, Wayne Gretzky, and others could visualize the performance before the moment of truth and then make that vision into reality during the heat of competition. So it needs to be for a change agent in charting the course for change in an organization.

Such visualization of the future is not always clear, which is why comfort with ambiguity is so important. Often, the first glimpse of the future will be fuzzy, unclear, and seem ludicrous. Think of John F. Kennedy's bold prediction of sending a man to the Moon. An inspirational moment, to be sure, but at the time he uttered those words the reality seemed incredible to most people and even for Kennedy must have been a bit of a stretch. However, this ability to go to the edge of present reality to define a future state demonstrates the brilliance of his leadership. Finally, to become a future shaper, break away from the certainty of the present. For a leader to rise above to see another higher plane, your feet must leave the solid ground of the present. Although we don't suggest taking hallucinogens, consider the concept of "taking a mental trip," as it is commonly termed.

> When we can see the present in terms of partial truth only, the fragmentary knowledge of the future is not seen as so sharp a contrast as when the knowledge of the present is seen as complete and solid. People who are dogmatic about the present are usually dogmatic about the future—and wrong. This is a curious line of reasoning, but I believe it is valid. To sharpen one's view of the future, one must first relax the certainty with which one views the present. (Greenleaf, 1996)

## Applying Visualization Techniques

Visualization involves mentally modeling a performance or set of activity, focusing on the positive steps necessary to achieve acceptable results while mental cues and feedback encourage mastery. There are two types of visualization techniques: forced analytical and open receptive (Gelb and Buzan, 1994). Forced analytical techniques involve observing the fundamental elements of an activity or performance, analyzing the execution of each step or task performed adequately, and identifying ways to improve them. The open receptive technique is a multisensory imaging process that allows one to use as many senses as possible (taste, touch, hearing, and so forth) when observing an activity or performance.

Visualization skills can be improved by making an honest, concerted effort to apply visualization techniques accurately. They also improve with multisensory visualization processes and practicing visualization on a regular basis. Further, visualization techniques improve when a change agent conducts both an outside-in (observation) and inside-out (reflection) activity, permitting him to analyze employees in action (observation) as well as allowing employees to develop insight about the execution of an activity or performance (reflection). Finally, visualization skills improve when you can distinguish between fantasy and visualization and remain positive and focused.

## Results Engineering

Future shaping change agents don't simply have their heads in the clouds, pondering their navels and dreaming dreams. The final competency of a change agent leader is a firm commitment, both personally and organizationally, to results. Once the future reality is defined, effective change agents are able to focus with laserlike precision on the journey to that reality.

The purpose of any organization is to secure results, from increasing market share or sales revenue to improving quality or profitability. The responsibility for securing desired results lies at your feet. Change agents are responsible for *getting results through people*. Therefore, it makes tremendous sense to reward people for the results they achieve. This simple philosophy works wonders in improving employee performance and achieving the results needed by the organization.

A future shaper has the responsibility of shifting the focus from performance activity to achieving results. As a result, helping employees understand their roles and responsibilities during performance improvement and change initiatives. To achieve this end, several questions should be asked prior to implementing any performance improvement or change initiative.

- What business need are we attempting to achieve?
- How will business needs be determined?
- What process was used to analyze the problem and derive the solution(s)?
- What data exist to support the solutions that were selected?
- How do we know that a change initiative will solve the performance problem? (Fuller and Farrington, 1999, 186)

Next, encourage employees to examine the role and impact of performance improvement and change within the organization. Ask the following strategic questions regarding human capital within the department:

- What are you doing to improve the performance/worth of our human capital?
- What measurable impact have you had on the business?
- What is the return on investment of your performance improvement efforts?
- How are your efforts driven by business strategy? (Fuller and Farrington, 1999, 186)

## Components of a Results-Oriented Reward Program

Historically, reward programs have been performance-based, with little consideration given to rewarding employees for achieving specific results (increased revenue, improved profitability, better quality, enhancing employee knowledge, skills, and competencies, as discussed in Chapter 7). Linking reward programs to specific results creates a mechanism for ever-increasing competitive readiness as opposed to mere performance achievement. The intent is not to mitigate the importance of performance, but to clarify that performance without results will ensure that organization performance does not stagnate or decline. As we have emphasized several times, shifting compensation and reward programs to encourage achieving specific results will allow employees to establish priorities and focus their efforts. Over time, the organization will benefit through enhanced business achievement and satisfied stakeholders.

Seven components comprise a results-oriented reward program, each of which is directly or indirectly linked to achieving organizational results (Figure 12.2). The components include goal setting, learning expectations, growth and development, reinforcement and feedback, performance improvement, and performance standards. This model serves as a comprehensive framework that change agents can use to facilitate learning (change) that brings about desired results.

Result-oriented reward programs are initiated by *setting goals* that employees are responsible for achieving. This process should be a collaborative activity between the change agent and employees. When completed, employees should have developed several specific, measurable, attainable, realistic, and time-based goals.

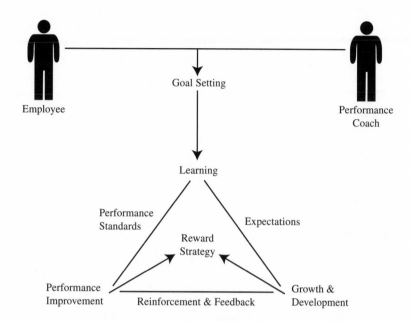

FIGURE 12.2   Components of a Results-Oriented Program (Gilley, Boughton, and Macunich, 1999, *Performance Challenge* Perseus Publishing.)

After goals are identified, employees should engage in the process of identifying the *learning* activities that will help them to achieve their performance goals. This requires employees to identify learning objectives, resources, and learning transfer strategies. Further, employees will need to identify the measurement critieria that they will use to determine whether learning occurred. To complete these activities, employees may interact with the change agent to solicit advice and recommendations on "what it will take" to reach their goals.

To transform learning from routine exercise to a real effort that produces growth and development, share *performance expectations* with employees. That is, communicate what employees are expected to be able to do differently as a result of learning and what specific outcomes are anticipated. These expectations may be in the form of measurable performance outputs, improved execution of performance activities, or demonstrations of new knowledge or skills. Thus, employee learning becomes more focused, meaningful, and valuable by establishing and communicating expectations.

As a future shaper, also provide employees with the *performance standards* by which performance outputs (deliverables) and activities (tasks used to generate deliverables) will be measured and evaluated. These standards serve as targets for employees as they attempt to acquire and integrate new learning. Once learning has been internalized, employees should be able to produce performance outputs that meet or exceed standards. Moreover, they can measure and evaluate their own performance outputs and activities once standards have been identified and communicated.

Performance improvement and growth and development are the anchors of results-oriented reward programs (Figure 12.2). These serve as the intermediate objectives of a result-oriented program, without which there would be no real, tangible outcomes by which to assign rewards. That is,

> Performance goals that are linked to an organization's reward strategy must produce some type of measurable outcomes that help the organization achieve its strategic business goals and objectives. Moreover, employee efforts to acquire new learning must result in performance improvement on the job or growth and development which increases overall organizational performance capacity. In either case, learning must be transferred to the job and demonstrated as performance improvement, or expended to the organization via the aggregate of employee growth and development. Regardless, the organization benefits from employee learning acquisition; therefore, they should be compensated and rewarded." (Gilley and Maycunich, 2000, 149–150)

Reinforcement and feedback is a common component used to bring about performance improvement and employee growth and development. By reinforcement and feedback, we mean sharing perceptions and opinions with employees regarding their performance and/or growth and development efforts. In this way, they know how you feel about their attempts to improve as well as know where they stand regarding future improvement activities.

Although each of the seven components is important in the application of a results-oriented reward program, emphasis on individual components varies depending on the employee's goals. For example, if an employee establishes a performance goal designed to improve their performance immediately, it would be most appropriate to proceed from the *top down, counter-clockwise,* focusing on learning acquisition and the role performance standards play in performance improvement (Figure 12.2). Additionally, provide positive reinforcement and feedback that will improve the employee's performance. Such an activity will help the employee continue to enhance overall growth and development over time.

Using the model this way allows the change agent and the employee to focus on the most appropriate components used in improving their immediate performance on the job. For example, new learning (skills or knowledge) helps employees to improve the delivery of deliverables (performance outputs) or the execution of tasks (performance activities), which are linked to performance standards (Figure 12.2). Hence, performance standards measure the depth and breadth of learning and its application to the job.

On the other hand, it is important to proceed from the *top down, clockwise,* when focusing on employees' long-term career development needs. Thus, employees can identify goals that are linked to learning activities based on the expectations of how learning will enhance their growth and development. In other words, growth and development targets require a different type of learning activity, one that is predicated on performance capacities not yet developed but critical to both the employee and the organization at some time in the future. This type of learning engagement requires a change agent to have a career development conversation with employees to share expectations, concerns, and recommendations. Although this approach is not intended to improve an employee's immediate performance, it may have a profoundly positive impact on productivity if reinforced. As a result, long-term growth and development plans often yield positive short-term effects.

Using this model to enhance growth and development requires change agents to identify performance expectations and link them to their employee's formal and informal learning efforts. In this way, results-oriented reward programs are always linked to learning. Furthermore, result-oriented reward programs incorporate seven integrated components, which are linked to an overall reward strategy. In the final analysis, result-oriented reward programs are meaningful, valuable, and produce positive organizational results.

### Linking Organizational Results to Guiding Principles

Guiding principles should be based on the collective values of every member of the organization. They provide insight into how decisions are made within the firm, how the organization is managed, and how people are treated and valued. Guiding principles are like an invisible hand that organizes scattered employees in a singular direction to help the organization achieve its strategic mission. Quite simply, they are beacons on moonless nights when the organization's future appears the darkest.

Certainly, guiding principles help identify the organization's strategic intent and how resources are allocated to achieve desired business results. They identify how people are perceived within the organization and how senior management values their commitment, involvement, and contributions. Finally, they indicate whether the organization is dedicated to the growth and development of its people and rewarding them accordingly. Result-oriented reward programs, therefore, should be linked to guiding principles because they are so essential to the direction and future of the organization. When linking such programs to the organization's guiding principles, the program must be designed to work in harmony with other vital systems within the firm, which ensures the consistent allocation of rewards. Avoided are the numerous, inconsistent changes that occur when organizations attempt to blindly incorporate insufficient motivational strategies and employee retention techniques.

## Conclusion

Without a doubt, change agents need to establish a vision for employees. In fact, it has been said that without a vision the people will perish. Employees want you to chart a course and lead the way; then and only then will they find the energy to participate collectively in an effort to reach the desired destination. As in *The Wizard of Oz*, Dorothy's vision was to somehow return to her beloved Kansas. By casting her eyes on that goal, she was able to energize and solicit support for friends and foes alike along her journey. In the end, she achieved her goal, as you will in your effort to *becoming a change agent.*

# References

Bell, C. R. *Managers as Mentors: Building Partnerships for Learning*. San Francisco: Berrett-Koehler Publishers, 1996.

Bellman, G. "Partnership Phase: Forming Partnerships." In *Moving from Training to Performance: A Practical Guide,* edited by D. G. Robinson and J. C. Robinson, 39–53. San Francisco: Berrett-Koehler Publishers, 1998.

Bibler, R. S. *The Arthur Young Management Guide to Mergers and Acquisition*. New York: John Wiley and Sons, 1989.

Block, P. *Stewardship*. San Francisco: Berrett-Koehler Publishers, 1992.

_____. *Flawless Consulting: A Guide to Getting Your Expertise Used*. San Diego: Pfeiffer, 1999.

Bolton, R. *People Skills: How to Assert Yourself, Listen to Others, and Resolve Conflicts*. New York: Simon and Schuster, 1986.

Boyett, J. H., and J. T. Boyett. *Beyond Workplace 2000: Essential Strategies for the New American Corporation*. New York: Dutton, 1995.

Briner, B. *The Management Methods of Jesus*. Nashville, Tenn.: Thomas Nelson, Inc., 1996.

Brookfield, S. D. *Developing Critical Thinkers: Challenging Adults to Explore Ways of Thinking and Acting*. San Francisco: Jossey-Bass, 1987.

Buckingham, M., and C. Coffman. *First, Break All the Rules: What the World's Greatest Managers Do Differently*. New York: Simon and Schuster, 1999.

Burke, W. W. *Organizational Development: A Process of Learning and Changing*. Reading, Mass.: Addison-Wesley, 1992.

Carlisle, K. E., and S. E. Murphy. *Practical Motivation Handbook*. New York: John Wiley and Sons, 1996.

Cascio, W. F. *Managing Human Resources: Productivity, Quality of Work Life, Profits*. New York: McGraw-Hill, Inc., 1995.

Clifton, D. O., and P. Nelson. *Soar with Your Strengths*. New York: Delacorte, 1992.

Conner, D. *Managing at the Speed of Change*. New York: Villard Books, 1992.

Deal, T., and A. Kennedy. *Corporate Cultures*. Cambridge, Mass.: Perseus Publishing, 2000.

De Pree, M. *Leadership Jazz*. New York: Dell Publishing, 1992.

Flannery, T. P., D. A. Hofrichter, and P. E. Platten. *People, Performance and Pay: Dynamic Compensation for Changing Organizations*. New York: Free Press, 1996.

Fuller, J. L. *Managing Performance Improvement Projects*. San Francisco: Jossey-Bass, 1997.

Fuller, J. L., and J. Farrington. *From Training to Performance Improvement: Navigating the Transition*. San Francisco: Jossey-Bass, 1999.

Gelb, M. J., and T. Buzan. *Lessons from the Art of Juggling: How to Achieve Your Full Potential in Business, Learning, and Life*. New York: Hannony Books, 1992.

Gilley, J. W. *Improving HRD Practice*. Malabar, Fla.: Krieger, 1998.

_____. "Taming the Organization: Lessons in Organizational Subordination." *Human Resource Development International* 4, no. 2 (2001): 1–17.

Gilley, J. W., and S. A. Eggland. *Principles of Human Resource Development*. Cambridge, Mass.: Perseus Publishing, 1989.

_____. *Marketing HRD Programs Within Organizations: Improving the Visibility, Credibility, and Image of Programs*. San Francisco: Jossey-Bass, 1992.

Gilley, J. W., and N. W. Boughton. *Stop Managing, Start Coaching: How Performances Coaching Can Enhance Commitment and Improve Productivity*. New York: McGraw-Hill, 1996.

Gilley, J. W., and A. Maycunich. *Strategically Integrated HRD: Partnering to Maximize Organizational Performance*. Cambridge, Mass.: Perseus Publishing, 1998.

Gilley, J. W., N. W. Boughton, and A. Maycunich. *The Performance Challenge: Developing Management Systems to Make Employees Your Greatest Asset*. Cambridge, Mass.: Perseus Publishing, 1999.

Gilley, J. W., and A. Maycunich. *Beyond the Learning Organization: Creating a Culture of Continuous and Development Through State-of-the-Art Human Resource Practices*. Cambridge, Mass.: Perseus Publishing, 2000a.

_____. *Organizational Learning, Performance, and Change: An Introduction to Strategic HRD*. Cambridge, Mass.: Perseus Publishing, 2000b.

Goleman, D. *Working with Emotional Intelligence*. New York: Bantam Books, 1998.

Greenleaf, R. K. *On Becoming a Servant Leader*. San Francisco: Jossey-Bass, 1996.

Gregory, J. M. *The Seven Laws of Teaching*. Grand Rapids, Mich.: Baker Book House, 1978.

Hale, J. *The Performance Consultant's Fieldbook: Tools and Techniques for Improving Organizations and People*. San Francisco: Jossey-Bass and Pfeiffer, 1998.

Heiman, M., and J. Slomianko. *Learning to Learn on the Job*. Alexandria, Va.: ASTD Press, 1990.

Heron, J. *The Facilitator's Handbook*. London: Kogan Page, 1989.

Hertzberg, F. *Work and the Nature of Man*. New York: World, 1971.

Hoppe, M. H. "Cross-Cultural Issues in Leadership Development." In *Handbook of Leadership Development*, edited by C. D. McCauley, R. S. Moxley, and E. V. Velsor. San Francisco: Jossey-Bass, 1998.

Hunter, D., A. Bailey, and B. Taylor. *The Art of Facilitation*. Auckland: Tandem Press, 1994.

Jick, T. *Managing Change*. Chicago: Richard Irwin Inc., 1993.

Katz, D., and R. Kahn. *The Social Psychology of Organizations,* 2d ed. New York: Wiley, 1978.

Katzenbach, J. R. *Real Change Leaders.* New York: Random House, 1995.

Killion. J. P., and G. Todnem. "A Process for Personal Theory Building." *Educational Leadership* 48, no. 6 (1991): 14–16.

Kissler, G. D. *The Change Riders: Managing the Power of Change.* Cambridge, Mas.: Perseus Books, 1991.

Knowles, M. S., E. F. Holton III, and R. A. Swanson. *The Adult Learner,* 5th ed. Houston: Gulf Publishing Company, 1998.

Kohlberg, L. *Meaning and Measurement of Moral Development.* Clark University: Heinz Weiner Institute, 1981.

Kotter, J. R. *Leading Change.* Boston: Harvard Business School Press, 1996.

Kouzes, J. M., and B. Z. Posner, B. Z. *The Leadership Challenge: How to Keep Getting Extraordinary Things Done in Organizations.* San Francisco: Jossey-Bass, 1996.

LeBoeuf, M. *Getting Results: The Secret to Motivating Yourself and Others.* New York: Berkeley Books, 1985.

Lewin, K. *Field Theory in Social Science.* New York: Harper, 1951.

Lucas, James R. *Fatal Illusions.* New York: AMACOM, 1997.

MacGregor, J. B. *Leadership.* New York: Harper and Row, 1978.

Maslow, A. H. *Motivation and Personality.* New York: Harper and Row, 1970.

_____. *Maslow on Management.* New York: Wiley, 1998.

Maxwell, J. C. *The 21 Irrefutable Laws of Leadership: Follow Them and People Will Follow You.* Nashville, Tenn.: Thomas Nelson Publishers, 1998.

McCauley, C. D., R. S. Moxley, and E. Van Velsor. *Handbook of Leadership Development [Center for Creative Leadership].* San Francisco: Jossey-Bass, 1998.

Meyer, E. C., and K. R. Allen. *Entrepreneurship and Small Business Management.* Mission Hills, Calif.: Glencoe/McGraw-Hill, 1994.

Mezirow, J. *Transformative Dimensions of Adult Learning.* San Francisco: Jossey-Bass, 1991.

Mills, G. E., R. W. Pace, and B. D. Peterson. *Analysis in Human Resource Training and Organization Development.* Cambridge, Mass.: Perseus Books, 1988.

Mink, O. G., P. W. Esterhuysen, B. P. Mink, and K. Q. Owen. *Change at Work: A Comprehensive Management Process for Transforming Organizations.* San Francisco: Jossey-Bass, 1993.

Nilson, C. *How to Start a Training Program.* Alexandria, Va.: ASTD, 1999.

O'Toole, J. *Leading Change.* San Francisco: Jossey-Bass, 1995.

Pascale, R. T. *Managing on the Edge.* New York: Touchstone, 1990.

Patterson, J. *Coming Clean About Organizational Change.* Arlington, Va.: American Association of School Administrators, 1997.

Peterson, D. B., and M. D. Hicks, M. D. *Leader as Coach: Strategies for Coaching and Developing Others.* Minneapolis, Minn.: Personnel Decisions International, 1996.

Pinto, J. K. *Power and Politics in Project Management.* Newtown Square, Pa.: Project Management Institute, 1998.

Preskill, H., and R. T. Torres. *Evaluative Inquiry for Learning in Organizations.* Thousand Oaks, Calif.: Sage Publications, 1999.

Randolph, A., and B. Posner, B. *Getting the Job Done: Effective Project Planning and Management.* Englewood Cliffs, N.J.: Prentice-Hall, 1992.

Renesch, J. *New Traditions in Business.* San Francisco: Berrett-Koehler Publishers, 1992.

Robinson, D. G., and J. C. Robinson. *Performance Consulting: Moving Beyond Training.* San Francisco: Berrett-Koehler, 1996.

Rokeach, M. *The Nature of Human Values.* New York: Free Press, 1973.

Rothwell, W. *Beyond Training and Development: State-of-the-Art Strategies for Enhancing Human Performance.* New York: AMACOM, 1996a.

_____. *The ASTD Models for Human Performance Improvement: Roles, Competencies, and Outputs.* Alexandria, Va.: American Society for Training and Development, 1996b.

Rothwell, W., and R. Cookson. *Beyond Instruction: Comprehensive Program Planning for Business and Education.* San Francisco: Jossey-Bass, 1997.

Rummler, G. A., and A. P. Brache. *Improving Performance: How to Manage the White Spaces on the Organizational Chart.* San Francisco: Jossey-Bass, 1995.

Schein, E. H. *Organizational Culture and Leadership.* San Francisco: Jossey-Bass, 1992.

Schon, D. A. *Educating the Reflective Practitioner.* San Francisco: Jossey-Bass, 1987.

Senge, P. M. *The Fifth Discipline: The Art and Practice of the Learning Organization.* New York: Doubleday, 1990.

Simonsen, P. *Promoting a Developmental Culture in Your Organization: Using Career Development as a Change Agent.* Palo Atlo, Calif.: Davies-Black Publishing, 1997.

Sofo, F. *Human Resource Development: Perspectives, Roles, and Practice.* New York: Business and Publication Inc., 2000.

Spitzer, D. R. "The Design and Development of Effective Interventions." In *Handbook of Human Performance Technology: A Comprehensive Guide for Analyzing and Solving Performance Problems in Organizations,* edited by H. D. Stolovitch and E. J. Keeps, 114–129. San Francisco: Jossey-Bass, 1992.

Thorndike, E. L. *Human Learning.* Cambridge, Mass.: MIT Press, 1931.

Ulrich, D. *Human Resource Champions.* Boston: Harvard Business School Press, 1997.

Ulrich, D., J. Zenger, and N. Smallwood. *Results-Based Leadership: How Leaders Build the Business and Improve the Bottom Line.* Boston: Harvard Business School Press, 1999.

Vaile, R. *Learning as a Way of Being.* San Francisco: Jossey-Bass, 1996.

Watkins, K. E., and V. J. Marsick. *Sculpting the Learning Organization: Lessons in the Art and Science of Systematic Change.* San Francisco: Jossey-Bass, 1993.

Weiss, J. W., and R. K. Wysocki. *5-Phase Project Management: A Practical Planning and Implementation Guide.* Cambridge, Mass.: Perseus Publishing, 1992.

Wren, J. T. *The Leader's Companion: Insights in Leadership Through the Ages.* New York: Free Press, 1995.

Zemke, R., and S. Zemke, S. "Adult Learning: What Do We Know for Sure?" *Training* 32, no. 6 (1995): 31–40.

# Index

change alignment process and, 237, performance management and, 145–146, results engineering and, 260–262

growth. *See* developmental philosophy

guiding principles. *See* principles; values

honesty, 123–124

hopeful adoption, change curve quadrant and, 46–47

human resources, 143, 194

humility, 225–228

"I" messages, 121

implementation

    change process model and, 41–42, implementer role on change team, 35–36, role of change agents in, 174–176

importation of energy, 189

industry experience. *See* technical skills

informal power structures, 63–67

    overview of, 63–64, rising stars, 65–66, technology and, 67, What's What, 66–67, Who Does What, 64–65, Who's Who, 64

information inputs, 191–192

information sharing, 161–162. *See also* communication

informed cynicism, change curve quadrant and, 46

instruction. *See* teaching

instrumental values, 219

internal change agents, 2–3, 9–11

involvement, 100–101, 116–117

jobs

    analyzing job designs, 195, basing on strengths, 92–93, career planning and, 196–197, improving job designs, 145–147, writing job descriptions, 93

journals, 92

language, 138

law of legacy, 227

leadership. *See also* servant leaders

    as center of organizational system, 160–161, change alignment and, 233–234, conceptual basis of, 247, development of, 251, as project management skill, 203, understanding styles/types of, 62–63, values and, 222, visualization and, 257

learning

    activities for, 261, analyzing, 194–195, engage employees in, 245, facilitating, 170–171, 244–245, needs for, 172, post-learning strategies, 140–142, preparatory strategies, 137–138, process of, 136, rapid, 89, slow, 90, strategies, 138–140, styles of, 113, use of questions for improving, 142–143

learning organizations, 251

listening, as relationship skill, 187

loyalty, rewarding, 103–104

Manager as Change Agent Blueprint, 22

managerial malpractice, 147–148

material resources, analyzing, 194

mentoring, 256–257. *See also* teaching

mission statements, 235

Model for Change Agent Excellence, 182–183

motivational philosophy, 96–104

    adopting principles of, 98, creating a climate for change, 112–113, developing, 97–98, rewarding commitment and loyalty, 103–104, rewarding

creativity, 102–103, rewarding employee development, 101–102, rewarding entrepreneurship, 99–100, rewarding involvement, 100–101, rewarding teamwork and cooperation, 102

myths, organizational change, 28–31

nonjudgmental evaluations, 241

nonverbal communication skills, 121–122

notes, relationship skills and, 188

objectivity, 8, 167

observing, as relationship skill, 187

obstructions. *See* barriers, to change

open receptive visualization, 258

operating talent, 247

organizational culture

    barriers to change and, 61–62, change process in, 25–26, 42–43, defined, 25, role in performance, 228, value accountability in, 221–222

organizational effectiveness

    change agent's expertise and, 128, change process and, 24–25, responsibility of change agent for, 177–178

organizational knowledge

    change agent's expertise in, 128–129, responsibility for demonstrating, 158–161

organizations

    crisis in, 1–2, 251, myths of change and, 30–31, systems and structure of, 158–160

outputs, 190–911

partnerships, 131–135

    building, 135, change partnerships, 134–135, overview of, 131–133, performance partnerships, 133, solution partnerships, 166, strategic partnerships, 133–134

passion, stewardship and, 217

performance

    analyzing needs and, 171, defined, 144, impact of organizational culture on, 228, sharing expectations and, 261, standards for, 93–94, 261

performance appraisal

    analyzing, 172–173, as developmental strategy, 95–96, organizational analysis and, 195–196, performance management and, 149

performance management, 143–151

    coaching and, 147–149, development plans and, 150, establishing goals, 145–146, job design and, 145–147, role of evaluation, 149, 194, sponsoring systems for, 144–145, use of compensation and rewards, 150–151

performance partnerships, 133

performance zones, 90

permanent white water, 1, 251

personality measuring instruments, 114

pitfalls, project management, 203–206

    changes in project scope, 203–204, excess/lack of detail, 204–205, lack of communication, 206, too many team members, 205–206

power, types of, 65. *See also* informal power structures

practice, learning process and, 139

principles. *See also* values

    change agents, effective communications, 14, change agents, employee advocacy, 14–15, change

# About the Author

Jerry W. Gilley is a Professor of HRD at Colorado State University and was previously the Director of Organizational and Executive Development at William M. Mercer, Inc. He has co-authored eleven books and over sixty articles, book chapters, and monographs. His books include Organizational Learning, Performance, and Change (Perseus Publishing), which was selected the HRD Book of the Year (2000) by the Academy of HRD. Other books include Beyond the Learning Organization, The Performance Challenge, and Strategically Integrated HRD (Perseus Publishing), and Stop Managing, Start Coaching (McGraw-Hill).

Scott A. Quatro is an Instructor of Management at Dordt College. He was previously Manager, Corporate Human Resources at Payless ShoeSource, Inc., and a change management consultant with American Management Systems, Inc. He is a Ph.D. candidate in Organizational Learning and Human Resource Development at Iowa State University. He received his MBA from the College of William and Mary.

Erik Hoekstra is the Director for People & Organizational Development at The Harbor Group, the parent company for a variety of firms in the construction, engineering, and factory automation industries. He holds an MBA degree from the Rotterdam School of Management in the Netherlands and is a Ph.D. candidate in Organizational Learning and Human Resource Development at Iowa State University. Prior to his current position, Erik led several companies in retail and wholesale distributions and was a member of the business faculty at Dordt College.

Doug D. Whittle is Director of Technology Development and Training at Pioneer Hybrid, Inc. He has a combined 30 years of experience as an educator and as a business manager for teams responsible for technology-related training and support. He has been published in several professional publications and frequently speaks at conferences about issues related to training, employee coaching, change management, strategic planning, and resource management. He is a Ph.D. candidate in Organizational Learning and Human Resource Development at Iowa State University.

Ann Maycunich is an Instructor in HRD at Colorado State University. Previously she was a performance consultant at Iowa State University and Marketing Training Manager at Foremost Insurance. She has co-authored four books including Organizational Learning, Performance, and Change (Perseus Publishing), which was selected the HRD Book of the Year (2000) by the Academy of HRD. Other books include Beyond the Learning Organization, The Performance Challenge, and Strategically Integrated HRD (Perseus Publishing). She is also a Ph.D. candidate in Organizational Learning and Human Resource Development at Iowa State University.

## Contributors

The following people were major contributors to this book:

**Joni Anderson** is an Instructor of Management at Buena Vista College and a Ph.D. candidate in Organizational Learning and Human Resource Development at Iowa State University.

**Cindi Cornelison** is the former Manager of Human Resources at Cobbs Manufacturing and is a Ph.D. candidate in Organizational Learning and Human Resource Development at Iowa State University.

**Deanne Gute** is now pursuing a doctorate in Educational Leadership and Policy Studies while serving as the Director of the Writing Center at Northern Iowa University. She is a freelance editor for Bedford/St. Martin's College Division.

**Laura Parker** is Manager, Customer Relations for Wells Fargo Mortgage and is a Ph.D. candidate in Organizational Learning and Human Resource Development at Iowa State University. She holds an MBA from Iowa State University.

**Susan G. Pickens** is Director, Training and Development at Grinnel Mutual Reinsurance Company and is a Ph.D. candidate in Organizational Learning and Human Resource Development at Iowa State University.